More Marylanders To Carolina

Migration of Marylanders to North Carolina and South Carolina Prior to 1800

Henry C. Peden, Jr.

Willow Bend Books
Westminster, Maryland
1999

Willow Bend Books and Family Line Publications

65 East Main Street
Westminster, Maryland 21157-5036
1-800-876-6103

Source books, early maps, CDs—Worldwide

For our listing of thousands of titles offered by hundreds of publishers see our website <www.willowbend.net>

Visit our retail store

First Published and Reprinted in 1999

Printed in the United States of America

International Standard Book Number: 1-58549-071-7

CONTENTS

Forward v

More Marylanders to Carolina 1

Index 137

FOREWORD

My first volume of *Marylanders to Carolina* was published by Family Line Publications in 1994. Since that time additional information has come to light from a variety of sources, so it was decided to publish a second volume and entitle it *More Marylanders to Carolina*. As in the first volume, the sources have been cited after each entry.

Additionally, a number of people have submitted information on the family lines that they have been researching over the years and I have added to their information in many cases. To encourage the exchange of genealogical information and to inspire additional research, the addresses of contributors have been included after each family group within the text. My appreciation is extended to the following researchers who have contributed information for this volume:

> Rosemary B. Dodd, of Maryland
> Vicki Doetsch, of South Carolina
> Patricia A. Fortney, of Maryland
> Virginia Heckel, of Kentucky
> Ira Helms, of Maryland
> Andrea K. Juricic, of Utah
> Donna Kirkman, of Florida
> Barbara Marvin, of Washington, D. C.
> James A. L. Miller, Jr., of North Carolina
> Dora W. Mitchell, of Maryland
> Donna J. Ottley, of Arizona and Alaska
> Carol L. Porter, of Maryland
> Margaret Walker, of Tennessee
> F. Edward Wright, of Maryland
> Ray A. Yount, of Maryland

It must be noted that the author assumes no responsibility for errors of fact or the opinion expressed or implied by the listed contributors, or the accuracy of the material published by others. Beware of family tradition and undocumented statements. With that in mind, I trust this second volume of Marylanders who migrated to North Carolina and South Carolina prior to 1800 will be helpful to researchers.

> Henry C. Peden, Jr.
> Bel Air, Maryland
> November 4, 1998

MORE MARYLANDERS TO CAROLINA

ADAMS

On August 6, 1795, William Adams, of Rockingham County, North Carolina, eldest son of Macnemarrow Adams, of the same county, conveyed to Abraham Lewis, of Dorchester County, Maryland, lands devised to said William Adams by his grandfather William Adams, late of Dorchester County, now in the possession of the Widow Jones, called *Adams's Lott*, containing 50 acres. Arthur Pritchett and Daniel Nicols, of Dorchester County, were named as attorneys for the grantor to acknowledge this deed. Witnesses were Aaron Lewis, John Groom, and Sarah Adams. Acknowledged before John Stevens and John Reed, Justices. [Ref: *Abstracts of the Land Records of Dorchester County, Maryland, Volume 34 (Liber HD#9)*, by James A. McAllister, Jr. (1967), p. 19.]

ANDREW-ANDREWS

"David and James Andrew (who bought 320 acres from Henry White in May, 1762) were evidently sons of John Andrew, who died somewhere in Rowan County [North Carolina] in 1757. Although inconclusive, the evidence suggests that John Andrew originated in Anne Arundel, Dorchester, or Queen Anne's County (where the name appears as early as 1724), and moved to the Middle Octararo settlement of eastern Lancaster County [Pennsylvania], where he was an elder in the Presbyterian Church in 1740. The deed to James Andrew was located '... on Gillespie's Creek, being a part of Henry White's place where he did live ...' David Andrew also acquired 137 acres in the forks of the Yadkin." [Ref: *Carolina Cradle*, by Robert W. Ramsey (1964), p. 96, citing North Carolina Land Grants VI:96, Rowan County Deeds IV:725, IV:668, and Rowan County Court of Pleas and Quarterly Session Minutes I:51.]

Dennis Andrew and Patrick Andrew were transported to Maryland in 1674 and Nathaniel Andrew and Mary Andrew were transported in 1677. There were also many people named "Andrews" who came to Maryland as early as 1656. [Ref: *The Early Settlers of Maryland*, by Gust Skordas (1968), pp. 9-10; *A Supplement to The Early Settlers of Maryland*, by Carson Gibb, Ph.D. (1997), p. 12.]

ARCHIBALD

John Archibald was a private in the Cecil County, Maryland militia (company of foot) in 1740 and his brother William was living in West Nottingham Township of Chester County, Pennsylvania at this same time. John subsequently migrated to Rowan County, North Carolina and settled in the Fourth Creek Settlement before 1750. [Ref: *Inhabitants of Cecil County, Maryland, 1649-1774*, by Henry C. Peden, Jr. (1993), p. 51; *Carolina Cradle*, by Robert W. Ramsey (1964), pp. 96-97, citing Cecil County Wills XXVII:393, Rowan County Wills A:3, 251, North Carolina Land

Grants VI:94, VI:95, and Chester County Tax Lists 1722-1727, 1735-1738, 1740-1747, 1753.]

ARNETT

On May 27, 1795, James Arnett, of Casuel [Caswell] County, North Carolina, conveyed to Moses Martin, of Dorchester County, Maryland, part of a tract called *Bell Field* located on the road from Cambridge to the head of Fishing Creek near the Presbyterian Meeting House, containing one acre more or less. Witnesses were Thomas Jones and John Williams. [Ref: *Abstracts of the Land Records of Dorchester County, Maryland, Volume 33 (Liber HD#8)*, by James A. McAllister, Jr. (1967), p. 35.]

On February 27, 1797, Valentine Arnett, late of Maryland but now of Stokes County, North Carolina, planter, granted to Gottlieb Shober, of Salem, Stokes County, North Carolina, power of attorney regarding land on Nanticoke River [in Dorchester County, Maryland] including Cratcher's Ferry and Walnut Landing, called *The Great Indian Town*, containing about 10,000 acres, bought by Arnett from the Nanticoke Indian Tribe. Witnesses were Christoph Rich and Adam Hepner. Acknowledged in open court. Robert Williams, Clerk of the Court, Stokes County, North Carolina. [Ref: *Abstracts of the Land Records of Dorchester County, Maryland, Volume 35 (Liber HD#12)*, by James A. McAllister, Jr. (1967), p. 8.]

On May 5, 1797, Valentine Arnett of the State of North Carolina, agent and attorney for the Nanticoke Indians, conveyed to Gottlieb Shober, of the same State and County, attorney at law, lease of the Indian land on Nanticoke River and Chickawan Creek, for the term of 1,000 years. Witnesses were William Wheatley and Lewis Blume. Acknowledged on May 29, 1797 by Valentine Arnett before Thomas Jones and John Williams, Justices for Dorchester County, Maryland. [Ref: McAllister, *loc. cit.*, p. 9.]

On May 11, 1798, Billy Nanticoke as Chief for himself and the Nanticoke Tribe, Elizabeth Nanticoke alias Gohunk, and Sarah Meyer of the Nanticoke Indians, conveyed to Gottlieb Shober, of North Carolina, Gentleman, a lease of the Indian lands on Nanticoke River for the term of one year. Witnesses were Daniel Hauser, John Sergeant Missionary [John Sergeant, missionary], Nicholas Cusick, and John Meloxen. Possession of the said land was delivered to Gottlieb on June 12, 1798, by Valentine Arnett, attorney for the Nanticoke Indians, in the presence of Nathan Bradley and Daniel Hauser. Acknowledged on June 13, 1798 by Valentine Arnett, attorney for the Indians, before Levin Woolford and John Reed, Justices of the Peace for Dorchester County, Maryland. A similar transaction was recorded on May 12, 1798. Further, on May 14, 1798, Billy Nanticoke as Chief for himself and heir and successor of Panquash and Annotoughquan, and for the whole tribe of Nanticokes, and Elizabeth Nanticoke alias Gohunk, and Sarah Meyers, now living in the State of New York, and town of Tuscarora, conveyed to Gottlieb Shober of North Carolina, the Nanticoke Indian lands on Chicakoon Creek and the Northwest Fork of Nanticoke River. Valentine Arnett was named as attorney for grantors to acknowledge deed. Witnesses were Daniel Hauser, John Meloxen and John Sargent Missionary [sic.] Acknowledged before James Dean, Judge of the Court of Common Pleas of Oneida County, New York. Sworn to by John Sargent before James Dean, Judge, and Mel T. Woolsey, Dy. Clerk. Sworn to by Daniel Hauser before Levin Woolford and John Reed, Justices of the Peace for Dorchester County, Maryland. H. Dickinson, Clerk. [Ref: McAllister, *loc. cit.*, pp. 60-61.]

ATTERBURY-ATTEBURY-ARTERBURY

William "Attebury" wrote his will on November 11, 1793 and it was probated on June 21, 1794 in Chester County, South Carolina. He named his wife Bridget "Attaberry" and sons Thomas, William, and James (eldest sons) and Nathan and Elijah (youngest sons), and daughters Mary Henderson and Sary, Ellender and Anney Attaberry. Witnesses were Thomas Attabery, Thomas Attebery, Brigget Attabery and Willson Henderson.

"Fragmented records from the states of Virginia, South Carolina and Kentucky, where the first three generations of Atteburys lived their lives, have made it most difficult to adequately trace family relationships. Also a penchant for calling their children by the same names has added to the difficulty. From the Virginia State Library's Auditors Account Book 27, p. 482, is a pay warrant to William Arterberry, October 10, 1785, for militia service during the Revolutionary War. We assume this is the same William Attebury who lived in Chester by 1790, when he appears on the Federal Census and died in that same county several years later. The location in Virginia of William's service has not been ascertained. However, we do know that the Attebury family lived in Loudoun County, Virginia from its formation in 1754 when they first appear in land records and the Tithables Lists."

"Family tradition gives William's wife Bridget the maiden name Murray. This is one tradition that has a ring of truth to it, although we find no records as proof. William Murray, possibly a brother, was executor of Bridget's husband's estate. Bridget had 3 Attebury grandsons named Zephaniah, one of whom was Zephaniah Murray Attebury. From census records we can estimate Bridget as being born 1750-55. We have definite information on only 2 of the offspring of this Attebury union and can only speculate on the others."

"[1] Thomas Attebury - Census records indicate his birth to have been between 1770-75. The biographical sketch of one of his sons states Thomas' wife to be Susannah Clemmons. Thomas and his mother Bridget Attebury both sold their land in the Sandy River area of Chester in 1805. Thomas next appears on the federal census of Hardin County, Kentucky in 1810. (The area of present day Hart County, Kentucky.) In 1812 we find Thomas Attebury on the tax list for Barren County, Kentucky and there he stayed until his death in 1836. Although he died intestate, a suit over his estate caused the following children to be listed. I have added birth dates and marriages which I have verified:

(1) William Pain Attebury or Atterberry (born 1804, married Susan A. Glazebrook on September 30, 1827);

(2) James Attebury or Atterberry (born 1810, married Elizabeth Bernard on October 25, 1827 or 1829);

(3) Stephen Attebury or Stephan Atterberry (married Martha Jane Ellis on January 8, 1835);

(4) Zephaniah Attebury (born 1817, married Eliza Jane Moore);

(5) Betsy Attebury or Atterberry (married John Boydston or Boydtseen on January 10, 1826, with William Atterberry as surety);

(6) Sarah Attebury or Sally Atterberry (married Arthur Williamson on October 24, 1822, with Thomas Atterberry as surety); and,

(7) Martha Jane Attebury (never married)."

[Ed. Note: I have added the dates of marriages, sureties' names and spellings from the marriage records, and the numbers prior to each name to assist in identification. It should be noted that there was also a Nancy Arterberry who married William Hall on October 25, 1821 in Barren County, Kentucky. HCP.]

"[2] Elijah Attebury - One of the 'younger sons' mentioned in his father's will. He was born 1785 according to census records and statements of family members. He married Mary Taylor, daughter of Isaac Taylor of Chester County, South Carolina and Hart County, Kentucky. Elijah was living several years later in Illinois. In 1834, he settled his family permanently in Monroe County, Missouri. His children were:

(1) Isaac Newton Attebury (born 1805, married Elizabeth Dowdy or Doddy on September 15, 1827),

(2) William Attebury (born 1808, married Nancy Grogan),

(3) James Attebury (born 1811, married Ellen Stroud), Seaman Attebury (born 1814, married first to Nancy Weatherford and second to Mary Dabney),

(4) Nathan Attebury (born 1819, married Harriet Holder),

(5) Zephaniah Murray Attebury (married Josephine Dabney), and Thompson Attebury (never married)."

"The James Attebury who was an early pioneer in Missouri may have been brother to Thomas and Elijah and one of the 'older sons' mentioned in William Attebury's will. Several branches of the Attebury family claim him. We have been unable to zero in on his ancestry. A biography of Greenberry Attebury was given in The Encyclopedia of Missouri History and published in 1801, almost 40 years after G. B.'s death in 1862. According to this account, Greenberry Attebury was born in South Carolina in 1799. In 1803, he was taken by his family to Kentucky where he lived until 1817. In that year he came to Missouri which would have been several years before Missouri's statehood. His father is stated to be James Attebury."

"In 1847, William Attebury's will was probated in Monroe County, Missouri. He leaves his estate to his wife Charity Attebury. No children are mentioned other than his 'natural and adopted son' Greenberry Attebury who is to receive his estate upon death of wife Charity. In the 1850 census of Monroe County, Missouri, Charity Attebury, age 78, born in South Carolina, is residing in the home of Nathan Attebury, age 30, her nephew and son of Elijah and Mary Taylor Attebury. I would be pleased to hear from anyone interested in this family. I would especially welcome information from those having ancestors who resided in Loudoun County, Virginia prior to their arrival in Chester County, South Carolina."

[Ref: Information compiled by Vicki Doetsch and published in *The Bulletin* of the Chester District Genealogical Society (P. O. Box 336, Richburg, South Carolina 29729) in March, 1983, Volume VI, No. I, pp. 5-6.]

Miscellaneous Atterbury deeds in Chester County, South Carolina:

(1) Abraham Myers conveyed 50 acres to Nathaniel Norward on July 29, 1793 "being part of an original grant to James Attebury of 641 acres made on September 4, 1786" and situated on Smith's Creek of Brushy Fork, in the section of Chester County known as "West Chest" County toward Union and Fairfield Counties.

(2) David Mitchell conveyed 100 acres to Abraham Myers on Brushy Fork on July 12, 1800 "being land formerly laid out by said David Mitchell to Edward Atterbury ... it being part of two tracts formerly granted to David Mitchell, Sr. and James Atterbury."

(3) Abraham Myers conveyed 100 acres of land "laid out by David Mitchell" to Edward Atterbury, being part of two grants made originally to David Mitchell, Sr. and James Atterbury."

[Ref: *The Bulletin* of the Chester District Genealogical Society, Volume X, No. IV (December, 1987), pp. 123-125; *Marriage Records of Barren County, Kentucky, 1799-1849*, by Martha Powell Reneau (1984), pp. 6, 21, 113, 282.]

From the foregoing information it becomes evident that there was an Atterbury-Mitchell connection in early Maryland prior to the migration to Loudoun County, Virginia, and subsequent to Chester County, South Carolina. The following clues are offered:

(1) John Mitchel or Mitchell, Sr. wrote his will on June 4, 1748 in Prince George's County, Maryland and it was probated on August 25, 1752, naming his wife Elizabeth Mitchel, daughter Mary Lee, son John Mitchel [Mitchell], Jr., son David Mitchell, daughter Sarah Atterbary [Atterbury], daughter Elizabeth Mitchell, Jr., and granddaughter Elizabeth Yaxley (minor under age 16). [Ref: *Maryland Calendar of Wills, Volume 10, 1748-1753*, pp. 234-235.]

(2) There was also a Thomas Arterbury, planter, of Calvert County, Maryland who died testate in 1749; however, he only names his wife Mary and "cousins" in his will; no children were named. [Ref: *Maryland Calendar of Wills, Volume 10, 1748-1753*, p. 37.]

(3) John Mitchell who died in 1752 was a son of John Mitchell and Susannah Burgess, daughter of Col. William Burgess and his third wife Ursula Puddington (who subsequently married Dr. Mordecai Moore). John's daughter Sarah Mitchell was born in Prince George's County, Maryland on August 31, 1720 and married first

to Robert Yackley or Yaxley in 1735 and second to William Atterbury (date and place unknown). This William Atterbury was born on June 21, 1710 in St. Giles, Cripplegate, London, England, a son of William Atterbury (1685-1741) and Sarah Rogers. James Atterbury, son of William Atterbury and Sarah (Mitchell) Yaxley, was born in 1758 in Loudoun County, Virginia, married Dorcas Wilkerson about 1780 in South Carolina, and died in 1843 in Monroe County, Missouri. Their son William Atterbury was born on December 11, 1789 in Chester County, South Carolina, married Mary Miller on November 10, 1811 in Hardin County, Kentucky, and died on September 28, 1839 in Monroe County, Missouri.

[Ref: Information compiled in 1998 by Mrs. J. Richard (Margaret) Walker, 4293 Nellwood Lane, Memphis, Tennessee 38117-2334; *Prince George's County, Maryland, Indexes of Church Registers, 1686-1885*, Volume I, p. 185; *Anne Arundel County Church Records of the 17th and 18th Centuries*, by F. Edward Wright, p. 13; *Anne Arundel Gentry, Volume One*, by Harry Wright Newman, pp. 1-9; *A Biographical Dictionary of the Maryland Legislature, 1635-1789, Volume I: A-H*, by Edward C. Papenfuse, et al., p. 182; *Kentuckians to Missouri*, by Stuart Seely Sprague, p. 14.]

AULD

James Auld was born circa 1665 in Ayrshire, Scotland and died testate in Talbot County, Maryland in 1721. He married Sarah Elliott, daughter of Edward Elliott, and she married second to William Lambdin. John Auld, son of James Auld and Sarah Elliott, died leaving a will dated April 20, 1765 in Talbot County. He married Mary Sherwood, daughter of Col. Daniel Sherwood and Mary Hopkins, and owned tracts called *Elliott's Folly* and *Cambridge* and *Grantham* and *Newport Glasgow* in Talbot County. The children of John Auld named in his will were James Auld, Mary Hambleton (deceased), and others were mentioned, but not named in the will. The others were John, Daniel, Edward, and Philemon.

In 1747 James Auld, son of John and Mary, married Rosanna Piper, widow of Howes Goldsborough, the clerk of the county who died in 1746, and then lived in Dorset [Dorchester] County. "Rose Ann" Piper was the daughter of Rev. Michael Piper, a clergyman of the Church of England, who lived in Annapolis at the time of her birth in 1723. In 1765 James Auld and family removed to Halifax, North Carolina.

On September 21, 1773 James Auld, of North Carolina, heir and devisee of John Auld of Talbot County, Maryland, deceased, and John Auld of North Carolina, grandson, conveyed to Matthew Tilghman, of Talbot County, gentleman, a 258-acre tract called *Newport Glasgow* according to patent. Rosanna Auld, wife of James, released her dower. Reference was made to the will of John Auld who devised to his wife Mary, his dwelling plantation during her widowhood, but in case of her death or remarriage, to his son James Auld, provided he appeared in person to claim the same; and if he did not, the land would go to his grandson James Auld. The aforesaid Mary, widow of John Auld, was still living; Matthew Tilghman had contracted to buy the land (except for 36 1/2 acres sold by John Auld, deceased) and Auld's dwelling plantation and the lands adjoining part of "Newport Glasgow." [Ref: *Maryland Genealogies* I:25-27, II:21-22.]

BAKER

"Henry Baker probably moved to North Carolina from Maryland. He was a wagon maker and married Barbara Bowers in Rowan County in 1758. In October, 1761, Henry Baker obtained Bowers' lot number three [in Salisbury] at a public auction conducted by Sheriff Benjamin Milner. A court ruling awarded Hugh Montgomery £8, 19s., 10d. proclamation money for damages incurred at the hands of James Bowers, Jr., hatter. Bowers' lot, also known as Bowers' shop, was sold to Baker as highest bidder. Bowers was placed in the sheriff's custody for his offense."

Earlier, in June, 1753, a John Baker petitioned the court that "whereas the said John Baker happened to be in a late affray with another person whereupon the person with whom he had the said affray ... bit the under part of his ear off ... he prays that his petition be recorded and granted and the court ordered the clerk to give him a certificate of the same." Ear-cropping was common punishment for larceny, and Baker was anxious to have a certificate to show that he was not a thief.

[Ref: *Carolina Cradle*, by Robert W. Ramsey (1964), pp. 165, 166, 182, citing Cecil County Judgments SK#3 (1723-1730) and SK#4 (1730-1747), Rowan County Court Minutes I:1, 66, 75, 151, Rowan County Deeds IV:399, V:274, X:274.]

There appears to have been several men named Henry Baker in Cecil County, Maryland, as early as 1740 when Henry Baker and Nathan Baker were privates in the militia (company of foot). Also, in 1741, one Henry Baker owned a tract called *Baker's Addition*. There was also a Henry Baker who was one of the commissioners in the fall of 1742 who were "appointed to carry out the act of incorporation of Charlestown, the town to be laid out at a place called Long Point on the west side of North East River." Henry Baker took a religious oath at St. Mary Ann's Protestant Episcopal Church in 1751, as did Peter Baker and Nathan Baker in 1742. There were also men named Henry Baker in Cecil County after 1758 by which time one Henry Baker had migrated to North Carolina and married, including one Henry Baker who was fined for assault in 1757. In fact, one Henry Baker represented Cecil County in the Lower House of the Maryland Assembly between 1749 and 1770. Additional research will be necessary before drawing conclusions. [Ref: *Inhabitants of Cecil County, Maryland, 1649-1774*, by Henry C. Peden, Jr. (1993), pp. 2, 7, 30, 33, 54, 58, 72, 89.]

BARRON

John Barron, wife Margaret and their family, moved from Talbot County, or possibly Cecil County, Maryland circa 1778 to the New Acquisition District of what became York County, South Carolina in 1785. John purchased "a 200-acre plantation on Broad River near Tate's Ferry and the mouth of Buffaloe Creek in 1778, a few days after Jane, widow of Adam Meek of Cecil County, Maryland, bought a plantation on Bullock's Creek from Daniel and Mary (Stephenson) McClaren.

The Barrons and Meeks were related, according to James Madison Hope, youngest son of Jane Barron (1767-1841) by her second husband James Hope, Jr., and this suggests that they may have come together from Cecil or a nearby county. In 1779 James Barron bought 250 acres on Bullock's Creek near the lands of John and Jane Stephenson and William Minter. He sold the tract in parts to Alexander Barron in 1782, to Samuel Barry in 1787, and to Richard Champion and wife Margaret in 1788. These deeds were witnessed severally by Samuel Barry, Alexander Barron, and Jane Barron's husband Robert Stephenson. When Stephenson died in 1798, his widow Jane and Samuel Barry were appointed to administer his estate. Two of the tutors of the Stephenson children were Minters, doubtless relatives of William Minter Hillhouse, husband of Sarah Barron.

When Richard Champion made his will in 1796 it was witnessed by Jane Stephenson and William Minter. Margaret and John Barron witnessed the deeds in 1785 when William McGowin of York County bought Hugh Quinn's 400-acre grant on the opposite side of Broad River. William Tate, Sr. brought suit against John and James Barron in 1787. John Barron and Peter Quinn were appraisers of the estates of Thomas Tate, Jr. and Sr. in 1785 and 1787.

During the War of the Revolution, John Barron held the rank of captain in the South Carolina militia, but because of his age he was given staff rather than field duty and was assigned to the commissary department and collected subsistence for Col. William Bratton's Regiment. His son James was a lieutenant in Capt. Jacob Barnett's Company of Bullock's Creek Horsemen, May 12, 1780 - March 1, 1781, and afterwards served 20 days in Capt. James Thompson's Company. After the war he was the first Under Sheriff of York when the county was formed in 1785. Another son Alexander drove a wagon and team for Colonel Bratton in the Stone Expedition in 1779, and lost a horse that was appraised by Samuel Barry and Isaac Lanay. Son-in-law William Hillhouse was captain of a company of horsemen. In January, 1781, the British Army under Lord Cornwallis camped for a week on his plantation on Turkey Creek. Robert Stephenson served under Captains Barnett and Thompson, and authorized James Barron to receive his service compensation.

John and Margaret Barron sold their land in 1787 and appear to have moved to Tennessee. Alexander sold his land in 1799 and bought in Pendleton County in 1801. The next year Hugh Barry died in York County without wife, or children, and his estate was distributed among his brothers and sisters, one of whom was Catharine, the wife of Alexander Barron. As they were living far away, Alexander got his brother-in-law Samuel Barry to collect his wife's share.

Alexander Barron sold his land in Pendleton in 1805 and moved to Giles County, Tennessee. A deed from him to his son Alexander, Jr. was witnessed and proved by Robert Stephenson (Jr.) and John Barron in 1814. Alexander's will was probated in Giles County in 1816 and it named as his executors his sons Alexander, Jr. and John. The latter had married his first cousin Dorcas Stephenson, daughter of Robert and Jane (Barron) Stephenson and had also moved to Giles County about 1808.

James Barron bought land next to Bullock's Creek Presbyterian Meetinghouse in 1785, sold it in 1798, and moved over Broad River to Union County where he died in 1800, survived by wife Martha and minor sons Adam, Samuel, and James Alexander Barron. Abraham Barron had an account with Francis King in 1781, sold his land on Turkey Creek, including William Hillhouse's great cowpen, in 1786, and moved to Giles County where he was residing in 1820.

Margaret Stephenson, daughter of Robert and Jane (Barron) Stephenson, married James Montgomery, and like her sister Dorcas and brothers Robert and Samuel, also moved to Giles County. Jane Barron was married at age seventeen to Robert Stephenson on December 3, 1784 and after his death in 1798 to James Hope, Jr. (1769-1840) on September 19, 1799.

[Ref: *The Bulletin* of the Chester District Genealogical Society, Volume IX, No. II (June, 1988), pp. 35-36, featuring an article entitled "The Barrons of Western York County, South Carolina" by Elmer Oris Parker.]

John Barron was a private in the foot company under the command of Capt. Peter Bayard in Cecil County, Maryland in 1740. [Ref: *Inhabitants of Cecil County, Maryland, 1649-1774*, by Henry C. Peden, Jr. (1993, p. 52.]

BARROW

John Barrow (Barron?) was born on October 3, 1749 in Talbot County, Maryland and married Susanna ---- on April 12, 1781 in Washington County, North Carolina (now Tennessee). He lived in Montgomery County, Virginia at the time of his enlistment in the Revolutionary War. After the war he lived in Washington County, Tennessee for 7 years, then to Franklin County, Georgia for 3 years. then back to Washington County, Tennessee for 3 years, and then to Pulaski County, Kentucky in 1797. John served in the North Carolina and Virginia Lines during the Revolutionary War. His oldest son James was born in 1791; no other children were mentioned in his pension claim on June 18, 1834. He died March 14, 1841 and his widow applied for and received pension W2987 on June 20, 1842, "aged 80 on September 17, 1842." She stated she had no record of their marriage by John Duncan, Justice of the Peace in Washington County, North Carolina, now in Tennessee, but it was recorded in the family Bible she had given to her oldest son James Barron. [Ref: *Genealogical Abstracts of Revolutionary War Pension Files, Vol. I: A-E*, by Virgil D. White (1990), p. 169.]

The foregoing information appeared in the first volume of my *Marylanders to Carolina*. It appears that the name could have been Barrow, Barron or Barrons, as these names are found quite often in the records of Talbot County, Maryland during the 1700's. For example, in St. Peter's Parish, John Barons *[sic]*, son of

Joseph and Elizabeth Barrons, was born on June 24, 1701 and baptized on August 3, 1701; Elizabeth Barron married James Merrick on December 10, 1713; John Barron married Sarah Stacy on January 9, 1722; and, Joseph Barron died on May 15, 1725. [Ref: *Maryland Eastern Shore Vital Records, 1648-1725*, by F. Edward Wright (1982), pp. 66, 69, 73, 86.] Also, in Talbot County in April, 1779, James and Margaret Barrow conveyed land to John Barrow (witnessed by Thomas Barrow) located on the northeast line of *Ashby*, a division between James Barrow and John Barrow. In January, 1782, Thomas and Anne Barrow conveyed land to their oldest son John and another son Thomas Jr., a gift of love, part of *Ashby* which had been conveyed by James Barrow, deceased, to the aforesaid John Barrow and located on the east side of the main road leading from Miles River Ferry to the Talbot County Courthouse. [Ref: *Talbot County, Maryland Land Records, Book Fourteen*, by R. Bernice Leonard (1989), pp. 19, 47.]

BARRY-BERRY

Andrew Barry was court commissioner for Cecil County, Maryland in 1736. He was commissioned a lieutenant in the county militia in 1740 (in a Company of Foot under Capt. Zebulon Hollingsworth), but "refuses to serve." He subsequently migrated to Rowan County, North Carolina. A Catherine Barry also migrated there from either Talbot or Cecil County. Although Andrew Barry had land on Fourth Creek, the evidence indicates that he lived in Anson County south of the Granville line. [Ref: *Inhabitants of Cecil County, Maryland, 1649-1774*, by Henry C. Peden, Jr. (1993), p. 51; *Carolina Cradle*, by Robert W. Ramsey (1964), pp. 96, 103, citing Cecil County Judgments SK#3 (1723-1730), p. 449, and SK#4 (1730-1747), p. 1; Rowan County Deeds III:215; *The May Wilson McBee Collection*, by May Wilson McBee (Greenwood, Mississippi: By the compiler, 1950), pp. 27, 127; and, *Maryland Calendar of Wills* III:205, which contains the will of William Berry in Talbot County written in 1685.]

Catherine Berry witnessed the will of Robert Spedden in 1742 in Dorchester County. [Ref: *Maryland Calendar of Wills, Volume VIII, 1738-1743*, p. 194.]

BARTON

"John Barton and Benjamin Barton may have removed to Frederick County, Maryland from Bucks County, Pennsylvania or Burlington County, New Jersey, or they may have originated in Somerset County, Maryland. They migrated to the forks of the Yadkin River in Rowan County, North Carolina circa 1750." [Ref: *Carolina Cradle*, by Robert W. Ramsey (1964), p. 77, citing Burlington Monthly Meeting of Friends, 1678-1865, pp. 10, 61; Hunterdon County Court Minutes, 173301736, IV:137; Testamentary Proceedings of Maryland, 1657-1777, XXI:441; and, Rowan County Court Minutes I:5, 50, 73.]

BARWICK

On November 7, 1768, John Barwick, of Johnson County, North Carolina, planter, son and heir at law of Edward Barwick, late of Dorchester County, Maryland, deceased, granted power of attorney to Nathan Barwick, of Dorchester County, planter, to sell lands in Dorchester County called *Tanton Deen* containing 200 acres, and 44 acres adjoining thereto, being part of *Forrest Range*. Witness: Thomas Curtis, proved by oath at New Bern, North Carolina on November 19, 1768 before Martin Howard, Esq., Chief Justice of said province. Will Tyron, Esq., His Majesty's Captain General and Governor in Chief in and over the said province.

On April 11, 1772, Nathan Barwick, of Dorchester County, Maryland, farmer, and John Barwick, of Johnson County, North Carolina, planter (the said Nathan Barwick being attorney for said John Barwick, son and heir of Edward Barwick, late of Dorchester County, deceased), conveyed to Joshua Barwick and Solomon Barwick, both of Dorchester County, a tract called *Tanton Deen* (or *Tanton Dean* or *Tenton Dean*) containing 200 acres, and part of *Forrest Range* containing 44 acres, located on the east side of the head of Choptank River, formerly in the possession of said Edward Barwick, the father, and devised by him to his wife Alice during her natural life. Acknowledged by Nathan Barwick, attorney for John Barwick, before Thomas White and Benson Stainton, witnesses and Justices of Dorchester County. [Ref: *Abstracts from Land Records of Dorchester County, Maryland, Volume H, 1772-1775*, by James A. McAllister, Jr. (1964), pp. 16, 21.]

BASHFORD

"Thomas Bashford, who probably moved to Salisbury, North Carolina from Anne Arundel County, Maryland, formed a partnership with Robert Gillespie for the purpose of speculating in town lots and county lands. They obtained lot number two in the south square (already fraudulently granted to Theodore Feltmatt) and lots three, eleven, and twelve in the east square."

"On February 21, 1759, the following information was included in the description of a deed transferring lots three, eleven, and twelve from Bashford to Alexander Dobbins and Henry Horah: '... whereas William Brandon ... died intestate and at the time of his death was possessed of a considerable personal estate, after whose death Anne Brandon (now Anne Bashford) widow and relic of said William Brandon administered on the said estate to secure the same for the use and benefit of the children of the said intestate, namely James Brandon and John Brandon, both infants, and whereas ... Thomas Bashford having from many casualties in his business become greatly indebted to sundry persons, and having from part of the money arising from the sale of the said William Brandon made many purchases of lands, and the remainder applied to his own interest and advantage ... [to] ... Alexander Dobbins ... are conveyed ... certain lands to sell in order to meet the obligation to James and John Brandon."

"There can be no doubt that Bashford engaged in questionable enterprises. That Gillespie was also involved is not clear, for he had previously dissolved his partnership with Bashford. William Brandon did not die intestate. His will was probated in 1799, causing an extended legal conflict among his heirs. Bashford evidently suppressed the will."

[Ref: *Carolina Cradle*, by Robert W. Ramsey (1964), pp. 162-163, citing Maryland Testamentary Proceedings 36:274; Rowan County Deeds II:363-365, III:533, IV:71, IV:382, XIII:309; Rowan County Minute Docket for the Court of Equity, March, 1799, pp. 173-178; and, *The Rowan Story, 1753-1953*, by James S. Brawley (Salisbury, North Carolina: Rowan Printing Company, 1954), p. 56.]

BEALL

Records at Queen Ann's Parish in Prince George's County, Maryland show that Zadock Beall, son of Robert and Jane Beall, was baptized on August 31, 1766. Records at Salisbury, North Carolina show his marriage to Nancy Begley on September 16, 1786. Zadock died in 1795 and is buried in the Lewis Graveyard in Iredell County, North Carolina. Nancy (Begley) Beall is believed to have married second to David Fitzgerald, as her grave is between his and Zadock Beall's. David Fitzgerald died in 1847, age 72. Nancy, his wife, died in 1840, age 74. Their daughter Cenith Fitzgerald, who married David Brandon, is buried in an unmarked grave. Also buried there is Brooke Beall (January, 1792 - June 30, 1792) and Henry Fitzgerald (died in 1841) and his wife Margaret Fitzgerald (died in 1878). [Ref: Information gleaned from "Lewis Graveyard With Mention of Some Settlers Along Fifth Creek, Iredell County, North Carolina" written in 1944 by Mary Elinor Lazenby (born 1875) in a booklet maintained in the Michigan Microfilm Collection (LH110) and published in the *Maryland Genealogical Society Bulletin*, Vol. 39, No. 1 (Winter, 1998), p. 94.]

BEARD

Andrew and John Beard of Anne Arundel County, Maryland (where both names appear as early as 1708) migrated south and settled in the Irish Settlement of Rowan County, North Carolina sometime between 1752 and 1762. John Beard moved to South Carolina following the death of Andrew in 1761. [Ref: *Carolina Cradle*, by Robert W. Ramsey (1964), p. 125, citing Rowan County Minutes I:77 and Rowan County Deeds VII:247.]

The will of Susannah Beard in Anne Arundel County, probated in October, 1708, mentions her sons John and Matthew Beard and daughter Rachel Beard. [Ref: *Maryland Calendar of Wills, Volume III, 1703-1713*, p. 114.]

BELL

"The Bells originated before 1720 in Cecil or Talbot County, Maryland, whence many of them removed to Philadelphia County sometime before 1739.

Accompanied by many of his kin, Thomas Bell removed to the Shenandoah Valley in 1741 or 1742, and thence to Carolina. The will of Robert Wilson of Augusta County, Virginia, written in 1745, mentions his daughter Catherine, the wife of Thomas Bell, and daughter Jennet, the wife of John Holmes. The family of John Holmes, Bell's brother-in-law, was evidently in Lower Dublin Township, Philadelphia County, between 1734 and 1741. Holmes himself moved on to Prince George's County [Maryland] in 1742 and proceeded from there to the Shenandoah Valley. Holmes was a man of considerable prominence, for he served as constable of Augusta County [Virginia] in 1747 and was appointed justice of the peace for Anson County [North Carolina] in September of the following year. Bell settled on Marlin's Creek, two miles south of James Cathey. Holmes' land was four miles to the northwest adjoining Thomas Gillespie on Sill's Creek." [Ref: *Carolina Cradle*, by Robert W. Ramsey (1964), p. 43, citing Augusta County Will Books I:1; Rowan County Deeds VI:351; Philadelphia County Court Papers, 1697-1749, 3 volumes; Philadelphia County Wills II:769, 833, 879; Prince George's County Deeds Y:503; North Carolina Land Grants VI:157, XI:5.]

The records of St. Peter's Parish in Talbot County, Maryland state that Thomas Bell, son of John Bell, died on November 22, 1708. Also, in Somerset County, Maryland, Thomas Bell, son of Anthony and Abigail Bell, was born on March 15, 1693 at Anamessex. [Ref: *Maryland Eastern Shore Vital Records, 1648-1725*, by F. Edward Wright (1982), pp. 79, 100.]

The records of St. Stephen's Parish (North Sassafras) in Cecil County, Maryland indicate that Thomas Bell, son of Richard and Jane Bell, was born on March 8, 1712. His older brother John Bell was born on February 18, 1710. [Ref: *Early Anglican Church Records of Cecil County*, by Henry C. Peden, Jr. (1990), p. 16.]

BENHAM

On "31 Oct 1767, Samuel & Tamlason Benham (Tamlason is the granddaughter and heir of Edward Carter, late of Baltimore Co., Maryland), planter, of Hanover Co., North Carolina, to Samuel Bond, miner, of Philadelphia, Pennsylvania, £0.25, to make good deed on 500 acres ... sold, 7 Oct 1750, by said Benham to Henry & Mary Garrett, (then of Johnston Co., North Carolina), who devised to Isaac Garrett, who sold to said Bond. Signed by Samuel Benham and Tamlason (x) Benham. Wit: William Ward and James Welsh, of North Carolina." [Ref: *Baltimore County, Maryland, Deed Records, Volume Four: 1767-1775*, by John Davis (1997), pp. 13-14.]

BENNET-BENNETT

In Dorchester County, Maryland, between November 14, 1769 and May 21, 1770, depositions were taken regarding the bounds of William Wheland's land called *Middleton's Grange*. The deposition of George Middleton, of Dorchester County, planter, aged about 51, mentioned the late Benjamin Wheland and William Bennet, an orphan brought up by old Richard Hart, who had been gone to Carolina about 25 years. [Ref: *Abstracts from Land Records of Dorchester County, Maryland, Volume G, 1767-1771*, by James A. McAllister, Jr. (1964), pp. 55-56.]

BENTLEY-BENTLY

On June 6, 1767, in Frederick County, Maryland, Jacob Banker recorded a deed made on June 5, 1767 between himself and Thomas Bently of County of Roan [Rowan] in the Province of North Carolina, £168 money of Pennsylvania, for a tract called *Carolina* and also one called *Addition to Carolina*, containing 108 acres and 35 acres respectively. The original tract *Carolina* contained 280 acres when taken up by Dr. Charles Carroll and was sold to Thomas Bentley in 1751. Signed by Thomas Bently before Joseph Wood and John Fee. Hannah Bentley, wife of Thomas, released her dower before Joseph Wood and Thomas Price. [Ref: *Frederick County, Maryland, Land Records Liber K Abstracts, 1765-1768*, by Patricia Abelard Andersen (1997), p. 100.]

BERRY

"James Berry, from Talbot County, Maryland, was evidently a candle maker. In 1756 [in Rowan County, North Carolina] he furnished candles for public use, receiving in payment 8s. 7d. out of the public money raised in this county." [Ref: *Carolina Cradle*, by Robert W. Ramsey (1964), p. 164, citing Maryland Wills, 1635-1777, XXIV:436, XXVII:60, and Rowan County Court Minutes I:34.]

James Berry may have been related to the William Berry who died testate in Talbot County between 1691 and 1711; his will mentioned sons William, James, and Thomas. [Ref: *Maryland Calendar of Wills, Volume III, 1703-1713*, p. 205.]

James Berry is mentioned in the will of William Goult in Talbot County in 1728. [Ref: *Maryland Calendar of Wills, Volume VI, 1726-1732*, pp. 90-91.]

One James Berry is mentioned as son-in-law and a James Berry is mentioned as a grandson in the will of Kenelm Skillington in Talbot County in 1733. [Ref: *Maryland Calendar of Wills, Volume VII, 1732-1738*, p. 240.]

James Berry is mentioned in the will of William Fookes, a Quaker, in Talbot County in 1740. [Ref: *Maryland Calendar of Wills, Volume VIII, 1738-1743*, p. 150.]

James Berry, a Quaker, died in Talbot County in May, 1746, and in his will mentioned his wife Sarah and sons John, James, Joseph, and Benjamin. [Ref: *Maryland Calendar of Wills, Volume 9, 1744-1749*, p. 69.] Also, see "Barry-Berry," q.v.

BILLETER-BILLITOR

Zebdiah Billeter married Anna Seward and served as a soldier in Maryland during the Revolutionary War. He subsequently moved to North Carolina and died after November 21, 1813. [Ref: *DAR Patriot Index, Centennial Edition, Part I* (Washington: 1990), p. 253.]

Zebdiah Billetor or Billitor enlisted as a private in the Maryland troops under Capt. Joseph Richardson in Caroline County, Maryland on August 31, 1776. James and Joseph Billetor (Billitor) also served in the 14th militia battalion. [Ref: *Revolutionary Patriots of Caroline County, Maryland, 1775-1783*, by Henry C. Peden, Jr. (1998), p. 13.]

BOSTICK-BOSTOCK

Thomas Bostick was a son of Thomas Bostick (Bostock) and his wife Mary, of Queen Anne's County, Maryland. Thomas Bostock, the father, died testate on June 5, 1732, aged about 64, and mentioned his children Samuel Bostock, Thomas Bostock, John Bostock, James Bostock, Jane Warde, Sarah Scotten, Mary Williams, Susannah Bostock, and Elizabeth Bostock in his will.

Thomas Bostick, the son, died testate in Queen Anne's County, Maryland. His will was dated September 21, 1765 and was probated on January 26, 1770. The heirs named were sons James and John and these grandchildren: James, son of son Solomon Bostick; Nathan, son of son Thomas Bostick; William Bostick; Rebecca Hadley; and, Sary Yoe. He also mentioned his wife Tamar Bostick and John Bostick, heir-at-law, now in Carolina. [Ref: Maryland Will Book 20, p. 595; Will Book 37, p. 607; Records of St. Luke's Parish, Queen Anne's County, Maryland.]

BOUDY-BONDY-BODRAY

John Boudy, Bondy or Bodray was a soldier in the Maryland Line during the Revolutionary War. He applied for a pension on January 4, 1834 in Orange County, North Carolina, aged 77, stating he had lived near Balfriar Ferry in Maryland [Bald Friar's Ferry was on the Cecil County side of the Susquehanna River in the northwestern corner of the county, across from Castleton in Harford County] at the time of his enlistment. He was born there in the fall of 1756 and in 1803 moved to Cumberland County, North Carolina. In the spring of 1804 he moved to the western part of Orange County, North Carolina and lived the first 3 years with George Albright and then with James McPherson. John died in 1836 and his widow Elizabeth applied for a pension (W5858) in Wake County, North Carolina on May 22, 1849, aged 75, stating they were married on February 4, 1793 in Wake County. An Alan Griffis signed the marriage bond with the soldier. [Ref: *Genealogical Abstracts of Revolutionary War Pension Files, Volume I: A-E*, by Virgil D. White (1990), p. 333.]

He may be the "John Bonnedy" who was a private in Major Harry Lee's Partizan Corps (Lee's Legion) in February, 1780. [Ref: *Revolutionary Patriots of Cecil County, Maryland*, by Henry C. Peden, Jr. (1991), p. 11.]

BOWERS

"James Bowers, a tavern-keeper, of Baltimore County, Maryland, bought lot number one in the south square, lot number three in the west square, and lot number one in the east square [of Salisbury, North Carolina.] Bowers lived in Salisbury in 1756 but returned to Maryland within seven years, for a deed of September, 1763, stated that James Bowers of Baltimore County, Maryland, sold lot number one in the south square of Salisbury to his son Bernard Bowers of Rowan County, North Carolina." [Ref: *Carolina Cradle*, by Robert W. Ramsey (1964), p. 163, citing Rowan County Deeds II:406, II:237-238, V:446, and Rowan Court Minutes I:38.]

"James Bower, of Baltimore County, conveyed to Bernard Beaver, son of James Beaver, for 10 pounds North Carolina money, lot #1 in south square of Salisbury on September 1, 1763. The witnesses were Benjamin Howard and Cornelius Howard." [Ref: *Rowan County, North Carolina, Deed Abstracts, Vol. II, 1762-1772*, by Jo White Linn (Salisbury, N. C.: Privately published, 1972), p. 37, citing Deed Book 5, p. 446.]

James Bowers, Nicholas Bowers, and Daniel Bowers appeared in the tax list of 1763 in Soldier's Delight Hundred, St. Thomas' Parish, Baltimore County. [Ref: *Inhabitants of Baltimore County, 1763-1774*, by Henry C. Peden, Jr. (1989), p. 1.]

BRAMBLE

Hackett or William Bramble [sic] applied for a pension (R1151) on April 27, 1819 in Cumberland County, North Carolina, stating that he had served in the Maryland Line during the Revolutionary War. In 1820 he was aged 61 and he died on the first Sunday in September, 1837. His widow Elizabeth Bramble died on March 1, 1840 and a son William Bramble, the only living child of the soldier, was aged 65 in 1855. [Ref: *Genealogical Abstracts of Revolutionary War Pension Files, Volume I: A-E*, by Virgil D. White (1990), p. 365.]

Hackett Bramble was a private in the 2nd Maryland Continental Line. He enlisted on May 4, 1778 and was still in service on November 1, 1780. Eton Bramble enlisted on May 1, 1778, David Bramble enlisted on June 7, 1779, William Bramble was discharged on April 3, 1779 (enlistment date not given), and Levin Bramble enlisted on July 16, 1780; all served in the 2nd Maryland Continental Line. [Ref: *Archives of Maryland, Volume 18*, "Muster Rolls of Maryland Troops in the American Revolution, 1775-1783," pp. 83-84.]

BRANNOCK

In March, 1734, David Brannock, of the Colony of Carolina, planter, conveyed to Walter Campbell, gentleman, of Dorchester County, a tract called *Brannock's Adventure* adjoining Peter Sharp's land on Fishing Creek in Little Choptank River, adjoining land of John Gather and containing 50 acres more or less. Also, the tracts *Addition to Brannock's Adventure* and *Chance*, both adjoining

Brannock's Adventure. Acknowledged on March 14, 1734 before Adam Muir and F. Money, Justices of Dorchester County. [Ref: *Abstracts from Land Records of Dorchester County, Maryland, Volume C, 1732-1745*, by James A. McAllister, Jr. (1962), pp. 20-21.]

BREEDEN-BREDING

On March 1, 1792, in Dorchester County, Maryland, John and Mary Breeden, of Marlborough County, South Carolina, granted to Abraham Lewis, of Dorchester County, power of attorney concerning a tract called *Cole's Venture* or *Cole's Regulation* on Cole's Creek. "(The said Mary Breding was formerly the wife of George Cole)." [See "Isaac Nichols," q.v.] Witnessed by Aaron Lewis and acknowledged before J. Winfield, Clerk of the Court, Marlborough County, South Carolina [Ref: *Abstracts of the Land Records of Dorchester County, Maryland, Volume 30 (Liber HD#3)*, by James A. McAllister, Jr. (1967), p. 63.]

BREVARD

"John G. Herndon, author of a number of articles containing references to early settlers of Carolina, has an excellent account of the history of the Brevard family. Of Huguenot origin, the Brevards made their way to Northern Ireland after the revocation of the Edict of Nantes and came to America sometime prior to 1711. They settled in Maryland, where, in 1726, John Brevard was an elder from Upper Elk [Cecil County] in attendance at a meeting of the New Castle Presbytery [Delaware.] Sometime after 1740, three of John Brevard's sons (Robert, John, and Zebulon) left Maryland (probably upon the death of their father) and set out for North Carolina. There, in 1747 or 1748, John and Robert entered upon land on the headwaters of Rocky River, located between the Davidson and Templeton families." [Ref: *Carolina Cradle*, by Robert W. Ramsey (1964), p. 48, citing "John McKnitt (c1660-1714) and Some of His Kinfolk: Alexanders-Brevards-Dales" in the *Publications of the Genealogical Society of Pennsylvania* XVI:92, and North Carolina Land Grants XI:4-5. II:10, X:310.]

For additional information on the Brevard family, see the first volume of *Marylanders to Carolina*, by Henry C. Peden, Jr. (Westminster, MD: Family Line Publications, 1994).

BROOKS

William Brooks applied for a pension (S6717) on April 22, 1834 in Rutherford County, North Carolina, stating that he was born in 1745 at "Yellowbritches" in Pennsylvania and lived in Frederick County, Maryland at the time of his enlistment in the Maryland Line. He also served in the North Carolina militia. After the war he lived in Guilford County, North Carolina for 9 years and then moved to Rutherford County. In 1834 he was aged 89 and was a resident of Sandy Run, North Carolina. He died on January 22, 1844, leaving a child (name not given in file). [Ref:

Genealogical Abstracts of Revolutionary War Pension Files, Volume I: A-E, by Virgil D. White (1990), p. 404; *Roster of Soldiers from North Carolina in the American Revolution*, published by the North Carolina Daughters of the American Revolution (Durham, 1932), pp. 433, 573.]

BROWNING

William Browning, son of Thomas Browning and Mary Ward, was born on October 20, 1709 and is probably the William who married Sarah Gooding on April 27, 1729 in St. Paul's Parish, Kent County, Maryland. They were the parents of John, William, and Mary. On November 12, 1763, William Browning, late of Kent County, Maryland, now of Craven County, North Carolina, planter, and his wife Sarah, conveyed a 105-acre tract called *Worton Mannor* to Shadrick Reed, of Kent County, Maryland, planter, it being part of a tract formerly conveyed by Richard Bennett, Esq., to Thomas Browning, father of William. [Ref: Kent County Land Records, Liber DD#1, f. 645, and Liber JS#X, f. 156; Records of St. Paul's Parish, Kent County.]

BUNDRICK-BUNDERICK-PUNDRICK-PENDRICK

"Johan Nicolaus Bundrick was born at Klein Steinhausen near Hornbach, Germany in 1717 and emigrated to Philadelphia in 1741. 'Nicholas Bundrick' married Anna Maria Miller [Mullerin] in 1744 at the German Monocacy Settlement in Frederick County, Maryland."

"In 1749 Nicholas 'Bunderick' was sued by George Valentine Matzger. The charge against him was that he owed £11 to Matzger. The warrant for arrest stated that it appeared to the Justice issuing it that Bunderick "had removed in a secret manner from the place of his abode." However, such was not the case. The final outcome was not that he had run away, but he appeared and made proper restitution as ordered by the court. During this time Nicholas Bundrick had petitioned the court for a license to keep "a publick house" in Frederick Town, and it was granted."

"In 1750 Mary Macknaul was tried for the theft of personal property from Nicholas 'Bundrick' and she was found guilty. She received five lashes as punishment and was ordered to make restitution."

"By 1754 Nicholas Bundrick was in Augusta County, Virginia as evidenced by a bill of sale for a horse which document was executed in Augusta County but recorded in Frederick County, Maryland (Book E, pp. 417-418). This record is also significant because it listed him as "ye J. Nicholas Bundrick" and stated he was a carpenter."

"By 1763 it appears that Nicholas had moved on to North Carolina. A burial monument was erected in the "Stranger's Section" of Dobb's Parish Cemetery in Winston-Salem, North Carolina and indicating "A. M. Bundrich, a married woman, who died in 1763." This appears to be the grave of Anna Maria [Miller] Mullerin Bundrick, wife of Nicholas."

"On May 16, 1763, Nicholas 'Pundrick' acquired a tract which was part of the McCulloh Grant, said land being then in Orange County, but now located between Burlington and Greensboro in Alamance County. Subsequent court records in 1763 and 1764 listed him as Nicholas 'Pendrake' and Nicholas 'Burndrake.'

"By 1767 Nicholas 'Pendriack' was in Newberry County, South Carolina near the fork of Cannon's Creek and Broad River. Nicholas Pendrick' became a loyalist during the Revolutionary War and was listed as a member of Capt. Faight Risinger's South Carolina Royalists, Savannah, Georgia, on December 1, 1778. The word "Old" was written by his name; at the time he was aged around 61 or 62 years."

"On April 18, 1782 a list of South Carolina casualties was sent to the King of England which named the men who had been murdered by "the winning side" of the Revolutionary War. Nicholas Bundrick's name appeared on this list."

[Ref: Information submitted in 1998 by Rosemary B. Dodd, 2 Oak Lane SW, Glen Burnie, Maryland 21061-3461; *The Bundrick Bunch*, by Max L. Tatum, pp. 6-7; *This Was The Life: Excerpts from the Judgment Records of Frederick County, Maryland, 1748-1765*, by Millard Milburn Rice, pp. 43-46, 58; *Monocacy and Catoctin*, by C. E. Schildknecht, ed., Volume I, pp. 102, 166, and Volume II, p. 43; *Loyalists in the Southern Campaign*, Volume I, by Murtie June Clark; *Genealogical Index to Frederick County, Maryland: The First Hundred Years*, Volume I, by John Stanwood Martin, p. 242.]

BURCH

Lincoln County, North Carolina historian Alfred Nixon, Esq., stated on February 22, 1902 in an address to the Anna Jackson Book Club in the hall of the Mary Wood School in Lincolnton entitled "Beattie's Ford, A Scotch-Irish Settlement on the Catawba" [See the *Charlotte Daily Observer*, June 1, 1902] that James King married Elizabeth Emmerson in Maryland. They settled on land adjacent to Unity Presbyterian Church in the Beatties Ford Community (in northeast Lincoln County near the Catawba River, now Lake Norman). Their daughter Elizabeth King married Richard Burch by a Lincoln County marriage bond dated July 21, 1800 and their children are listed in Elizabeth's petition for dowry rights in 1838 (North Carolina Archives in Raleigh).

Elizabeth Burch's petition was filed in the January Session, 1838 of the Lincoln County Court and stated, in part, "that since the last term of this court Richard Burch, her husband, died and left your petitioner his widow and Richard, John, James, William, Sarah, Mary Randall his heirs at law, that he died seized of a tract of land in Lincoln County aforesaid on the waters of Sligh's Creek, joining Abram Wamack [Womack] and Charles Ragan ... [and] ... her said husband died intestate ..."

From census and other records, Thomas F. Burch also appears to have been a son. The 1880 U. S. Census entry for James Burch in Lincoln County, North Carolina states that his parents were born in Maryland. They were likely from the Prince George's, Charles, and Calvert Counties since Kings, Emersons, and Burches were all in this area.

[Ref: Information compiled in 1998 by Ray A. Yount, 10031 Shortest Day Road NW, La Vale, MD 21502-6011, or E-Mail: alby6@juno.com.]

BURCHFIELD

"At the July 20, 1784 estate sale of Robert Burchfield in Lincoln County, North Carolina, the buyers included Elizabeth Burchfield, Ezekiah Hyatt, Edward Letherhood, Thomas Young, Christopher Sewel, Nicholas Trosper, I---. Cunningham, Lydia Burchfield, Elisha Sheril, John Oliphant, Robert Burchfield, Joseph Allen, and James Henry. This Robert Burchfield was killed by the Cherokee Indians in 1783. His administrators were Elizabeth Burchfield and James Henry."

"A son, also Robert (whom I will call Robert III), applied for a Revolutionary War pension and stated he was born in 1759 [December 18, on Pipe Creek] in Baltimore County, Maryland [lived in Rowan County, North Carolina at the time of his enlistment and married Elizabeth Hill in March, 1787 in Burke County, North Carolina] and his father (not named) was killed about 1783 [Robert, the son, moved to Ripley County, Indiana and died on October 29, 1844.]"

"I believe the Robert who died in 1783 (whom I will refer to as Robert Jr.) was the son of the Robert Burchfield who was born February 27, 1710 (St. George's Parish, Baltimore County) in Maryland who married Ann Clark on December 3, 1735. Robert, Jr. sells land in Frederick County, Maryland on Sam's Creek on March 27, 1772 to Jacob Crumbecker. His wife, Elizabeth, relinquishes her dower rights. Robert Barnes (in a communication to Loretta Berry in the mid 1980's) believes the 1772 deed refers to Robert, Sr. and that Elizabeth, surname Justice according to him, was a second wife."

"However, I interpret this deed differently. When he transfers 'Robert Burchfield's interest' I believe he is referring to his father rather than to himself. The fact that the wife of the Robert, Jr. in North Carolina was named Elizabeth is consistent with this interpretation. Furthermore, it seems unlikely that the Robert killed by Indians while on a scouting party in 1783 would be the one born in 1710. Seventy-three years of age seems rather old for such an activity. The Ezekiah Hyatt who buys at the sale was the brother-in-law of Robert Burchfield, Jr. Ezekiah Hyatt married Mary Burchfield on February 16, 1769 at Evangelical Lutheran Church in Frederick, Maryland."

"A brother of Elizabeth Justice Burchfield, Hans Justice, may have also gone to North Carolina. A Hans Justice received a land patent on the east side of Buffalo Creek in what is now western Lincoln County, near Burke County, North Carolina, January 30, 1773 (NC Crown Patent B22-223, 225). John Justice in a Frederick County, Maryland will, October 18, 1775, probated October 22, 1776, names both a daughter Mary Burchfield and a son Hans Justice among other heirs. The Burchfields in North Carolina moved from Lincoln County to Burke County. There, Burchfield and Justices appear near each other in many land transactions."

"There was also a Thomas Burchfield in Burke County who lived near the Robert Burchfield family, who I believe to have been a brother of Robert, Sr., but no proof. Thomas is said to have married Sarah Ledgerwood. His family was involved in an Indian massacre about 1765. One son was killed, a daughter was abducted and never heard from again, and another daughter Lydia (my ancestor), about 2 1/2 years old, was scalped. However, she survived and raised a large family. The story is told about how she always wore a cap on her head, and how friendly Indians in later years would visit her to see the scar, considering it a miracle that she had survived."

"There were other Burchfields appearing in southwestern North Carolina and northwestern South Carolina records having the given names Adam, Joseph, James, and John. These could be half brothers of Robert Burchfield, Sr. In Robert Barnes' *Baltimore County Families, 1659-1759* he states that Thomas Burchfield married (2) Joanna ---- and had sons John, Joseph, and James. There was also a son Adam by the first marriage who is said to have died young. Thomas may have named a later son Adam from this second marriage."

[Ref: Information compiled by Ray A. Yount, 10031 Shortest Day Road NW, La Vale, MD 21502-6011, or E-Mail: alby6@juno.com.]

Additional information on Burchfields in North Carolina was compiled by Ray A. Yount (cited above) as follows:

Sgt. Adam Burchfield was paid in 1771 for service against the Cherokees under an officer of Tryon County.

Thomas Burchfield signed a petition to form a new county (Burke) from Rowan.

Joseph Burtchfield and James Burtchfield signed a petition concerning the North Carolina-South Carolina boundary.

Adam Burchfield witnessed the will of David Robertson of Tryon County in October, 1771.

Robert Burchfield deeded land to Francis Cunningham of Lincoln County, on July 12, 1784, in Burke County. This land had been granted to Robert Burchfield, Sr. on March 14, 1780.

Adam Burchfield was in Mecklinburg [sic] County before 1767 and was granted land in Tryon County on Thickety Creek in 1773, as was Joseph Burchfield in 1771 and James Burchfield in 1772.

Nathaniel Burchfield, a Revolutionary War soldier, settled in Greasy Cove near Erwin, Tennessee and was said to have died in 1863, aged 107.

Thomas Burchfield in North Carolina may have had a son Nathan.

[Ref: Information gleaned by Ray A. Yount (cited above) from these sources: *North Carolina Colonial Records*, Vol. 8, p. 517; Vol. 9, p. 91; Vol. 9, pp. 1260-

1262; Vol. 11, pp. 250-252; *North Carolina Land Grants in South Carolina*, by Brent Holcomb; *Tennessee Cousins*, by Worth Ray; *Deed Abstracts of Tryon, Lincoln, and Rutherford Counties, 1769-1786*, by Brent Holcomb.]

Meshack Burchfield applied for a pension (S16668) in Marion County, Missouri on May 7, 1833, stating he was born in 1762 in Baltimore County, Maryland, lived in Burke County, North Carolina during the war, and there his father was killed by Indians. Meshack later moved to Warren County, Kentucky and Lincoln County, Missouri and Marion County, Missouri. It should be noted that the pension application (R1444) of Robert Burchfield was rejected (probably due to lack of proof of military service). His widow Elizabeth Burchfield (neé Hill) also applied in 1845 and died on September 20, 1848, leaving children Mary Roberts, Sally Kelly, Betsey O'Neal, John Burchfield, Nancy Whitam or Whitain, Kitty Smith, and Robert Burchfield.] [Ref: *Genealogical Abstracts of Revolutionary War Pension Files, Volume I: A-E*, by Virgil D. White (1990), p. 466.]

BURGES-BURGESS

James Lindsey recorded a power of attorney in Frederick County, Maryland on September 19, 1760, as follows: "I, John Burges, of Orange County, North Carolina, formerly an inhabitant of Frederick County, Maryland, for diverse good causes appoint well beloved friend James Lindsey of the County of Frederick, colony of Virginia, to act as attorney for me, to make a deed for 50 acres of land called *Stoney Hall*, which tract I, the said John Burges, bought of from William Davis, 19 May 1753." Signed John Burges (his mark) before Benjamin Stone, George Nickelson, and John Lindsey, Jr. Benjamin Stone and George Nickelson attested to power of attorney before Thomas Prather and Moses Chapline.

On September 17, 1760, James Lindsay, of Frederick County, Colony of Virginia, for £90 current money of Maryland paid by Thomas Kelly, sold, by a power of attorney from John Burges, of Orange County, Province of North Carolina, a 50-acre tract called *Stoney Hall*. Signed by James Lindsay before Thomas Prather and Moses Chapline. Recorded by Thomas Kelly in Frederick County, Maryland on September 19, 1760. [Ref: *Frederick County, Maryland Land Records, Liber F Abstracts, 1756-1761*, by Patricia Abelard Andersen (1995), p. 108.]

BURK

James Burk and Thomas Burk may have originated in Baltimore County or Kent County, Maryland, or they may have moved west from Bradford Township, Chester County, Pennsylvania. Thomas Burk was in Frederick County by 1749, and apparently James Burk as well, as both were in the Shenandoah Valley by 1750. From there they migrated to the forks of the Yadkin River in western North Carolina. [Ref: *Carolina Cradle*, by Robert W. Ramsey (1964), p. 78, citing Probate Records of Maryland, 1635-1776, 18:164, 20:466, 28:208; Chester County Warrants II:307, 542; Surry County Wills II:1, V:105.]

It is interesting to note that a Thomas Burke was named as the father of the child of Sarah Owings in June, 1733 in Baltimore County, Maryland. [Ref: *Baltimore County Families, 1659-1759*, by Robert W. Barnes (1989), p. 85.]

BUTTNER

"Adam (and probably Peter) Büttner was in Frederick County, Maryland between 1743 and 1752. His disappearance from Frederick County records in 1753 may mark the year of his departure for Rowan County," North Carolina. [Ref: *Carolina Cradle*, by Robert W. Ramsey (1964), p. 91.]

In Frederick County, August Court, 1750, the Grand Jurors presented Micajah Plummer for stealing a colt belonging to Adam Büttner on the information of Joshua Barton, John Carmack, John Martin, Jr., William Beatty, Catherine Büttner, Anna Büttner, James Büttner, Jeremiah Elroade, Benjamin Barton, Leah Büttner, Adam Büttner, and Martha Büttner. [Ref: *This Was The Life: Excerpts from the Judgment Records of Frederick County, Maryland, 1748-1765*, by Millard Milburn Rice (1979), p. 49.]

CALDWELL

John Caldwell, mariner, died in Somerset County, Maryland and left a will dated March 28, 1775 which was proved on April 25, 1775. In his list of legatees (which included nieces and nephews with the surnames of Venables, Caldwell, Hitch, and Sanford) he bequeathed land to his nephew Spencer Caldwell, of North Carolina. [Ref: *Maryland Calendar of Wills, Volume 16, 1774-1777*, p. 65.]

CAMPBELL

Moses (Mosess) Campbell married Rebecca Hughson (Hughston) in June, 1751, in St. John's Parish, Baltimore County, Maryland. John Hughston wrote his will in Harford County, Maryland on October 3, 1784 (probated October 23, 1784) and mentioned his mother Jane Hughston (lot in town of Joppa), son Thomas Waltham Hughston, daughter Elizabeth Hughston, and "the children of my sister Rebecca Hughston in North Carolina." [Ref: Harford County Wills Liber AJ#2, f. 331; *Maryland Marriages, 1634-1777*, by Robert W. Barnes (1975), p. 28.]

The children of Moses and Rebecca Campbell, born in Baltimore County, Maryland, were as follows:

(1) William Campbell, born in September, 1753;
(2) John Campbell, born in October, 1755; and
(3) Mary Campbell, born in October, 1757.

[Ref: *Baltimore County Families, 1659-1759*, by Robert W. Barnes (1989), p. 91]

Moses Campbell witnessed the will of William Hughes of Baltimore County on February 14, 1765 (probated in Harford County on March 26, 1776). Moses also witnessed a lease between William Hughes and James Bonar on January 10, 1765. [Ref: Harford County Wills Liber AJ No. 2, f. 271; *Baltimore County, Maryland Deed Records, Volume Three: 1755-1767*, by John Davis (1996), p. 290.]

CARTER

"James Carter was probably the son of James and Susannah Carter of Southampton Township in Bucks County, Pennsylvania. Sometime prior to 1736 he made his way into the Appoquinimink Creek district on the border between Pennsylvania (now Delaware) and Maryland. A certain William Williams, then living in the area, made the following statement on April 28, 1739, when interrogated regarding the boundary controversy between Maryland and Pennsylvania:

"About two years ago and since, part of the said land within the fork of the main branch of Appoquinak [sic] Creek has been entered on by one Mathew Donohue, James Carter, Augustine Noland, and James Poor, pretending to be tenants of one Mr. James Paul Heath of Cecil County and Province of Maryland." The deposition of Thomas Rothwell, living in the same area, was to the effect that "a certain James Carter, also pretending to be a tenant of the aforesaid James Heath, entered on the aforesaid tract of land (though often required to forbear) and built a house about 200 yards within the line and cleared some of the said land, and after left it when said small settlement was entered on about four months ago by one James Poor."

"In 1740, James Carter was caught in the midst of this turmoil [a veritable hotbed of religious conflict] and found himself 'a languishing prisoner [for debt] in the Cecil County Gaol.' Late the same year, due largely to the influence of William Rumsey, Carter was released. The association between the two men was very close; indeed, the prominent Marylander may be regarded as Carter's patron. Rumsey loaned considerable sums of money to the vigorous millwright and taught him the secrets of surveying. Moreover, Carter witnessed Rumsey's will, which was probated in 1743."

"Bereft of his patron, Carter moved to Augusta County, Virginia in 1744 and settled in the Shenandoah Valley on the Great Calfpasture River. He built a mill and apparently prospered before moving on to the Yadkin in 1747. Carter seems to have located at first on the river itself, but obtained a 350-acre tract on the future site of Salisbury in 1753. He spent the remainder of his life in Rowan County [North Carolina] and died there in 1765."

"Of the other initial settlers, at least seven were close friends of Carter and had known him for many years before moving to North Carolina. They were Gamble, Dunn, Bryan, Davis, Hughes, Forbush, and Linville. Robert Gamble, originally from Bucks County, Pennsylvania, was James Carter's son-in-law. He was in Augusta County in 1746 and removed to North Carolina in 1747 or 1748, undoubtedly with

Carter. Gamble settled on the west bank of the Yadkin near the trading ford, but moved to South Carolina sometime between 1756 and 1765."

[Ref: *Carolina Cradle*, by Robert W. Ramsey (1964), pp. 26-28, citing Bucks County Will Abstracts, 1685-1795, p. 19; Calendar of New Jersey Wills, XXX:47, 184, and XXXIII:461; Rowan County Court of Pleas and Quarterly Session Minutes I:31; Rowan County Wills A:43; Pennsylvania Archives, First Series, I:563-564; *Maryland Calendar of Wills, Volume VIII, 1738-1743*, p. 200.]

James Carter was a private in Capt. Zebulon Hollingsworth, Company of Foot in Cecil County in 1740. [Ref: *Inhabitants of Cecil County, Maryland, 1749-1774*, by Henry C. Peden, Jr. (1993), p. 51.]

Mary Carter, daughter of James and Dinah Carter, was born on November 11, 1740 in St. Stephen's (North Sassafras) Parish in Cecil County. [Ref: *Early Anglican Church Records of Cecil County*, by Henry C. Peden, Jr. (1990), p. 38.]

CATHEY

"James Cathey's first place of residence seems to have been Cecil County, Maryland, where he purchased a tract of land from James Scott sometime between 1719 and 1724. In the latter year he was referred to as James Cathey of Chester County, Pennsylvania, but his son George was living in Cecil County as late as 1734. By 1736, James and George were in Lancaster County [Pennsylvania], the home of John Cathey. Accompanied by his sons George, William, and Andrew, James Cathey removed to the Shenandoah Valley in 1738, where the family settled on a tract of land adjoining the northern boundary of the Beverly Patent. John Cathey died in Lancaster County in 1743, whereupon his son Alexander joined the other Cathey's in Virginia. Sometime prior to 1751, William Cathey died, leaving his land in the Shenandoah Valley to an older brother (John) still living in Ireland. The latter came to America to claim the land, but moved to North Carolina [present day Mecklenburg County] upon discovering that the rest of the family had done so. John Cathey made his home on the east bank of the Catawba near the mouth of Davidson's Creek." [Ref: *Carolina Cradle*, by Robert W. Ramsey (1964), pp. 37-38, citing Cecil County Deeds IV:128; Lancaster Common Pleas, Volume 11, 1731-1732; Lancaster County Wills A-1:77; Orange County Deeds III:7; *The Tinkling Spring, Headwaters of Freedom: A Study of the Church and Her People*, by Howard M. Wilson (Richmond, VA: Garrett and Massie, Inc., 1954), p. 472.]

CHAMBERS

"Members of the Chambers family settled by 1726 in the Cumberland Valley and in Derry Township, Lancaster County, Pennsylvania. Henry Chambers left one of these groups and proceeded to Prince George's County, Maryland, before 1739. He was in Carolina by April, 1752, where he bought 640 acres on Third Creek from Thomas Gillespie." [Ref: *Carolina Cradle*, by Robert W. Ramsey (1964), pp. 125-

126, citing Prince George's County Judgments, 1739, p. 512, and Anson County Deeds 1:169.]

CHAMNESS

On "31 Aug 1764, Anthony & Sarah Chamness, gentleman, of North Carolina to Joseph Ensor, of Maryland, £10, 100 acres ... east side of Jones Falls. Signed by Anthony (x) Chamness and Sarah (x) Chamness. Wit: William (x) Cole, Thomas Stevens and Joseph Chamness." On the same day a similar conveyance was transacted between Anthony and Sarah Chamness and William Cole, of Baltimore Co., Maryland, for 220 acres. [Ref: *Baltimore County, Maryland, Deed Records, Volume Three: 1755-1767*, by John Davis (1996), pp. 281-282.]

Anthony Chamness married Sarah Cole, daughter of Joseph Cole, on November 24, 1735 in Baltimore County. Anthony may have been born circa 1713 in London. Sarah was born on May 1, 1718. They moved to Frederick County, Maryland, and then to Orange County, North Carolina. [Ref: *Baltimore County Families, 1659-1759*, by Robert W. Barnes (1989), p. 103.]

Anthony Chamnis and Sarah Coale married on November 24, 1735 in St. Paul's Parish, Baltimore County, Maryland. [Ref: *Records of St. Paul's Parish, Volume I*, by Bill and Martha Reamy (1988), p. 32.]

CHANCE

Samuel Chance applied for a Revolutionary War pension on January 25, 1834, aged 86, in Wayne County, Indiana, stating he was born in 1748 in Queen Anne's County, Maryland. At the age of 14 he moved with his father (unnamed) to North Carolina and settled between the Neuse and Kent Rivers, now Wayne County, North Carolina. He lived there 6 or 7 years and also enlisted in the war in North Carolina. In 1797 he moved to Richmond County, North Carolina and in 1831 moved to Wayne County, Indiana. His pension application (R1846) was rejected. [Ref: *Genealogical Abstracts of Revolutionary War Pension Files, Volume I: A-E*, by Virgil D. White (1990), p. 594.]

Samuel Chance resided in Centreville, Indiana. His pension was rejected because six months' service was required in order to be eligible for benefits and he served only five months. [Ref: *Rejected or Suspended Applications for Revolutionary War Pensions* (Report of the Secretary of the Interior, 1852), p. 406.]

CHEW

Thomas S. Chew wrote his will in Harford County, Maryland on January 12, 1820 (probated on March 13, 1821). He stated, in part, "I bequeath to my son Thomas S. Chew my farm in North Carolina, Carteret County, with all and singular my claim, interest and title which I hold to the same, the same being derived by the devise of my grandfather Col. Henry Chew, deceased, as willfully appears by

referring to the records in Carteret County Court, to him, his heirs and assigns forever, and a riding horse saddle, and no more
of my estate." [Ref: Harford County, Maryland Wills Liber SR No. 1, ff. 234-236.]

It appears that Thomas Chew, son of Thomas, may have sold the land in North Carolina (or lived there a short time) because he later moved to Mississippi, as noted here: Thomas Sheredine Chew, son of Joseph Chew (1719-1753) and grandson of Henry Chew (born 1693, ancestor of the Harford County Chews), married Elizabeth Morgan, daughter of William and Cassandra Morgan, and died on February 15, 1821. His son Thomas became a physician in Baltimore, moved to Mississippi, and died unmarried. [Ref: "The Chew Family," by Francis B. Culver (1935), published in *Maryland Genealogies, Volume II* (1980), pp. 254-272.]

CLARK

On October 9, 1734, a power of attorney was recorded at the request of William Clark in Prince George's County, Maryland, as follows: William Trewher, of Edgecomb, North Carolina, guardian of Thomas Clark, aged about 15 years, son of Thomas Clark, deceased, appoints William Clark to take 100 acres into his possession until Thomas Clark arrives at full age of 21. Signed by William Trewher, guardian, and witnessed by J. Edwards and Richard Clark (made his mark) on September 30, 1734.

On March 8, 1734/5, the following was recorded at the request of William Clark in Prince George's County, Maryland: September 30, 1734: Indenture between Richard Clark, living in South Carolina, near Charles Town, Edestone County, planter, and William Clark, planter, for £25, a parcel called *Clark's Fancy*, containing 72 acres. Richard Clarke made his mark and witnesses were Margery Belt and Thomas Sprigg.

On March 8, 1734/5, the following was recorded in Prince George's County, Maryland at the request of William Clark: The land of Daniel Clark, late of Anne Arundel County, deceased, called *Clark's Fancy*, willed to his 3 sons, Thomas, William and Richard Clark; Richard being the youngest divided *Clark's Fancy* as follows (diagram of tract division). Memorandum: September 19, 1733 - Richard Clark surveyed the above land and divided according to his father's last will and testament. William Clark the second brother being constituted attorney to act for the orphan Thomas Clark, son of Thomas Clark, the oldest brother, deceased, by William Trunker, guardian of said orphan. William Clark and Richard Clark made their marks, and witnesses were Richard Isaac and Joseph Peach.

On March 26, 1755, the following was recorded in Prince George's County at the request of William Clark: Indenture between George Iams, of Anne Arundel County, Maryland, planter, and Thomas Clark, of Edgecomb Precinct, North Carolina, orphan; for £20 Thomas Clark, deceased, father of Thomas Clark, orphan, and £2.10 paid by William Clark, uncle, deputed to act for the orphan; tract called *James' Choice* on the southwest side of Patuxent River near Henry Fitch's wading place; mentions George Iams and Richard Iams and *Charles' Marsh*; containing 100 acres. Signed by George Jiams and witnessed by James Beck and Conrad Schomaker. Acknowledged by George Iams and Elizabeth his wife, March 26, 1735. [Ref: *The Land Records of Prince George's County, Maryland, 1733-1739*, by Elise Greenup Jourdan (1996), pp. 35, 44, 45, 47.]

CLARY-CLAREY

Daniel Clary, son of John Clary and Elizabeth Haly, was born circa 1710 in Maryland and married Eleanor Deveron or Devern, daughter of William Deveron or Devern, by 1733 in Prince George's County, Maryland, at which time the said William had died testate. Daniel and Eleanor had the following children:

(1) Ruth Clary (born April 10, 1734 or 1735);

(2) William Clary (born 1736);

(3) Eleanor Clary (born 1738, married Joseph Summers, and migrated to South Carolina);

(4) Elizabeth Clary (born January 11, 1740 and probably died young);

(5) Mary Clary (born March 23, 1742); Levine Clary (born March 3, 1744);

(6) Sarah Clary (born March 1, 1746 and married Samuel Swearingen in Maryland; their children included Massom Swearingen, born December 19, 1761 in Maryland);

(7) Daniel Clary, Jr. (born 1748); Ann Clary (born May 2, 1750);

(8) Kasandra Clary (born April 7, 1752, married Timothy Thomas, and died March 23, 1827; both are buried in Newberry County, South Carolina);

(9) Vachel Clary (born 1755);

(10) Basil Clary (born December 25, 1756);

(11) Linny Clary (born July 12 or 14, 1761).

Daniel Clary was listed as a resident of Prince George's County in 1740 as noted in his brother John Clary's testamentary proceedings in Anne Arundel County (John Clary's widow Mary married Benjamin Browne by 1743 as noted in an administration account filed that year). The Rock Creek area where Daniel lived became Frederick County in 1748 and he acquired a 100-acre tract called *Buck Bottom* in 1749. During the 1750's he acquired tracts called *Clary's Delight* and *Valley of Strife* and in 1755 Daniel Clary of Frederick County sold part of *Buck Bottom* to his younger brother Benjamin Clary of Baltimore County. In 1763 he sold the rest of this tract to Charles Hammond, Jr. of Anne Arundel County.

After 1773 Daniel disappears from the Frederick County debt books and is last mentioned in Maryland as a debtor to the estate of Col. William Young of Baltimore County in 1774. Migrating southward to the Ninety-Six District in South Carolina, he made his home in what is now Newberry County and acquired land on the Saluda River. At the time of the Revolutionary War, sentiment in the Carolinas was divided. In the backcountry, such as Ninety-Six District, many citizens wanted no part of the Revolution and were disaffected with the American cause. Those who lived in the Dutch Fork between the Broad and Saluda Rivers were among them. A brigade of loyalists was organized in Ninety-Six District and six regiments were formed in

1775, one being the Dutch Fork Regiment of Col. Daniel Clary. Among the records of South Carolina under the Acts of 1783-1784, which were acts to rescind the order to confiscate property because of Tory sympathy, Daniel Clarey is listed. Also in the South Carolina Act of 1784 is a list of persons taken off the confiscation list and disqualified from holding office and Daniel Clarey is listed. He died around 1795 in Newberry County.

[Ref: Information compiled before 1998 by Rosemary B. Dodd, 2 Oak Lane SW, Glen Burnie, Maryland 21061-3461, citing *Clary Genealogy: Four Early American Lines and Related Families*, by Ralph Shearer Rowland and Star Wilson Rowland; *Provincial and General Court Deed Index 139* (1658-1790), Liber DD, No. 2 (17266), folio 78; *The Maryland Gazette, 1727-1761*, by Karen Mauer Green, page 133; Frederick County Will Book A, No. 1, page 187; *South Carolina Loyalists in the American Revolution*, by Robert S. Lambert, page 111; *Loyalists in the Southern Campaign*, Volumes I and III, by Murtie June Clark.]

The will of William Deveron was written on April 9, 1733 and probated in Prince George's County, Maryland on October 11, 1733. He mentioned his wife Eleanor Deveron, daughters Eleanor Clary and Mary Clary, and sons-in-law John Clary and Daniel Clary. [Ref: *Maryland Calendar of Wills, Volume VII, 1732-1738*, p. 45.]

The will of Eleanor Deveron was written on December 12, 1743 and probated in Prince George's County on November 19, 1744. She mentioned her daughter Eleanor Clary, son-in-law Daniel Clary, granddaughters Ruth Clary and Mary Clary (daughters of Daniel Clary), and grandson William Clary. [Ref: *Maryland Calendar of Wills, Volume 9, 1744-1749*, p. 3.]

CLYMER

Sara Clymer was born in 1795 in North Carolina and died in 1865 in Smith County, Tennessee. She married Alexander McClanahan, son of Thomas Marshall McClanahan, probably in 1814 or 1815 in Bourbon County, Kentucky. He was born in 1785 and died in 1855 in Smith County, Tennessee. Their oldest son Phillip McClanahan was born in 1816 in Kentucky and they moved to Smith County, Tennessee circa 1829. Sarah Clymer may have been the daughter of Cain Clymer (born 1781) or James Clymer (born 1750) in Queen Anne's County, Maryland. [Ref: Query from Forrest G. Gregory, 1310 Estatewood Drive, Brandon, Florida 33511 in *Kentucky Pioneer Genealogy and Records*, Volume 2, No. 3 (July, 1980), p. 162.]

There is no mention of the aforementioned Sarah Clymer, Cain Clymer, or Alexander McClanahan in the exhaustive study entitled *The Clymer Clan of Maryland, Delaware and Points West* as published in 1987 by Anita L. Ockert (8818 Higdon Drive, Vienna, Virginia 22181). It should be pointed out, however, that although there were families named Clymer, Clymor, or Climer on the Eastern Shore of Maryland as early as 1669, they were also in Kent County, Delaware and

Bucks County, Pennsylvania before 1790 (as evident by the First U. S. Census taken in that year).

COMMINS-CUMMINS

Harmon Commins applied for a pension (S21701) on March 25, 1819 in Pendleton District, South Carolina, stating that he had lived in Frederick County, Maryland when he enlisted at Sharpsburg in Washington County, Maryland for service in the Virginia Line during the Revolutionary War. In 1832 he was living in Anderson District, South Carolina. [Ref: *Genealogical Abstracts of Revolutionary War Pension Files, Volume I: A-E*, by Virgil D. White (1990), p. 724.]

"Harman Cummins, or Harmond Commins, or Commonds" served in the 8th Virginia Continental Line during the Revolutionary War. [Ref: *Historical Register of Virginians in the Revolution, 1775-1783*, by John H. Gwathmey (1938), pp. 171, 199.]

"Harmon Cummin" was taken prisoner and kept aboard a prison ship. [Ref: *Roster of South Carolina Patriots in the American Revolution*, by Bobby Gilmer Ross (1983), p. 224.]

COOK

Jesse Cook was born circa 1763, probably in Maryland (possibly in present-day Caroline County) and migrated to North Carolina where he married Prudence Cranor circa 1793, probably in Guilford County. She was a daughter of Moses and Sarah Cranor who migrated from Caroline County to North Carolina between 1778 and 1783. The children of Jesse and Prudence Cook were as follows:

(1) John C. Cook (born on November 10, 1783 in North Carolina; married first to Elizabeth Selvin or Selivan, second to Lucinda McQuary, and third to Elizabeth Cushman; John died on January 26, 1847 in Green Township, Hancock County, Indiana and was buried in the Cook Cemetery);

(2) Prudence Cook (born circa 1785-1790, married first to William Manlove and second to John McKinkey in 1824; Prudence died after 1856 in Fayette County, Indiana and was buried in Lick Creek Cemetery); and,

(3) Pheba or Phoebe Cook (born on June 5, 1792 in North Carolina, married William Gilliam on December 16, 1815; she lived with James B. Gilliam and wife Christina in 1860, and died on May 24, 1870 in Whitley, Indiana).

Jesse Cook appears in the 1790 and 1798 censuses for the Salisbury District of Guilford County, North Carolina; his second wife was named Sarah. They moved to Fayette County, Indiana by February 27, 1830 (land record) and were original landowners in Rush County in 1831 (Certificate #10777; Deed Book E:104). In November, 1835, Jess and Sarah Cook sold 27 acres of their first property to Absalom Manlove. If this Jesse Cook was the father of Prudence Cook Manlove, then Absalom Manlove would be his grandson.

[Ref: Information compiled by Mrs. Donna J. Ottley, 12011 Portage Drive, Anchorage, Alaska 99515 (winter address: 2132 Leisure World, Mesa, Arizona 85206) in 1998.]

COVINGTON

Sarah Hopper, widow, died in Queen Anne's County, Maryland and left a will dated January 25, 1774 and probated February 8, 1775. Among her list of legatees (no relationships were given), she bequeathed £25 to Sarah Covington, daughter of John and Hannah Covington, now in Carolina. [Ref: *Maryland Calendar of Wills, Volume 16, 1774-1777*, p. 49.]

CRAIG-CRAGH-CRAGE

"The Craig or Cragh family settled in Freehold, Monmouth County, New Jersey, before 1721. Members of this family were in Kent County, Maryland by 1733. Archibald and Mary Craig, with their son James, left Maryland (probably accompanied by John Howard) sometime prior to 1756 and proceeded to the Yadkin Valley" in western North Carolina. [Ref: *Carolina Cradle*, by Robert W. Ramsey (1964), p. 107, citing *Calendar of New Jersey Wills, in Documents Relating to the Colonial History of the State of New Jersey*, 1st Series, Volumes XXX and XXXIII; Maryland Testamentary Proceedings 30:353.]

The children of Arcabil (Archabil) and Elizabeth Crage were born in Shrewsbury Parish, Kent County, Maryland, as follows:

(1) Mary Crage (born March 27, 1725);
(2) William Crage (born March 7, 1728); and,
(3) Elizabeth Crage (born March 11, 1729/30).

[Ref: *Maryland Eastern Shore Vital Records, 1648-1725*, by F. Edward Wright (1982), p. 45; *Maryland Eastern Shore Vital Records, 1726-1750*, by F. Edward Wright (1983), p. 2.]

There were Craigs in Cecil County, Maryland, by May, 1733, at which time James Craig was an executor of Humphry Alcock, deceased, who, by his will, assigned his son John Alcock to James Craig to learn "the joyner's trade." Also, James Craige witnessed the will of Dr. Peter Bouchelle in Cecil County on August 22, 1735. [Ref: *Maryland Calendar of Wills, Volume VII, 1732-1738*, pp. 38, 186.]

CRANOR-CRANER

"It appears that the Cranors may have migrated to Maryland from Delaware and then to North Carolina. Moses Cranor gave his age as 41 in a deposition in Caroline County in 1774 and he appears in the census for Choptank Hundred in 1778. He subsequently appears on the membership rolls of Abbott's Creek Baptist Church in Rowan (now Davidson) County, North Carolina in 1783, and in Cheraw District, South Carolina in the 1790 census (with 2 white females). Moses died testate by June 22, 1793 in Marlboro County, South Carolina (Will Book A:20).

His wife Sarah ---- was born circa 1739 in Talbot County, Maryland and died testate between July, 1797 and May, 1801 in Guilford County, North Carolina. Their children were as follows:

(1) Thomas Cranor (born circa 1754 in Maryland, married Hannah Trotter, and died testate on April 5, 1795 in Guilford County, North Carolina);

(2) Elizabeth Cranor (married Henry Ford); Prudence Cranor (married Jesse Cook; not mentioned in her mother's will when recorded in 1801);

(3) Sarah Cranor (married ---- Lister); and,

(4) Moses Cranor (born December 28, 1769, married Jane Trotter, died on May 9, 1858 in Christian County, Kentucky, and buried in Christian Privilage Cemetery)."
[Ref: Information compiled in 1998 by Mrs. Donna J. Ottley, 12011 Portage Drive, Anchorage, Alaska 99515 (winter address: 2132 Leisure World, Mesa, Arizona 85206), and Irma Harper's *Heirs and Legatees of Caroline County* (Westminster, MD: Family Line Publications, 1989), p. 8.]

Charles Craner, Sr., planter, of Mispillion Hundred, died testate in Kent County, Delaware between August 6, 1781 and April 19, 1783. His heirs were wife Elizabeth Craner, daughters Lucresey Jester, Mary Craner and Dorcas Craner, and sons Charles, Thomas, Samuel, and Moses Craner. [Ref: *Calendar of Kent County, Delaware Probate Records, 1680-1800*, by Leon deValinger, Jr. (1944), p. 348; reprinted by Family Line Publications in 1994.]

Sarah Cranor died in Guilford County, North Carolina, leaving a will dated July 15, 1797 and probated in May, 1801. Her named heirs were: grandson Joshua Cranor (son of Moses Cranor); son Moses Cranor (to whom she left the family Bible); grandson John Cranor; granddaughters Prudence and Phebe Cranor; grandson Joseph Listor; granddaughter Mary Lister; daughter Elizabeth Ford; granddaughter Prudence Ford; son Thomas Cranor's estate; grandsons William Cranor, Moses Cranor, and Thomas Ford. Executor: Henry Ford. [Ref: *Guilford County, North Carolina, Will Abstracts, 1771-1841*, compiled, indexed and published by Irene B. Webster, p. 12.]

Thomas Cranor died in Guilford County, North Carolina in 1796, leaving a will dated April 5, 1795 and probated in May, 1796. His named heirs were his wife Hannah, sons Joseph and Moses, and other children (not named). Executor: brother, Moses Cranor. [Ref: Webster, *loc. cit.*, p. 10.]

CUSICK-CUSACK

Edward Cusick settled in the Trading Camp Settlement in western North Carolina sometime between 1750 and 1762. His ancestors were in St. Mary's County, Maryland as early as 1703. [Ref: *Carolina Cradle*, by Robert W. Ramsey (1964), p. 110, citing Rowan County Deeds IV:107, VI:541.]

Michael Cusack died testate in St. Mary's County in August, 1703, and mentioned his brother George Cusack in his will. [Ref: *Maryland Calendar of Wills, Volume III, 1703-1713*, p. 14.]

DARBY

Asa Darby, son of George and Anne Darby, was born in Anne Arundel County, Maryland on April 13, 1756. He served in the Revolutionary War as a private in the 6th Company of Montgomery County militia in the Upper Battalion. On November 30, 1779 he married Dorcas Goore (Gore or Goar) who born on May 3, 1759 (in South Carolina) in Craven County, South Carolina. Their children were born at Baton Rouge, Chester County, South Carolina as follows:

(1) Nancy Darby (born September 15, 1780, married Edward Sealy);

(2) George Darby (born April 11, 1783, married ---- Clark);

(3) Anne Darby (born April 5, 1785, married Thomas Sanders);

(4) Lydia Darby (born July 9, 1788, married John Sanders);

(5) John Darby (born February 28, 1792, married first to Mary Ann Smith, second to Leonora Foote, and third to Mary Kidd);

(6) Elizabeth Darby (born July 3, 1796, married Thomas Estes);

(7) James Darby (born January 29, 1799, married Elizabeth Estes);

(8) Mary Darby (born August 9, 1801, married ---- Humphries);

(9) William Jefferson Darby (born September 22, 1808); and,

(10) Thomas Darby.

Asa Darby lived in Sugarland Hundred, Montgomery County, Maryland in 1777, at which time he served in the militia. He died in Chester County, South Carolina on December 30, 1833.

[Ref: *The Bulletin* of the Chester District Genealogical Society, Volume V, No. 1, March, 1982, p. 15 (Darby Bible Records); *Revolutionary Patriots of Anne Arundel County, Maryland, 1775-1783*, by Henry C. Peden, Jr. (1992), p. 41; *Old Southern Bible Records*, by Memory A. Lester (1974), pp. 97-98; *The Maryland Militia in the Revolutionary War*, by S. Eugene Clements and F. Edward Wright (1987), p. 194.]

George Darby, father of Asa, was born on June 12, 1726, married Ann (Anne or Anna) ----, and lived in the Upper Part of Newfoundland Hundred in Montgomery County, Maryland in 1777. George and Asa Darby both took the Oath of Allegiance in 1778. George also rendered aid by providing wheat for the use of the military in 1781.

George Darby wrote his will on February 27, 1788 and died on March 29, 1788. His will was probated on May 5, 1788, naming his wife Anna Darby and sons Rezin Darby, Basil Darby, John Darby, Caleb Darby, Zadock Darby, Samuel Darby, and Aden Darby. He did not mention his son Asa or his daughters in his will. Likewise, the will of George's widow "Ann Darby, of Anne Arundel County" (written on June 10, 1809) was probated in Montgomery County on March 5, 1818, naming sons Samuel Darby, John Darby, Aden Darby, and Zadock Darby, daughter Ann Blowers, granddaughters Rada Darby, Drusillar Darby, Ann Darby (daughters of Samuel Darby) and Martha Ann Ray, and grandsons James Ray, William Alford Ray, George Washington Ray, and Asa Ray. Ann's son Asa was not listed; however, the final administration account on November 28, 1822 mentioned her other children as follows: Asa Darby, Basil Darby, Caleb Darby, Elizabeth Allnutt, and Rezin Darby.

[Ref: *Revolutionary Patriots of Montgomery County, Maryland, 1775-1783*, by Henry C. Peden, Jr. (1996), pp. 83-84; *Abstracts of Wills, Montgomery County, Maryland, 1776-1825*, by Mary Gordon Malloy, Jane C. Sween and Janet D. Manuel (1977), p. 38.]

DAVIS

"Although inconclusive, the evidence strongly suggests that Samuel Davis migrated from Cecil or Kent County, Maryland to the back parts of Prince George's County in 1738 or earlier. He was still there in 1747 and, like John Dunn, seems to have proceeded directly from western Maryland to [Rowan County] North Carolina. His 579-acre tract (lying directly opposite that of George Forbush) in the bend of the Yadkin passed into the hands of Edward Hughes in 1752, and Davis moved out of the region. It is possible that Davis operated a mill for some time prior to 1758 on Dutch (lower) Second Creek, nine miles southeast of Salisbury." [Ref: *Carolina Cradle*, by Robert W. Ramsey (1964), p. 34, citing Prince George's County Judgments, 1738, p. 154, and 1747, pp. 113-114; Rowan County Deeds II:321, V:529.]

One Samuel Davis was the son of Phillip Davis, yeoman, of Kent County, Maryland, who wrote his will on August 8, 1735 and it was probated on June 14, 1740. Another Samuel Davis was the son of Edward Davis, of Somerset County, Maryland, who wrote his will on February 6, 1739/40 and it was probated on March 20, 1739/40. Another Samuel Davis witnessed the will of Sarah Bass in Cecil County, Maryland on January 22, 1737/8. [Ref: *Maryland Calendar of Wills, Volume VIII, 1738-1743*, pp. 71, 91, and *Maryland Calendar of Wills, Volume VII, 1732-1738*, p. 237.]

DEACON

"In 1731, Thomas Sharp of Duck Creek, Kent County, Maryland, referred in his will to his friend Elizabeth Deacon. Although the available evidence is insufficient, it indicates that James and Elizabeth Deacon came from the narrow strip of territory lying between the bounds of two Kent Counties, one in Delaware, the other in Maryland. On June 24, 1751, the Deacons obtained a 640-acre tract of land ... [in Rowan County, North Carolina] and part of the 4,480 acres acquired by James McManus of Northampton County, North Carolina, situated on Sill's Creek less than three miles downstream from Thomas Gillespie." [Ref: *Carolina Cradle*, by Robert W. Ramsey (1964), pp. 60-61, citing *Maryland Calendar of Wills* III:241 and North Carolina Land Grants XI:8.]

The debt books of Kent County, Maryland indicate that Thomas Deacon owned a tract called *Friendship* on which he paid taxes between 1741 and 1747. [Ref:

Inhabitants of Kent County, Maryland, 1637-1787, by Henry C. Peden, Jr. (1994), p. 10.]

DEDMON-DEADMAN

On May 9, 1765 David Jones, of Rowan County, North Carolina, conveyed to Edmond Dedmon, of Baltimore County, Maryland, for £15, 200 acres on Elisha's Creek, adjoining John Pasinger, who was granted it on May 6, 1757. The witnesses were John Barton, John Williockson and Daniel Lewis.

[Ref: *Rowan County, North Carolina, Deed Abstracts, Vol. II, 1762-1772*, by Jo Linn White (Salisbury, N. C.: Privately published, 1972), p. 68, citing Deed Book 6, pp. 240-241.]

Edmund Deadman married Elizabeth Corbin on January 30, 1753 at St. John's Protestant Episcopal Church in Baltimore County. He was probably a brother of Thomas Deadman who married Sarah Griffith in that same parish on October 2, 1749. [Ref: *St. John's and St. George's Parish Register, 1696-1851*, by Henry C. Peden, Jr. (Westminster, MD: Family Line Publications, 1987), pp. 90, 95.]

Edmund Deadman and Thomas Deadman do not appear in the 1737 tax list of Baltimore County, but Nathaniel Dedman does. They were probably related to Thomas Deadman who was transported to Maryland by 1674. [Ref: *The Early Settlers of Maryland*, by Gust Skordas (1968), p. 128; *Inhabitants of Baltimore County, 1692-1763*, by F. Edward Wright (1987), p. 20.]

DENT

On March 4, 1781, Thomas Beall of George, Georgetown, wrote to the Governor of Maryland, Thomas Sim Lee, as follows: "I have been repeatedly called on by Detachments of Continental as well as State Troops on their march to Southern Army, for Provisions and Forage &c. it has so happened that high Winds and badness of wether prevented them getting to a Regular post to draw the same. Shall Esteem it a particular favour for your Orders how to proceed on like occations, I have Issued some Forage to Capt. Golder & Capt. Brown of Artiry. [Artillery.] Inclosed is a Coppy of Orders from Brigr. Genl. Morgan in favour of Mr. Willm. Dent Formerly a Resident of this County [Prince George's] -- who is now here -- drove by the Enemy with his Wife & many small Children he applied to me for Corn & flour &c. but shall not deliver any till I receive your Orders, on this head. "William Dent of Guilford County and State of North Carolina having furnished the Troops of the United States with two Thousand pounds of Salt Pork -- Two hundred Bushells of Indian Corn and Ten bushells of Meat on Conditions of being furnished with the like quantity on his way to Maryland or in that State I do therefore hereby request all Commissarys and Forage Masters to Issue to the said William Dent or his order (not exceeding the Quantity above mentioned) taking his receipt for what each may Issue and Certifying the same on the back of this order -- given under my hand at Guilford Court House in the State aforesaid this 6th Feby. Anno Domini 1781. Signed: Daniel

Morgan, Brigr. Genl." [Ref: *Archives of Maryland, Volume XLVII*, "Journal and Correspondence of the State Council of Maryland (Letters to the Governor and Council), 1781," pp. 102-103.]

William Dent, son of Peter Dent and Mary Brooke, married Verlinder Beall, daughter of Samuel Beall and Eleanor Brooke, circa 1758 and lived in Frederick County, Maryland before migrating to North Carolina. William Dent's children were: Mollie Dent (married first to ---- Campbell and second to Smythe Moore); William Dent (born in Prince George's County, migrated to western North Carolina with his parents in 1772; in 1790 he lived in Guilford County, North Carolina, with 5 males (under 16) and 3 females in his household); Peter Dent (born March 16, 1761); and, Ann Dent (born December 10, 1767, married Risdon Moore and died in St. Clair County, Illinois). [Ref: *Early Families of Southern Maryland, Volume 6*, by Elise Greenup Jourdan (1998), pp. 156-157, 219-221.]

DICKEY

John Dickey migrated from Charles or St. Mary's County, Maryland to Rowan County, North Carolina and settled in the Davidson's Creek Settlement circa 1755. [Ref: *Carolina Cradle*, by Robert W. Ramsey (1964), pp. 102-103, citing North Carolina Land Grants VI:137-138, and John Dickey's Store Account Book (1755-1786), at the Duke University Library.]

DILL-DELL

John and Peter Dill were in the Shenandoah Valley of Virginia in 1746 and sometime after 1750 they "settled on the bank of the South Yadkin River at the spot where it flows into the Yadkin. The Dill family was in Maryland before 1675." [Ref: *Carolina Cradle*, by Robert W. Ramsey (1964), pp. 106-107, citing Maryland Testamentary Proceedings 6:436.]

William Dell immigrated to Maryland in 1655; Mary Dell, wife of William, was transported in 1656; John Dell or Dill was transported in 1659; and, a William Dell was transported in 1658. [Ref: *The Early Settlers of Maryland*, by Gust Skordas (1968), p. 130; *A Supplement to The Early Settlers of Maryland*, by Carson Gibb, Ph.D., (1997), pp. 66, 68.]

John Dill married Sarah ---- in St. Peter's Parish, Talbot County, Maryland on April 7, 1702. James Dill recorded his cattle mark in Kent County, Maryland on January 26, 1724. [Ref: *Maryland Eastern Shore Vital Records, 1648-1725*, by F. Edward Wright (1982), pp. 9, 63.]

William Brown died testate in Kent County, Maryland in February, 1729, and among his heirs was a daughter Mary Dill, wife of James Dill, to whom he bequeathed 5 shillings. [Ref: *Maryland Calendar of Wills, Volume VI, 1726-1732*, p. 146.]

In Dorchester County, Maryland, Rev. Thomas Dill owned a tract called *Exeter* in 1732. [Ref: *Settlers of Maryland, 1731-1750*, by Peter Wilson Coldham (1996), p. 63.]

John Dill married Mary Earley in St. Luke's Parish, Queen Anne's County, Maryland on June 17, 1732. [Ref: *Maryland Eastern Shore Vital Records, 1726-1750*, by F. Edward Wright (1983), p. 49.]

DIMMITT-DEMMETT

James Dimmitt, son of William, was born circa 1707; "age 60 in 1767 when he was stated to have gone to Carolina." He married Barbara Broad on March 27, 1733 and their children were: Mary (born December 29, 1734); Athaliah (born February 21, 1738); Elizabeth Ann (born August 26, 1740); Mary (born in December, 1744); and, James (born February 17, 1748). In 1742 James leased 200 acres of Gunpowder Manor in Baltimore County, Maryland, for the lifetimes of himself, Athaliah (born 1738), and Elizabeth (born 1740). In July, 1761, he was conveyed the right to 10 acres of *Dimmitt's Delight* and 160-acre *Addition to Dimmitt's Delight* by William Dimmitt who was a son of William. By August, 1765, he was in Leesburg, Virginia, when he and wife Barbara assigned a lease to William Lux. [Ref: Baltimore County Families, 1659-1759, by Robert W. Barnes (1989), pp. 173-174.]

As to the rest of the story, we find that in Baltimore County Court on "1 Aug 1765, came Charles Walker, clerk and storekeeper to William Lux, merchant, of Baltimore Co., Maryland, [who] stated that James Demmett has run away to Carolina and is in debt to said William Lux; the said William being gone to Norfolk, Virginia, this disponet employed Nicholas Gardner to go with him in quest of said James Demmett and they over took him in Leesburg, Virginia and said James gave them the negro man Jack and negro woman Judy, for debt. Signed: Charles Walker and Nicholas Gardner. Wit: Benjamin Rogers." [Ref: *Baltimore County, Maryland, Deed Records, Volume Three: 1755-1767*, by John Davis (1996), p. 339.]

DORSEY

The following Dorsey and related family information was prepared and submitted to the author for publication by Virginia Heckel, 1047 Franelm Road, Louisville, Kentucky 40214-4626:

"There are a number of people who have been working on Cornelius Dorsey of Chester, South Carolina. If all the people interested in Cornelius ever get together, we might be able to figure out who his parents were. He is in the Camden District, Chester County, South Carolina, 1790 Census. Nobody ever seems to realize it is him because it is listed as Cornelius Dawson. There is one white male 16 years or above. Four free white males under 16. Five free white females. According to his will of 1820, he had children John, Alexander, Peggy, Robert

Walker, Peggy, Rebecca, Patsy, Cornelius, and James. I suspect James is the oldest or one of the older sons."

"In the 1850 Talledega, Alabama census:
>   Alexander Dorsey, Sr., age 70, born Maryland
>   Patsy Dorsey, age 64, born Virginia
>   Margaret Dorsey, age 27, born South Carolina
>   Alexander Dorsey, Jr., age 23, born South Carolina
>   Wesley Dorsey, age 20, born South Carolina
>   Martha Brakefield, age 12, born South Carolina
>   Lila Ann Brakefield, age 10, born South Carolina
>   Margaret Brakefield, age 8, born Alabama."

"I have found documents that place Cornelius Dorsey in Chester, South Carolina by 1786. I think it is very likely that James, John, Alexander, and possibly a couple of his daughters, were born before South Carolina. I don't know yet if any except Alexander were born in Maryland, but it seems likely."

"There was interaction in Chester, South Carolina between Cornelius and Nicodemus Barnes who you have in your Marylanders to S. C. and Kentucky. You say Nicodemus Barnes claimed to be from an area no farther than 20 miles from Baltimore. He claimed to have served under a Colonel Lacy in the Rev. War for 6 months before going to North Carolina and then Chester, South Carolina. There is also a Caleb Barnes with Nicodemus."

"I have not yet found Nicodemus Barnes or Cornelius Dorsey in Maryland records. There is a Col. Edward Lacey in the Chester, South Carolina 1790 census. I keep thinking that if I find Nicodemus and Caleb in Maryland, I might have a better idea of where to look for Cornelius."

"Cornelius seems to be closely connected to Robert Walker in South Carolina and the son I descend through was named Robert Walker Dorsey, who moved to Hart County, Kentucky. Cornelius' wife Martha may have been a Walker. The father of Robert Walker was Alexander."

"A Leakin Dorsey, of Georgia, sold a slave to one of the Walkers. I have seen no other connection to a Dorsey yet. There was a James, John and David Dorsey who moved to West Virginia from Maryland who have the same given names, but that might mean nothing. John Dorsey married Arah Stockdale in Baltimore. There are two James Dorsey's in the 1790 Baltimore census. John and David were in the 1790 Frederick County census."

"I think Cornelius was from Maryland, but the most I'm sure of is that his son Alexander was born there. If you can use him in your *More Marylanders to Carolina*, I don't mind if you say you got this from me and list my address."

"I don't know if this will be of any interest, but I have run across this information while looking for my Cornelius and Martha Dorsey prior to 1785 or 1786 when they appeared in Chester, South Carolina."

"In your *Inhabitants of Baltimore County, 1763-1774*, in Delaware Hundred, 1763, is Andrew Dorsey. Also, the Index to Aquila Hall's Assessment Ledger lists an Andrew Dorsey, 1762-1765. In the *St. Thomas Parish Register, 1732-1850*, in 1764? in Delaware Hundred is Andrew Dorsey and Charles, Edward, John, Lanslot, Nicholas Jr., Nicholas Sr., and Vachel Dorsey. Also, in Barnes' Baltimore County [Families, 1659-1759] is Andrew Dorsey who owns 50 acres called *Dorsey's Prospect*."

"In the *Maryland Genealogical Society Bulletin* they talked about a page of Dorsey records mixed into a Tevis Family Bible. That Dorsey page in the Tevis Bible is mostly the family of Orlando G. Dorsey:

    Luke Dorsey, born January 22, 1780
    Elizabeth Dorsey, born November 8, 1784
    Beal Dorsey, born February 20, 1786
    Deborah Dorsey, born July 24, 1787
    Nicholas Dorsey, born February 3, 1789
    Henry C. Dorsey, born July 10, 1790
    Orlando Dorsey, born March 10, 1792
    Mary Dorsey, born January 10, 1794
    John Hood Dorsey, born September 16, 1796."

"The first entry on that page looks like it is in a different handwriting. You can't really tell what the child's name is but it is for a son of Andrew and Patience Dorsey, born November 30, 1748. I received this from Nancy Pearre Lesure. I have seen it speculated the name might be Charles and I was hoping it was Cornelius, but you can't tell. I doubt it is Cornelius."

"I think Andrew and Patience went to Rowan County, North Carolina. Some of this is from *Abstracts of the Minutes of the Court of Pleas and Quarter Sessions of Rowan County, North Carolina, 1775-1789, Volume III*, by Jo White Linn (1982); also, *Abstracts of the Deeds of Rowan County, North Carolina, 1753-1785, Volumes 1-10*, by Jo White Linn (1983):

A:258 -	Will of Endymon Dorsey, Nov. 14, 1777; wife and children mentioned, not named.
A:254 -	Will of Indimion Dorsey proved by oath of William Gibson, and Letters Testamentary issued to Ann Dorsey, widow and relict.
4:136 -	Admin. on estate of Andrew Dorsey issued to Patience Dorsey, widow of dec., who gave bond with Jason Frizle and William Gibson.
5 May 1778 -	Inventory and Account of Sales of estates of Indymon Dorsey and Andrew Dorsey returned.
4:208 -	Settlement of estate of Endemean Dorsey 8 May 1779: £151.48. Balance £211.4.10.
4:215 -	Patience Dorsey, admx. of Andrew Dorsey 5 Aug 1779: £66.13.8. Balance £369.4.3.

Rowan County, N. C. Vacant Land Entries, 1778-1779:
#724 -   Patience Dorsey, 400 acres on draught of

	Buffalow Creek adj. Jonas Brown's entry and Andrew McClanahan [9:591.]
#401 -	James Gibson, 200 acres on Buffelow Creek adj. improvements of late Indimon Dorcey on s., running along William Gibson and his own lines [9:216.]
Deeds:	
9:591 -	10 Oct 1783. State Grant #236 at 50 sh. the 100 acres to Patience Dorsey, 396 acres on Buffalo Creek adj. Jones Brown and George Gibson and Joseph Justice.
10:176 -	18 Mar 1785. Patience Dawsey of Lincoln County, N. C. to William Wilkie for £85, 396 acres on Buffalo Creek adj. Absalom Taylor, Jonas Brown, George Gibson, and Joseph Justice, granted 10 Oct 1783.
4:496 -	7 May 1785 [10:179.] Patience Dorsey to Will Wilkie, 396 acres.

"Going back to that birth record of a child for Andrew and Patience Dorsey, it could be Indimion, I guess. If this seems to connect up, you might look at Rowan County, N. C. records. There are Howards and Bakers and Todds and Gaithers. It sounds like a lot of Marylanders could have ended up there at some point. I have been looking at everything trying to see some Dorsey connection to my Cornelius, but I don't find him in Rowan. There was also a George Dorsey there: 1787 - orphans of George Dorsey: Elizabeth, Nacey and infant. 1789 - Lincoln County Court ordered Bazil Dorsey to take to court Elisha Dorsey, an orphan of Indimion Dorsey. So, who do you think Andrew, Patience and Indimion were connected to in Maryland? Orlando G. Dorsey? There was also a James Dorsey in the area buying and selling land. In 1791, Sept. 20, Phillip Howard married Nancy Dorsey (George Dorsey's child?). I hope you find something you can use in your *More Marylanders to Carolina*. Thank you so much for the work you are doing to help us make connections to Maryland."

Addendum: "We have long considered that his [Cornelius Dorsey] wife may have been a Walker as the son we are descended through was named Robert Walker Dorsey. There are several documents which mention both Robert Walker and Nicodemus Barnes with Cornelius. In *Camden District, South Carolina, Wills and Administrations, 1781-1787*, abstracted by Brent H. Holcomb and Elmer O. Parker, is a bill of sale of various items from Nicodemus Barnes to Cornelius Dorcey, both of Chester. Wit: Phillip Walker, Caleb Barnes. 24 Jan 1794. Also, in Robert Barnes' *Maryland Marriages, 1778-1800* is a marriage for Caleb Barnes and Margaret Walker, 12 Oct 1780, in Frederick County. This is the same year Nicodemus claimed he served six months and it is the same year Cornelius' son Alexander claimed to be born in Maryland." [Ref: Information submitted in 1998 by Virginia Heckel, 1047 Franelm Road, Louisville, Kentucky 40214-4626.]

DUNN

"John Dunn, a lawyer, was registrar of deeds for Anson County and first clerk of the court for Rowan County [North Carolina.] It is evident that he originated among the numerous Dunns of Kent and Queen Anne's Counties in Maryland. He was a member of the Cecil County colonial militia in 1740 and, like his friend James Carter, was a tenant or servant of William Rumsey of Bohemia. After Rumsey's death in 1743 [John Dunn and James Carter witnessed his will], Dunn accompanied Carter as far as Prince George's County, Maryland, where he remained until 1747. He removed to the Yadkin Valley before the summer of 1748 and settled near a commanding eminence four miles south of the site of Salisbury. After the town's establishment in 1755, Dunn established a law practice which he maintained until the Revolution." [Ref: *Carolina Cradle*, by Robert W. Ramsey (1964), pp. 28-30, citing the *Maryland Historical Magazine* VI:51; Anson County Deeds I:240, 272; Rowan County Deeds IV:351, VII:4; Prince George's County Judgments, 1738, p. 63; *Maryland Calendar of Wills, Volume VIII, 1738-1743*, p. 200; and, Jethro Rumple's *A History of Rowan County, North Carolina, Containing Sketches of Prominent Families and Distinguished Men* (Salisbury, N. C.: J. J. Bruner Co., 1881), p. 165.]

DWIGGINS-DWIGANS

Robert Dwiggins or Dwigans was born in Maryland circa 1745, married Lydia ----, served as a second lieutenant, rendered patriotic service during the Revolutionary War in Caroline County, Maryland, and died before May, 1789, in North Carolina. [Ref: *DAR Patriot Index, Centennial Edition, Part I* (Washington: 1990), p. 907.]

In addition to Robert, the following family members served in the Revolutionary War in Caroline County, Maryland: Daniel Dwigans or Dwigens, corporal, 1776; James Dwigans or Dwiggans, lieutenant, 1777-1778; James Dwigans or Dwiggans, Jr., private, 1777; John Dwigans or Dwiggans, private, 1777; Nathan Dwigans or Dwiggans, private, 1777; Samuel Dwigans or Dwigens, corporal, 1776; and, James Dwigans or Dwiggans, Sr. took the Oath of Allegiance in 1778. [Ref: *Revolutionary Patriots of Caroline County, Maryland, 1775-1783*, by Henry C. Peden, Jr. (1998), pp. 52-53.]

DWIRE-DWYER

Thomas Dwire applied for a pension (R13913) on July 17, 1835 in Anderson District, South Carolina, aged about 75, stating that he had enlisted at Baltimore, Maryland "at the age of 12 to 14" and served in the Maryland Line. [Ref:

Genealogical Abstracts of Revolutionary War Pension Files, Volume I: A-E, by Virgil D. White (1990), p. 1059.]

Although his pension application was rejected, one "Thomas Dwyer" was a drummer in the 4th Maryland Continental Line on March 16, 1778, and became a private on June 1, 1778. "Thomas Dwier" was listed as a defective who reportedly "deserted" on July 3, 1780. His relationship, if any, to a "Thomas Dwyer" who was a sergeant in the 6th Maryland Line under Capt. Peter Adams on January 30, 1776 is not known. It appears, however, that this company was from Maryland's Eastern Shore, rather than Baltimore where "Thomas Dwire" stated he had enlisted. [Ref: *Archives of Maryland, Volume 18,* "Roster of Maryland Troops in the American Revolution, 1775-1783," pp. 13, 105, 415.]

EATON

John Eaton, a Baptist, moved westward from Pennypack, Philadelphia County, Pennsylvania to Frederick County, Maryland sometime between 1749 and 1754. During this same time frame he migrated to the forks of the Yadkin River in western North Carolina. [Ref: *Carolina Cradle*, by Robert W. Ramsey (1964), pp. 76-77, citing Frederick County Judgments, 1750-1751, p. 283; Rowan County Deeds V:383; and, tombstones in the cemetery of Eaton's Baptist Church in Davie County, North Carolina.]

ECKERT

Adam Eckert was born circa 1730 and married twice, first to Eva Reisz (Rice) on August 16, 1757 at the Evangelical Reformed Church in Frederick County, Maryland, and second to Anna Maria ---- before 1762. Their children were as follows:

(1) Martin Eckert (born August 22, 1759 in Frederick County, Maryland, married Catherine Traffenstaat (1759-1842), and died November 20, 1830 in Lincoln County, North Carolina);

(2) Catherine Eckert (born circa 1760 and married ---- Miller);

(3) Peter Eckert (born December 21, 1763, baptized February 12, 1764);

(4) Maria Elizabeth Eckert (born November 27, 1765 or 1766, married John Null (1754-1831), and died in Lincoln County, North Carolina on May 11, 1852, aged 86 years, 5 months and 13 days);

(5) Simon Eckert (born April 14, 1768, married ---- (perhaps a Hartle or Hartlie), and died November 26, 1835 in Lincoln County, North Carolina);

(6) Adam Eckert, Jr. (born circa 1768, perhaps a twin of Simon, married ----- (perhaps a Hartle or Hartlie), and died before 1850 in North Carolina);

(7) Margaret Eckert (born circa 1771 in North Carolina, married William Coonse, and died June 30, 1848); and,

(8) Barbara Eckert (born circa 1773 and still single in 1797 when her father wrote his will).

"In October, 1942 eight or ten graves were found about a mile from Conover, North Carolina, east of the road leading to the Lail School, but only had three markers, Hans Adam Eckert 1775, Magdalen Eckert 1799, Daniel Eckert 1803 ... By July, 1944 these stones had been removed and cemetery was destroyed."

[Ref: *German Speaking People West of the Catawba River in North Carolina, 1750-1800*, by Lorena Shell Eaker (1994), pp. 156-157.]

EDWARDS

The Edwards family who lived in southern Maryland most likely had some members who migrated to North Carolina and South Carolina, as noted in Walter Whatley Brewster's article entitled "The Ancestry of the Edwards Brothers: Jarrott, Joseph, John and Stourton" in *The Bulletin*, a quarterly publication of the Chester District Genealogical Society, Volume XVIII, Number 2 (June 1994), pp. 46-51. Brewster reaches logical and documented conclusions from existing land and probate records in St. Mary's County Maryland, most of which were lost long ago in a courthouse fire. He states, in part, that it is his belief that Joseph Edwards, of Halifax County, North Carolina, is indeed Joseph Edwards, Jr., the son of Joseph Edwards, Sr., who died testate in St. Mary's County, Maryland in 1746. Brewster writes: "To support my contention, I searched the Tax Lists of St. Mary's County to 1762 and found that Mary Edwards, the widow of Joseph Sr., paid the taxes on the 110 acres tract called *Diamond's Adventure* through 1761. On the 10 April 1762 list, the tax on *Diamond's Adventure* was paid by Benjamin Edwards, co-heir with his brother Joseph Edwards, Jr., to this tract of land. The tax he paid was for the entire 110 acres. Joseph paid his tax on two other tracts he owned in 1761 and does not appear in the lists after that year. It appears that he must have sold his interest in *Diamond's Adventure* soon after his mother's death and moved from St. Mary's County. Joseph Edwards, his wife Maryan, and their children may have arrived in North Carolina as early as 1765. According to a deed registered in Edgecombe County, North Carolina, a Joseph Edwards purchased a 100-acre tract of land on the north bank of Town Creek in that year." For additional information, see the aforementioned quarterly.

In August, 1755, Mary Edwards petitioned the Frederick County, Maryland Court "that having been imposed upon by the wives of Matthew and Mark Edwards in bringing to her counterfeit money to carry to buy saddles with, she not knowing anything of their fraudulent design, they having brought the money to her at dark and she not knowing anything of it nor much of the nature of the money whether good or bad, begs therefore that Your Worships would be so good as to take into consideration and acquit your petitioner, a poor prisoner left here destitute of either friends or money, her husband having gone to Carolina ever since last February and she being intended to follow him before now if she had not been unluckily stopped by passing the abovesaid counterfeit money which she was entirely innocent and ignorant of or of any other felonious or fraudulent action and in hopes of Your Worships' clemency remains as in duty bound will always pray." The record also noted that "the honest and good behavior of the above petitioner is attested by us the subscribers who have known her these several years: Isaac Eltinge, Arthur Hickman, George Jack, Isaac Baker, Moses Jewell, Robert Lamar, William Hickman, Nehemiah Ogden, and Henry Hickman." The record indicated that "upon reading which petition, nothing further was done in the premises." [Ref: *This Was the Life: Excerpts from the Judgment Records of Frederick County, Maryland 1748-1765*, by Millard Milburn Rice (1979), pp. 166-167.]

Regarding Mary Edwards, it is interesting to note that in June Court, 1753, she had petitioned "that her husband James Crumton Edwards grossly abuses her in such manner as can be made apeir [appear] and has turned her out a dores [out of doors] and says she shall not live with him ... if Your Worhips would take into consideration to alowe [allow] your petitioner maintenance of the said James Edward's estate ..." The record indicated that "the Court rejects the petition." [Ref: Rice, *loc. cit.*, pp. 119-120.]

ELLIOT-ELLIOTT

George Elliott migrated to western North Carolina and settled in Rowan County before 1750. He seems to have originated in Queen Anne's County, Maryland, where a George Elliot died testate in December, 1729; one of his sons was named George. [Ref: *Carolina Cradle*, by Robert W. Ramsey (1964), p. 96, citing Queen Anne's County Deeds R.T.(A):17-18; North Carolina Land Grants VI:143; Rowan County Wills B:214; *Maryland Calendar of Wills, Volume VI, 1726-1732*, p. 140.]

EMERSON-EMMERSON

George Emmerson or Emerson, Sr. left a will in Rowan County, North Carolina which was probated in November, 1825. He named his sons Richard Emmerson, George Emmerson, William Emmerson, and Phendle Emmerson who received a legacy from his brother-in-law William Dickson's estate in Maryland, and daughters Catherine Emmerson, Sarah Emmerson, and Anney Emmerson. In Prince George's County, Maryland in 1777 a John Emmerson died and named his sons John, Richard and George Emmerson. [Ref: Information compiled in 1998 by Ray A. Yount, 10031 Shortest Day Road NW, La Vale, MD 21502-6011, or E-Mail: alby6@juno.com.]

In Prince George's County in 1763 John Emerson and Richard Emerson witnessed the will of Elizabeth Halley who subsequently died in 1773. It is also interesting to note that Adam Hoops, of the Falls, Bucks County, Pennsylvania, wrote his will in 1771 and named a number of legatees, including "to Mary Emerson, wife of James Emerson, £100" (date and place of probate in Maryland were not stated). James Emerson was also one of the witnesses. [Ref: *Maryland Calendar of Wills, Volume 15, 1772-1774*, pp. 23, 97.]

There were also several Emerson or Emmerson families in the register of King George's Parish (Protestant Episcopal Church of Prince George's County) which listed births between 1762 and 1796. Although some of the children of a George and Mary Emerson are listed, however, there is no mention of a son George. [Ref: *Prince George's County, Maryland, Indexes of Church Registers, 1686-1885, Volume 1*, p. 20.]

ENNALLS

On August 20, 1785, in Dorchester County, Maryland, Joseph Ennalls, of North Carolina, conveyed to Bartholomew Ennalls, of the State of Maryland, a tract called *Ennall's Timber Yard*, containing 80 acres more or less. Witnesses: Joseph Richardson and James Shaw, Justices. On that same date, Joseph Ennalls, of North Carolina, son of Col. Bartholomew Ennalls, late of Dorchester County, Maryland, deceased, conveyed to Bartholomew Ennalls, brother of said Joseph, of Dorchester County, Gentleman, part of a tract called *Ennalls' Outlett* on Dumpling Creek Beaverdam. [Ref: *Abstracts of the Land Records of Dorchester County, Maryland, Volume 27 (Liber NH#5)*, by James A. McAllister, Jr. (1967), p. 32.]

ENOCHS

On September 17, 1766, in Frederick County, Maryland, John and David Jones recorded a power of attorney from Enoch Enochs, Jr., now of Rowan County, North Carolina, appointing them his lawful attorneys to sell a plantation in Frederick County called *Enochson's Lot* which was sold by order of said Enochs to David Tice. The tract had been patented to Gabriel Enochs and made over to Enoch Enochs according to law. Signed by Enoch Enochs before Jonathan Hunt and Morgan Bryan, Justices of Rowan County, North Carolina, on September 30, 1765. On September 17, 1766, David Tice, of Lancaster County, Pennsylvania, recorded a deed made September 4, 1766 between John Jones and David Jones, of Frederick County, Maryland, appointed by a power of attorney from Enoch Enochs, of North Carolina, to sell the tract *Enochson's Lot* for £210 money of Pennsylvania, containing 100 acres. Signed by John and David Jones. Receipt acknowledged. [Ref: *Frederick County, Maryland, Land Records Liber K Abstracts, 1765-1768*, by Patricia Abelard Andersen (1997), pp. 62-63.]

ENYART

Silas Enyart lived in Hunterdon County, New Jersey before 1739 and sometime between 1749 and 1754 he was in Frederick County, Maryland. In 1752 he was "committed for indecent behavior to the court" in the case of Silas and John Enyart against Joseph Wood. During or after this time it appears that he migrated to western North Carolina, settling north of the South Yadkin. [Ref: *Carolina Cradle*, by Robert W. Ramsey (1964), p. 76, citing the Minutes of the Court of Common Pleas of

Hunterdon County, 1713-1756; Frederick County Judgments, 1748-1750 (p. 617), 1750-1751 (p. 170), 1752-1753 (p. 540); Rowan County Deeds IV:697.]

ERWIN

"The Erwins migrated from Cecil County, Maryland and from Chester County, Pennsylvania. George Erwin lived in Nantmeal or London Britain Township before 1747, while Christopher Erwin obtained a warrant for land in the Middle Octararo settlement as early as 1733. A William Erwin was residing in West Nottingham Township, Chester County, in 1740 and departed within seven years. The records of Sadsbury Township of the same county reveal a William Erwin in 1747." George Erwin settled in the Fourth Creek Settlement in Rowan County, North Carolina before 1752. [Ref: *Carolina Cradle*, by Robert W. Ramsey (1964), pp. 95-97, citing Chester County Tax Lists in 1740 and 1747, Donegal Presbytery 1A:9, and North Carolina Land Grants VI:143-145.]

EVANS

Thomas Evans settled in the Trading Camp Settlement in western North Carolina between 1750 and 1762. "The progenitors of Thomas Evans settled in Calvert, St. Mary's, and Somerset Counties in Maryland between 1677 and 1714." [Ref: *Carolina Cradle*, by Robert W. Ramsey (1964), p. 110, citing Maryland Land Warrants 19:392, Testamentary Proceedings 23:179, 180, 277, 295, 300; North Carolina Land Grants VI:135; James S. Brawley's *The Rowan Story, 1753-1953* (Salisbury, N. C.: Rowan Printing Co., 1954), p. 352.]

John Philips, planter, Kent County, Maryland, write his will in 1737 (exact date not given) and was accidentally shot to death. The will was found on his body and probated on November 24, 1739. To his niece Elizabeth Morgan he left his 555-acre dwelling plantation called *Friendship*. If she should die without issue, the tract was to pass to his nephew Thomas Evans, son of William, now in Cape Fair, North Carolina, providing he immediately be sent to his mother's relatives in Pennsylvania to be raised. If he should die without issue or the aforesaid condition was not met, the land would pass to testator's cousin John David. [Ref: *Maryland Calendar of Wills, Volume VIII, 1738-1743*, p. 92.]

FEIGLEY-FIGELY

Johannes Feigley (Faiglin, Fikele, Figely), Jr. was the son of Johannes Faiglins, shoemaker, of Winterlingen, Germany. He married Ursula Schneckenberger, daughter of Christian Schneckenberger, of Addingen Tuttlengen. Both families arrived on the ship *Forest* at Philadelphia on October 27, 1752 and they settled in western Maryland. A delayed baptismal certificate for daughter Catherine reads: "Catherina Schell was born June 7, 1751. She was born in Winterlingen, Wurttemberg, Germany. Her parents are Johannes and Ursula Feigley." In 1785 John Feigley gave power of attorney to his father-in-law Christian Schneckenberger in

Hagerstown, Maryland to sell his belongings there. On August 10, 1785 John purchased 180 acres on Henry's River in Lincoln County, North Carolina from his son-in-law John Shell of which he sold 52 acres on May 15, 1788 to Lodowick Bonner. "John Feigley doesn't seem to appear in North Carolina records after 1794. He just fades away." Peter Feiglee of Washington County, Maryland sold his inheritance from John Figlee, deceased, to John Wilfong, of Lincoln County, North Carolina, on September 2, 1809. [Ref: *German Speaking People West of the Catawba River in North Carolina, 1750-1800*, by Lorena Shell Eaker (1994), p. 164, citing Deed Book 17:105 and Deed Book 25:78-79.]

John Figely and Christian Schnegenberger took the Oath of Allegiance and Fidelity to the State of Maryland in Washington County before the Hon. Henry Schnebley in 1778. George Figely and Peter Figley (1758-1845) were privates who were enrolled by Capt. Henry Hardman on July 19, 1776 in the part of Frederick County that became Washington County later that year. [Ref: *Revolutionary Patriots of Washington County, Maryland, 1776-1783*, by Henry C. Peden, Jr. (1998), pp. 115-116, 329.]

FELLOW

John Fellow was probably a son of Robert and Pheby Fellow of Talbot County, Maryland. On July 7, 1720, Robert Fellow and John Fellow conveyed to their sister Sarah Fellow, now Sarah Ratcliffe, a 100-acre part of a tract called *Goughton* located between the branches of Tredhaven and a branch of King's Creek called Galloway Branch in Talbot County, Maryland. On the 25th day of the 10th month, 1734, John Ratclif and John Fellows requested certificates of removal as "they intend to remove themselves and families in some part of the government of Carolina." On May 6, 1735, John Fellow and wife Pheby conveyed to their sister Mary James, now wife of John James, Jr., a gift of 58 acres, part of the tract called *Abraham's Lott* located on the north side of *Pitts his Bridge* branch. John died before August 6, 1746 when his son returned to Talbot County and sold some land. [Ref: Talbot County Land Records, Volume 12, p. 404, Volume 14, p. 76, Volume 16, p. 305, and Third Haven Monthly Meeting Records, Talbot County Society of Friends. For information on the Ratcliffe family, see my first volume of *Marylanders to Carolina*.]

FEW

William Few, son of Isaac Few of Wiltshire, England and wife Hannah Stanfield, was born on the 16th day of the 5th month, 1714, in Chester County, Pennsylvania and later moved to Baltimore County, Maryland. In 1743 he married Mary Wheeler, daughter of Benjamin, and their children were: Benjamin (b. 1744); James (1746-1771); William (1748-1828, married Catherine Nicholson); Elizabeth (1755-1829, married thrice: first to Greenberry Lee, second to Benjamin Andrew, and third to Thomas Bush); Hannah (married Rhesa Howard); and, Ignatius. In 1750 William owned a 200-acre tract called *Three Sisters* and a 100-acre tract called *Harris' Trust*. By 1760 he was in North Carolina when he and wife Mary conveyed a 200-acre tract called *Bond's Gift* to William Perrine. [Ref: *Baltimore County Families, 1659-1759*, by Robert W. Barnes (1989), pp. 216-217.]

Regarding the foregoing, please note the following:

On "21 Oct 1760, William & Mary Few, late of North Carolina, but now of Baltimore Co., Maryland, to William Perrine, of Baltimore Co., Maryland, £120, 200 acres of 800 acres ... north side of little falls of Gunpowder River ... surveyed for Edmund Talbot, who devised to his son John Talbot. Signed by William Few. Wit: E. Andrews and Peter Perrine." [Ref: *Baltimore County, Maryland, Deed Records, Volume Three: 1755-1767*, by John Davis (1996), pp. 123-124.]

FLETCHALL

In June, 1755, John Smoot petitioned the Frederick County, Maryland Court, stating "that Thomas Fletchall has the estate of Edward and Barton Smoot in his hands and is now going to move to Carolina. Therefore your petitioner prays Your Worships would make some order in behalf of said Edward and Barton Smoot." The Court ordered that a bench warrant issue returnable immediately for Fletchall and that the "Sheriff go immediately to execute the same." [Ref: *This Was the Life: Excerpts from the Judgment Records of Frederick County, Maryland, 1748-1765*, by Millard Milburn Rice (1979), pp. 160-161.]

FORBUSH

"George Forbush seems to have moved northward from Somerset County or St. Mary's County [where there were families named Forbes], Maryland. He was in Lancaster County, Pennsylvania in 1735, and in the back parts of Prince George's County, Maryland four years later. Before the summer of 1743 he settled in the Shenandoah Valley, where his daughter Mary evidently married one of the sons of Morgan Bryan. Forbush moved to North Carolina in the fall of 1748 and established his residence overlooking a beautiful, mile-long meadow on the west (or south) bank of the Yadkin, two miles north of the shallow ford. Forbush's land was probably located in Brock's Gap in the northwestern portion of present-day Rockingham County." [Ref: *Carolina Cradle*, by Robert W. Ramsey (1964), pp. 33-34, citing *The Black Books: Calendar of Maryland State Papers, No. 1*, pp. 60-61; Rowan County Wills A:58; North Carolina Land Grants VI:147; John W. Wayland's *The German Element of the Shendandoah Valley of Virginia* (Charlottesville, VA: By the author, 1907), p. 70.]

Jacob White, of Worcester County, Maryland, left a will dated November 13, 1775 which was probated on November 14, 1775. Among his legatees he mentioned Bathshaba Forbush, granddaughter of Isaac Forbush in North Carolina, to whom he left three slaves that were to be sold and the money sent to her. [Ref: *Maryland Calendar of Wills, Volume 16, 1774-1777*, p. 82.]

FOY

Thomas Foy appeared on a list of taxables in the Upper Hundred, north of Gunpowder, in Baltimore County in 1737. [Ref: *Inhabitants of Baltimore County, 1692-1763*, by F. Edward Wright (1987), p. 16.]

"Thomas Foy, Sr. and wife Rebecca moved from Baltimore County, Maryland about 1749 and settled on the Trent River in Craven County, North Carolina. James Foy, Sr., son of Thomas and Rebecca, was born in 1737 in Baltimore County and died in Onslow County, North Carolina on November 11, 1822. There is a Thomas Foy who married Rebecca Poteet (Potee, Peteet) on or by January 18, 1726. She was the daughter of Peter and Rebecca Poteet. Thomas Foy sold his land in Baltimore County to George Haile in November, 1748, which would fit with his having moved to North Carolina in 1749. Joseph Franklin Foy was born in Angola, Onslow County, North Carolina in 1871, the son of Enoch E. Foy and Marinda Shepard." [Ref: Information compiled in 1998 by Patricia A. Fortney, 2730 Barrick Road, Finksburg, Maryland 21048-1423, citing *The Heritage of Onslow County, North Carolina*, by the Onslow County Historical Society (1983), p. 145, and *Baltimore County Families, 1659-1759*, by Robert W. Barnes (1989), pp. 227, 513, 514.]

It must be noted that John Foy, son of Thomas and Rebekah Foy, was born on January 18, 1726 in Baltimore County. There is no record of the birth of their son James in 1737 in this register. [Ref: *St. John's & St. George's Parish Registers, 1696-1851*, by Henry C. Peden, Jr. (1987), p. 11.]

FRY-FREY

Nicholas Fry was born about 1724 and "there is some evidence suggesting this family may have been in Frederick County, Maryland, at least briefly. The baptismal records of most of the children appear in Bucks County, Pennsylvania records, although I did not find a baptism for the oldest child, at the Moselem Lutheran Church in Berks County, Pennsylvania: Hannah Frey, daughter of Joh. Nicolaus Frey and wife Elizabeth Papstin, born ----, baptized Trinity 14, 1745. Sponsors: Michael Hauer and Hannah Hillin. The marriage of Nicholaus Frey and Mary Elizabeth Pabst are also recorded in the Moselem records, which, fortunately, gives their fathers' names: 1744, ----, Nicholaus Frey, son of Johannes Frey, to Mary Elizabeth Pabst, daughter of Henry Pabst. Mrs. Eaker [referring to Lorena Shell Eaker's book in 1994 entitled *German Speaking People West of the Catawba River in North Carolina, 1750-1800*] states that Nicholas Fry, Jr. (born 1746) married (1) Catharine ----, and (2) Margaret Anselt/Onsell."

"In the records of the Evangelical Reformed Church, Frederick, Maryland, a Nicholas Frey married Catharine Schnector on August 20, 1767. If my supposition that this is the Lincoln County, North Carolina family is correct, the second marriage may also have occurred in Frederick County, Maryland. The Ansell/Onsell name appears in Frederick County civil and church records (it often appears as Unseld/Unselt in the church records). Mrs. Eaker also mentions that there is no further record of the daughter, Elizabeth, of Nicholaus Fry, Sr., after her baptism in Bucks County, Pennsylvania in 1754. Again, no proof, but there is an Elizabeth Frie who married Henrich Valentine at the Frederick Evangelical Lutheran Church, September 21, 1779."

[Ref: Information gleaned from an article in *Catawba Cousins* (Journal of the Catawba County Genealogical Society), Vol. 12, No. 1 (June, 1997), pp. 5-8, by Ray A. Yount, entitled "Some Pre-1800 Emigrants from Frederick County, Maryland to Old Lincoln County" which was contributed by Ray A. Yount, 10031 Shortest Day Road NW, La Vale, MD 21502-6011, or E-Mail: alby6@juno.com.]

GALLION

Elizabeth Gallion wrote her will in Harford County, Maryland on April 28, 1797 (probated December 16, 1799), naming daughters Rachel and Elizabeth Gallion, and also "daughter Hanna Gallion who is in Carolina." [Ref: Harford County Wills Liber AJ No. 2, f. 266.]

GIBBON-GIBBENS

Maryland Will Book No. 4 contains the will of "Edmond Gibbon, of Delaware River," which was written on February 21, 1685 and probated on June 4, 1686. The name of the Maryland county is not stated, but it could have been either Cecil or Kent. The heirs named included the testator's youngest brother Francis Gibbon to whom he left "all land on the Pennsylvania side except *Mulberry Swamp*" and also "lands at Carolina and on Rariton River; also various interests in the Barbadoes." To Edmond Gibbon, son of the testator's eldest brother George Gibbon of Bemendon in Kent, he left part of *Mulberry Swamp* at Dover, Kent County [Delaware.] To his eldest brother George Gibbon he left "all land at Covansey in Phenixes Colony" and to his brother's George and Francis Gibbon he left land at Smith's Valley in New York. It is not known whether or not Francis Gibbon who inherited land "at Carolina" actually moved there from Delaware or Maryland, or sold the land. Additional research will be necessary before drawing conclusions. [Ref: *Maryland Calendar of Wills, Volume II, 1685-1702*, p. 5.]

Thomas Studes, of Back Creek, Somerset County, Maryland, wrote his will on January 28, 1720 (proved June 28, 1721). He named John Gibbens as his executor and left his "entire estate in either Maryland or Carolina" to him. [Ref: *Maryland Calendar of Wills, Volume V, 1720-1726*, p. 65.]

GILES

The Giles family of Somerset County, Maryland is the subject of an article written by Lewis F. Giles entitled "The Giles Family of Old Somerset" in the *Maryland Genealogical Society Bulletin*, Vol. 35, No. 1 (Winter, 1994), pp. 3-21. He states, in part, that "on 12 March 1730 Thomas Giles married Ann Harris, daughter of William and Frances Harris, in Stepney Parish. In his will, written on 6 October 1769 and probated on 22 November 1769, Thomas Giles left a one third life estate to his wife Ann and divided *Giles' Lott*, which was inherited from his father William, between his sons Jacob, Isaac, Thomas and William. His personal estate was divided between his children, his son John's share being contingent on his returning home to accept it. This he apparently did as the accounting of Thomas Giles' estate by his executor, William, shows John's share disbursed to him ..." (Somerset County Administrative Accounts Liber EB#10, f. 157).

In a letter in 1996 from David W. Bishop, 715 S. Moss Street, Leesburg, Florida 34749-5631, he states that it is his belief and he is searching for documentation that John Giles, son of Thomas Giles of Maryland who died testate in 1769, migrated to Buncombe County, North Carolina. A John Giles appears in the 1800 census for that county. Mr. Bishop also believes that Elijah Giles (born in Maryland in 1778 and living with his son Nathaniel in 1880 in Colquett County, Georgia) was a son of John Giles and grandson of Thomas Giles of Somerset County, Maryland. He thinks that Elijah Giles followed the Desota Trail from western North Carolina down to Augusta, Georgia, then went to Jones County, Georgia and finally to Houston County, Georgia. Perhaps someone reading these pages will be able to assist Mr. Bishop in his quest for documentation.

GILLESPIE

Rev. George Gillespie, son of Rev. George Gillespie (1613-1648) and Catherine Murray, of Ulster, Northern Ireland, was born in 1644 and came to America in 1700. He married a daughter of John Garner, of Ulster, and was mentioned in the will of said John Garner which was written in Cecil County, Maryland on March 7, 1723/4 and probated on October 22, 1725. [Ref: *Maryland Calendar of Wills, Volume V, 1720-1726*, p. 204.]

George Gillespie and Miss Garner had the following children [births may not be in order]:

(1) Patrick Gillespie (married Ann Denniston, daughter of Daniel and Sarah, had 6 children, and died sometime after 1747 in Winchester, Virginia);

(2) Rev. George Gillespie (born about 1687 in Ulster, married Rebekah Allison, served as pastor at White Clay Presbyterian Church in 1712, had 7 children, and died in Cecil County, Maryland in 1760);

(3) Robert Gillespie (born about 1724, married Elizabeth Maxwell, had children, died 29 days after he was scalped by Indians, March 21, 1760, and buried

in Thyatira Cemetery in Rowan County, North Carolina; his widow married William Steele);

(4) James Gillespie (moved to New Castle County, Delaware); Thomas Gillespie (born in 1719 in Chester County, Pennsylvania, married Naomi Thompson (1728 - December 12, 1797) on January 1, 1745, had 10 children, died on December 12, 1797 (the same day as Naomi), and buried in Thyatira Cemetery in Rowan County, North Carolina; they were the great-grandparents of President James Knox Polk (1795-1849);

(5) Joseph Gillespie (born about 1725, died July 2, 1800, and buried beside his second wife Ruth --- at Coddle Creek ARP Church in Iredell County, North Carolina); and,

(6) John Gillespie (bought land on Sill's Creek on the east side of Thyatira Church in Rowan County, North Carolina).

[Ref: "Gillespie Ancestors and Relatives of James Knox Polk, The President," compiled in 1978 by Rollin Wilson Gillespie, 1540 Longfellow Court, McLean, Virginia 22101, and contributed by Ray A. Yount, 10031 Shortest Day Road NW, La Vale, MD 21502-6011, or E-Mail: alby6@juno.com.]

"Thomas Gillespie was born in 1719 either in Cecil County [MD] or in New London Township, Chester County [PA.] The Gillespies, like so many other families at the head of Chesapeake, moved westward after 1730, first into Lancaster County and then through the Cumberland Valley into the Shenandoah. Thomas Gillespie's eldest son James was baptized in the valley of Virginia by the Reverend James Craig in 1741, and his son William in 1747, shortly before Gillespie departed for Carolina.

"The late Professor Walter L. Lingle, in his book on Thyatira Church, included an item gleaned from the *North Carolina Journal* (January 9, 1797) to the effect that Thomas Gillespie and his wife Naomi were the first people to settle in Rowan County west of the Yadkin River, but the date of their arrival was not given. There seems little doubt that Gillespie was among the earliest settlers, for it is recorded in the Augusta County, Virginia, court proceedings for September, 1747, that 'Thomas Gillespie, about to remove an orphan boy of William Humphrey's, deceased, out of the Colony, is ordered to deliver said orphan to the church wardens.' The first record of Gillespie's presence in North Carolina is a land grant dated June 24, 1751, but it is clear that he was there before the summer of 1749 -- and possibly before the winter of 1747-1748. The Gillespie homeplace was located on Sill's Creek, approximately one mile west of James Cathey's house."

[Ref: *Carolina Cradle*, by Robert W. Ramsey (1964), pp. 40-41, citing Cecil County Deeds X:468; Chester County Wills IV:223; Rowan County Deeds XII:180-190; "The Taylor Papers" at the Historical Society of Pennsylvania; Tombstone of Thomas Gillespie at Thyatira Presbyterian Church.]

"The story of Elizabeth Gillespie is an interesting one. Her husband, Robert Gillespie, the former business partner of Thomas Bashford, was scalped and killed by the Cherokees during the Indian uprising of 1759. In June, 1760, the widow bought part of the lot number two in the north square [of Salisbury, North Carolina] which had previously been conveyed by John Ryle to William Williams. She operated an inn on this lot, probably one built by Ryle in 1755. In 1761, widow Gillespie acquired lot number eleven in the north square and a 275-acre tract adjoining the town land on the north. The following year she bought the remaining portion of Ryle's old lot. The extent and location of her purchases indicates that she was a shrewd, capable woman and that her husband had left her financially well established. In 1763, the widow married William Steele, of Lancaster County, Pennsylvania, who obtained sixteen lots in the north square of Salisbury 'adjoining Elizabeth Gillespie.' Their son, John Steele, became a prominent figure in the early history of the State of North Carolina. In 1787, he entered the state legislature and, three years later, became a member of the first Congress of the United States under the Constitution. Margaret, daughter of the widow by her first husband Robert Gillespie, married Samuel Eusebius McCorkle, a co-founder of the University of North Carolina."

[Ref: *Carolina Cradle*, by Robert W. Ramsey (1964), pp. 168-169, citing James S. Brawley's *The Rowan Story, 1753-1953* (Salisbury, N. C.: Rowan Printing Co., 1954), p. 27; Rowan County Deeds IV:241, IV:763, V:307-308, VI:160; and, C. L. Hunter's *Sketches of Western North Carolina, Historical and Biographical, Illustrating Principally the Revolutionary Period of Mecklenburg, Rowan, Lincoln and Adjoining Counties, Accompanied With Miscellaneous Information, Much of It Never Before Published* (Raleigh, N. C.: Raleigh News Steam Job Print, 1877), p. 185.]

GILMORE

On October 18, 1763, Stephen Gilmore, of Cumberland County in the Province of North Carolina, assigned and appointed Robert Wood, of Frederick County, Maryland, his true and lawful attorney, to ask, recover and receive such cattle as shall be hereafter mentioned [and described] that he understood were killed by a certain Peter Ryer-- [part of name missing in margin of record.] Signed by Stephen Gilmore before Joseph Wood and John Harlan. On October 22, 1763, Stephen Gilmore appeared before Joseph Wood, one of his Lordship's Justices of the Peace for Frederick County, and made oath that the above mentioned cattle were his property and they were driven from Carolina in order to be driven to Pennsylvania and sold, and he understood by the man that drove said cattle, that they left the road between Frederick Town and Pipe Creek in July in the year 1762. [Ref: *Frederick County, Maryland, Land Records Liber G & H Abstracts, 1761-1763*, by Patricia Abelard Andersen (1996), p. 99.]

GIVEN-GIVAN

"The Given (or Givan) family settled in Somerset County, Maryland, where the name appears as early as 1709 [when James Givan was the co-executor of the will of William Langsden in Stepney Parish.] Samuel Given, who received a Blunston license to settle in the Cumberland Valley in 1735, was in the Shenandoah Valley three years later. Edward, John, and James, probably his sons, were there by 1747. Edward Given went to the Catawba Valley in 1748 or 1749 and settled on the west bank of the Catawba near Davidson's Creek where it crossed the Granville line. It is not clear whether Samuel Given belonged to the Somerset County family. He may have emigrated from Ulster to Pennsylvania." [Ref: *Carolina Cradle*, by Robert W. Ramsey (1964), p. 50, citing Orange County Deeds III:12, IV:88; North Carolina Land Grants V:308, VI:152; *Maryland Calendar of Wills* III:152, IV:49, V:164.]

A Michael Givin who was transported to Maryland in 1658. [Ref: *The Early Settlers of Maryland*, by Gust Skordas (1968), p. 183.]

In 1689, James Given and Robert Givan each owned 350 acres in Somerset County. [Ref: *Settlers of Maryland, 1679-1700*, by Peter Wilson Coldham (1995), p. 63.]

In 1721, a Robert Givan appeared in Somerset County Court as an "evidence" (his age was not given). In 1755, a Robert Givvins gave his deposition in Cecil County, stating he was 46 years old. [Ref: *More Maryland Deponents, 1716-1799*, by Henry C. Peden, Jr. (1992), pp. 42-43.]

William Given witnessed the will of John Caldwell in Somerset County in 1742. Thomas Given witnessed the will of George Wetherell in Kent County in 1743. [Ref: *Maryland Calendar of Wills, Volume VIII, 1738-1743*, pp. 228, 245.]

GORE

"For several years before the Revolutionary War, eight years would be a good estimate, James Gore, Sr. was a resident of Chester District, South Carolina. He was baptized on November 7, 1707 in St. Barnabas Church, Queen Ann Parish, Maryland, and was the son of James Gore I and Mary (Burke) Gore Tomlinson. [Burke has not been proven, but with most Gore researchers, it is accepted with the understanding that hard proof must still be sought.] He came to South Carolina from Frederick County, Maryland. The last date of reference that I have for him in Frederick County, Maryland is in 1768 when James Gore sold land to one Samuel Beggs in that same county. This is found in the General Index for Frederick County, Md. 1748-1778."

"In the next General Index with the dates 1778-1803, no Gores are listed, so we may assume that sometime between 1768 and 1769, the move to South Carolina was accomplished. James Gore, Sr. signed his will in Kershaw, South Carolina on April 3, 1783 and his wife Elizabeth Dowden Gore signed her will five years later on November 25, 1788 in Chester County, South Carolina. [This will may be found in Apt. 21, Pkg. No. 327, recorded in Will Book A at pages 19 and 20.]"

"Elizabeth (Dowden) Gore, from all research available, was the daughter of John Dowden and Esther Ashford. She was baptized on August 9, 1718 in St. Barnabas Church, Queen Anne Parish, Maryland. Her brother, John Dowden, married

Mary Gore, the sister of James Gore, Sr., or II, as I shall now refer to him. From the legatees mentioned in both of these wills, we have a list of their children and some, if not all, of their grandchildren. Children: James Manning Gore, Clement Gore, Michael Gore, John Ashford Gore, Eleazar Gore, Sarah Wornell [daughter or grand daughter], Mary Sanders, Easter (Esther?) Wood. Granddaughters: Elizabeth Noland, Fillinda Gore, and Elizabeth Sanders who was the daughter of Easter Sanders Wood or the daughter of the above mentioned Mary Sanders and her husband James Sanders I. Grandsons: Michael Dowden and Davis Gore. [Michael Dowden Gore, no doubt, brother of Davis. Naming them together, he used the last name of Gore only with the name of the last grandson named, i. e. with married couples: Ray and June Smith, etc..]"

"Ruth Blakely Powers of Irving, Texas is a descendant of Thomas Gore [brother of James Gore, Sr.] and she tells us the following: James and Elizabeth moved to South Carolina around 1788. His brother Thomas had gone to South Carolina in 1757. In 1790 there were thirteen Gore families living in South Carolina, mostly in Chester and Newberry Counties. By the early 1800's they started a movement to Kentucky, at least one family went to Georgia and another to Claiborne County, Mississippi. A son of James and Elizabeth, Thomas, was killed during the American Revolution at the Battle of Fort McIntosh in 1777. James furnished supplies for the Continentals in 1779 in South Carolina: Issued July 9, 1785 to James Gore, £29, 19s., 7p. 1/4, for a waggon and 2 horses for Continentals in 1779 per account audited."

[Ref: *The Bulletin* of the Chester District Genealogical Society, Volume XVI, No. 3 (September, 1992), featuring an article entitled "The Gore-Sanders Connection of Chester District, South Carolina" by Ann Lynch Boyer, pp. 80-84; article continued in December, 1992 and March, 1993 issues.]

From the Judgment Records of Frederick County, Maryland, we find these entries:

(1) November Court, 1750: "Margaret White was convicted of bastardy and fined £3. James Gore, planter, paid Margaret's fine and also posted bond of £40 as indemnity that her child would never become a public charge."

(2) James Gore served as a Grand Juror in 1750 [1751], 1759, and 1761.

(3) Thomas Gore served as a Grand Juror in 1760.

[Ref: *This Was The Life: Excerpts from the Judgment Records of Frederick County, Maryland, 1748-1765*, by Millard Milburn Rice (1979), pp. 64, 66, 201, 209, 222, 234.]

GRAFTON

On July 2, 1770, Francis Jenkins, husband of Casander, daughter of William Grafton, and Thomas Smith, husband of Margaret, another daughter of said William, of Rowan County, North Carolina, sold to John Love, of Baltimore County, Maryland, for £60, slaves: Ceasar, Nam, Jack, Sall, Easter, Salt and Hannah and Tom with Sarah Grafton. Signed by Francis Jenkins and Thomas Smith. Wit: John Harris and William Morgan. [Ref: *Baltimore County, Maryland, Deed Records, Volume Three: 1755-1767* (1996), p. 208.]

William Grafton, son of William, of Baltimore County, died leaving a will dated August 19, 1769 and proved on September 11, 1769. His heirs were wife Sarah and children: William, Samuel, Daniel, Aquila, Nathaniel, Cassandra, Margaret and Priscilla. All were mentioned also in the will of their grandfather William Grafton who died just two years earlier in October, 1767. [Ref: *Maryland Calendar of Wills, Volume 14, 1767-1772*, pp. 17, 18, 102.]

GRAHAM

"Richard Graham married Hannah Cathey in 1736 and was a resident of Cecil County, Maryland, seven years later. He was closely related to the numerous Grahams in the northern part of the adjoining Delaware County of New Castle, and at least three of them accompanied him to North Carolina. On April 11, 1749, Richard Graham petitioned for a tract of land in Anson County and nine years later received a 567-acre tract on each side of Second Creek, commonly called Withrow's Creek. James and John Graham, brothers or cousins of Richard, probably took up residence in the 'Irish Settlement' at the same time as he, though proof of their presence in 1749 is lacking. John Graham resided on a branch of the South Yadkin eleven miles north of George Cathey. James Graham's grant, dated June 24, 1751, was described as being 'on the headwaters of cold water joining a branch of Cane Creek about two miles from his own house southeast between him and the trading path.' Graham thus lived six miles southeast of George Cathey and (as the above description indicates) might well have been there in the spring of 1749." Also, a tombstone in Thyatira Cemetery bears the inscription "James Graham, died January 1, 1758, age 88." [Ref: *Carolina Cradle*, by Robert W. Ramsey (1964), p. 39, citing Records of the Donegal Presbytery 1A:12-13; Lancaster County Commissioner's Minute Book, 1729-1770, pp. 39-41; Rowan County Deeds II:253; North Carolina Land Grants XI:10.]

Richard Graham and Hannah Kathi [Cathey?] were married on December 12, 1736 in Holy Trinity (Old Swedes) Church in Wilmington, New Castle County, Delaware. [Ref: *Early Church Records of New Castle County, Delaware, Volume 2* (1994), p. 66, a reprint of the original register, 1713-1799, as translated by Horace Burr circa 1890.]

GRANGER

On October 8, 1782, in Dorchester County, Maryland, a deed was recorded between Benjamin Granger, of Guilford County, North Carolina, and Levin Cator, of Dorchester County, Maryland, for part of a tract called *Hard Grove* on Taylor's Island near the land of John Avery on Purnall's Cove, adjoining *Purnall's Land* and containing 50 acres more or less; also, conveyed half of tract called *Granger's Chance* containing 50 acres. Witnesses: John Dickinson and Joseph Richardson,

Justices of Dorchester County. [Ref: *Abstracts of the Land Records of Dorchester County, Maryland, Volume 26 (Liber NH#2)*, by James A. McAllister, Jr. (1965), p. 7.]

On October 29, 1782, Benjamin Granger, John Granger and Mary his wife, of Guilford County, North Carolina, conveyed to Matthias Traverse, of Dorchester County, a tract called *Avery's Lott* on Taylor's Island on the east side of Oyster Creek (containing 36 acres more or less), two-thirds of a tract called *Hog Pen Neck* on the east side of Oyster Creek on Taylor's Island (containing 100 acres more or less), and one-half of a tract called *Granger's Chance* on the said island and creek (containing 25 acres more or less). Witnesses: Thomas Jones and Benjamin Keene, Justices of Dorchester County. [Ref: McAllister, *loc. cit.*, p. 9.]

GREEN

On October 24, 1786, in Dorchester County, Maryland, a bond of conveyance was recorded by Henry Green and his wife Priscilla, of Guilford County, North Carolina, planter, to Daniel Godwin, of Dorchester County, Maryland, for the following tracts: part of *Walker's Lott*, sometimes called *Walker's Chance*, containing 100 acres; part of *Goodridge's Choice*, containing 51 acres; and, part of *Cheesman's Gore*, containing 13 acres. [Ref: *Abstracts of the Land Records of Dorchester County, Maryland, Volume 28 (Liber NH#9)*, by James A. McAllister, Jr. (1967), p. 16.]

On October 22, 1787, Henry Green, of North Carolina, now residing in Dorchester County, Maryland, conveyed to Daniel Godwin, of Dorchester County, the following tracts: part of *Goodridge's Choice* between Hunting Creek and Trots Creek, containing 51 acres more or less; part of *Walker's Lott* or *Walker's Chance* on Hunting Creek, containing 100 acres more or less; and, *Chesum's Gore* on Hunting Creek, containing 13 acres more or less. Witnesses: John Eccleston and R. Stevens, Justices. [Ref: McAllister, *loc. cit.*, p. 49.]

GUNNELL

On "2 Jul 1685, George Gunnell, of Chyrusgson, Cellemack Co., Carolina to James Miles, of Baltimore Co., Maryland, said Miles to pay Vincent Lowe, of Maryland, 5,000 pounds tobacco, a certain debt due from Edward Gunnell, deceased, brother to the said George Gunnell ... also 500 pounds of tobacco to Daniel Clocker and 773 pounds of tobacco to John Bloomfield, 100 acres ... Bush River ... line of John Collier ... Edward Gunnell, purchased of Joseph Gallion. Signed: George Gunnell. Wit: John Taylor and John Hathaway." [Ref: *Baltimore County, Maryland, Deed Records, Volume One: 1659-1737*, by John Davis (1996), p. 16.]

Regarding the foregoing, please consider the following:

"2 July 1685: George Gunnell, of Allemack Co., NC, conv. to James Mills 100 a. *Galliarbe*, formerly belonging to Joseph Gallion, and sold by him to Edward Gunnell, bro. of the grantor (RM#HS:175)."

"6 June 1687: James Mills conv. to James Phillips his interest in the 100 a. tract *Galliarbe*, which formerly belonged to Joseph Gallion, and later to said George Gunnell (RM#HS:227)."

"12 Dec 1691: George Gunnell, chirurgeon, heir and admin. of Edward Gunnell, conv. to Cornelius Boyce 100 a. *Gallard's Bay*, which was once sold by Joseph Gallion to Edward Gunnell, dec. (RM#HS:336)."

Also, this interesting entry regarding the tract *Gunnell's Devotion*: "12 April 1680: 60 a. surv. for George Gunnell, near the mouth of Rumley Creek; it appears to be no such land, Gunnell dead (MRR:29)."

[Ref: *Baltimore County, Maryland, Deed Abstracts, 1659-1750*, by Robert Barnes (1996), pp. 78, 89.]

"Edward Gunnell, poss. brother of William, imm. to Md. c1673; on 6 Feb. 1676/7 purch. 100 a. *Gallar's Bay* from Joseph and Sarah Gallion; was summ. to the Prov. Court in June 1677; d. by 14 Aug. 1680 when his est. was inv. by Edward Reeves and William Osborn, and val. at 17,186 lbs. tob.; est. was admin. 25 Feb. 1680 by George Gunnell, who also had to appear in court for the debts of his bro. Edward, in Sept. 1682. George Gunnell, bro. of Edward, imm. to Md. in 1673; m. by 1677/8 Jane, widow and admnx. of Thomas Overton; by 1678 was in Cecil Co., but by 1692 was back in Balto. Co. as a taxable in Spesutia Hund.; on 11 June 1694 admin. the est. of Edward Gunner." [Ref: *Baltimore County Families, 1659-1759*, by Robert W. Barnes (1989), pp. 286-287.]

HALL

On "17 Apr 1764, Joseph Hall, of Craven Co., North Carolina to Charles Wells, of Maryland, £70, 200 acres ... patented 10 Apr 1730 by Smith, who sold to his grandson John Hall and descended to said Joseph ... line of Edward Stevenson. Signed: Joseph Hall. Wit: Thomas Agnis and James Low." [Ref: *Baltimore County, Maryland, Deed Records, Volume Three: 1755-1767*, by John Davis (1996), p. 273.]

HAMILTON

"Archibald Hamilton settled at the source of Gillespie's Back Creek [in Rowan County, North Carolina] in 1750. He seems to have originated in Prince George's County, Maryland, and to have entered the valley of Virginia sometime between 1740 and 1747." [Ref: *Carolina Cradle*, by Robert W. Ramsey (1964), p. 56.]

Archibald Hamilton may have originated in Prince George's County, Maryland as Ramsey has suggested, but he is found neither in the land records nor the probate records nor the protestant episcopal church registers between 1686 and 1743 in that county. The only reference that I have found is for "Archibald Hambleton" who appears on a long list of persons who paid money owed to the estate of Col. John Baker, deceased, of St. Mary's County, Maryland on May 1, 1735. [Ref: *Abstracts of the Administration Accounts of the Prerogative Court of Maryland, 1731-1737*, by V. L. Skinner, Jr. (Westminster, MD: Family Line Publications, 1996), p. 92.]

HAMPTON

"The Hamptons, like the Craigs and Gardiners, have a history which includes both Maryland and New Jersey. One branch of the family lived in Cecil County, Maryland (whence John and David Hampton removed to Carolina) in 1722; another was in Freehold, Monmouth County, New Jersey, before 1710." John and David Hampton settled in the Trading Camp Settlement of Rowan County, North Carolina sometime between 1750 and 1762. [Ref: *Carolina Cradle*, by Robert W. Ramsey (1964), p. 110, citing North Carolina Land Grants VI:164.]

David Hamton [sic] witnessed the will of John Lewis in Cecil County in 1735. [Ref: *Maryland Calendar of Wills, Volume VII, 1732-1738*, p. 167.]

David Hampton was a private in the militia in 1740 in Capt. Zebulon Hollingsworth's Company of Foot. [Ref: *Inhabitants of Cecil County, Maryland, 1649-1774*, by Henry C. Peden, Jr. (1993), p. 51.]

HARMON

John Harmon originated in either New Castle County, Delaware or in Talbot County, Maryland. He migrated to North Carolina and settled on the Yadkin River in Rowan County circa 1750. [Ref: *Carolina Cradle*, by Robert W. Ramsey (1964), p. 83, citing Rowan County Deeds V:91, Testamentary Proceedings 1:105.]

HARRISON

William Harrison, who was in western North Carolina by April, 1752, and settled in the Trading Camp Settlement, originated among the Harrisons of Charles and St. Mary's Counties, Maryland. The family was in Charles County by 1654. [Ref: *Carolina Cradle*, by Robert W. Ramsey (1964), pp. 107, 110, citing Anson County Deeds 1:202-203; Rowan County Deeds V:529; Rowan County Marriage Records in 1762, noting the marriage of a Joseph Harrison on June 30th; Maryland Land Warrants AB&H:416.]

One William Harrison was a son of Col. Richard Harrison, of Nangemoy, Charles County, and his wife Dorothy (Hanson) Harrison who died on March 5, 1752. [Ref: *Charles County Gentry*, by Harry Wright Newman (1940), p. 224.]

For additional information on the Harrison family, see *Early Charles County, Maryland Settlers, 1658-1745*, by Marlene Strawser Bates and F. Edward Wright (Westminster, MD: Family Line Publications, 1995), and *Early Families of Southern*

Maryland, Volume 4, by Elise Greenup Jourdan (Westminster, MD: Family Line Publications, 1995).

HARTLE

Peter Hartle was born before 1755 in Maryland or Pennsylvania. He married twice, first to Elizabeth Reiter on February 25, 1778 in Washington County, Maryland by Rev. Jacob Wiemar, and second to Elizabeth Masters, daughter of Jacob Masters and Elizabeth Clubb, in Lincoln County, North Carolina circa 1795. There are deeds in his name dated January 27, 1780 for 100 acres on Snow Creek and April 16, 1785 for 61 acres on Howard's Creek in Lincoln County, North Carolina. On March 18, 1802 he sold his land and moved to (now) Cape Girardeau County, Missouri. His known children were as follows:

(1) Simon Hartle (born circa 1779 in either Washington County, Maryland or Burke County, North Carolina, married Margaret ----, and died before 1825 in Cape Girardeau County, Missouri);

(2) Mary Hartle (born 1797 in Lincoln County, North Carolina, married Christopher Seabaugh (1794-1866) in 1818, and died in 1891 in Bollinger County, Missouri);

(3) Jacob Hartle (born circa 1799, married Sarah Ann Smith, daughter of Daniel Smith and Elizabeth Hahn, and died before 1826 in Cape Girardeau County, Missouri; his widow married Joseph Miller in 1829);

(4) Sarah Hartle (born circa 1800, married Philip Smith, son of Daniel Smith and Elizabeth Hahn, and died after 1850 in Cape Girardeau County, Missouri);

(5) Joseph Hartle (born circa 1803, married Sarah Masters, daughter of Jacob Masters, and died before 11826 in Missouri; his widow married Philip Wise);

(6) Elizabeth Hartle (born circa 1805, died before 1826, single);

(7) Michael Hartle (born circa 1808, died before 1826, single);

(8) George Hartle (born 1813, married Mary Niswonger, daughter of Joseph Niswonger and Catherine Limbaugh, and died in 1869 in Missouri);

(9) Jesse Hartle (born 1814, married Sarah Seabaugh, and died in 1877 in Missouri); and,

(10) Solomon Hartle (born in 1816, married Jane Davis, and died in 1863).

[Ref: *German Speaking People West of the Catawba River in North Carolina, 1750-1800*, by Lorena Shell Eaker (1994), pp. 215-216.]

HEFNER

"Another Frederick County, Maryland family that came to Lincoln County, North Carolina was that of Melchoir Hefner (born about 1730). Mrs. Eaker [referring to Lorena Shell Eaker's book in 1994 entitled *German Speaking People West of the Catawba River in North Carolina, 1750-1800*] lists the baptism of his children in Frederick County, Maryland. She states that his oldest daughter, Anna Maria, is supposed to have married Dr. Johann Michael Raub; however, she said she could not verify this. There certainly was an Anna Maria Hefner who married Dr. Johann Michael Rauh (several different spellings appear in the records). Based on the dates, and the fact that she came to 'Carolina,' it is very probable that she indeed is the daughter of Melchoir Hefner. The following obituary for her husband, which is not very flattering of her, appears in the records of Evangelical Lutheran Church in Frederick, Maryland: "April 3, 1792. Sunday after Palm Sunday (Why didn't the Pastor say Easter?), Dr. Johann Michael Rauh, born Dec. 20, 1728 in *'Durr im Durlachischen Pfortzheimer Amts.'* Father Jacob Rauh, a shoemaker, and mother Elisabeth. He married Maria Ursula ---- in 1753 in Wurttemberg and had 8 children with her, of whom 1 son and 2 daughters are alive. After her death, he married Anna Maria Hoeferin in 1769 and had 6 children with her of whom one son is dead and one is here with Gottlob Muller. The others were taken by his wife, who was unfaithful, with her to Carolina. Died of an infection the 2nd at 9 p.m., aged 63 years, 3 months, 3 days."

The children of Melchoir Hefner of Frederick County, Maryland and Lincoln County, North Carolina were as follows:

(1) Anna Maria Hefner (baptized February 4, 1753, and probably married Dr. Johann Michael Raub);

(2) John Hefner (born October 9, 1754 in Maryland, married three times (third wife was Catherine ----), and died before July, 1837 in North Carolina);

(3) Maria Margaret Hefner (baptized October 21, 1759, married Sebastian Bolick on February 18, 1776);

(4) Jacob Hefner or Hafner (born November 1, 1763); Maria Catherine Hefner (born August 16, 1766);

(5) Philip Hefner (born January 16, 1768 or 1769 in Maryland, married twice, first to Elizabeth Keller (1765-1822) and second to Elizabeth Bolick (1785-1864), and died February 11, 1858 in North Carolina); and,

(6) Dorothea Hefner (born September 9, 1771).

[Ref: *German Speaking People West of the Catawba River in North Carolina, 1750-1800*, by Lorena Shell Eaker (1994), p. 220, and information gleaned from an article in *Catawba Cousins* (Journal of the Catawba County Genealogical Society), Vol. 12, No. 1 (June, 1997), pp. 5-8, by Ray A. Yount, entitled "Some Pre-1800 Emigrants from Frederick County, Maryland to Old Lincoln County" which was contributed by Ray A. Young, 10031 Shortest Day Road NW, La Vale, MD 21502-6011, or E-Mail: alby6@juno.com.]

HELMS-HELMES-HELME

In the first volume of *Marylanders to Carolina* published in 1994 there was a brief mention of a John Helms born circa 1690 in Maryland (possibly on the Eastern Shore) who married ---- Tilghman, went to Anson County, North Carolina circa 1748, raised a large family including sons Tilman Helms, Jonathan Helms, Moses Helms, and a daughter unnamed, and died in 1760. His wife was probably related to Richard Tilghman (1672-1738) who was the Chancellor of the Province of Maryland in 1722. Although nothing new has been uncovered about this family, the following information has been shared from a family member in hopes of finding out more about the early Helmses just mentioned:

"As you probably know, there were two documented John Helmes in Maryland in the 1660's-1670's in Charles County. Also, a Sarah Helme, daughter of John Meaks of Prince George's County in 1694 settling her father's estate. Earlier [in 1663] one John Helme had been a servant to Meaks [Meekes] on land in the Seward grant in Charles County. That John died about 1666 leaving a wife Penelope. Perhaps there was a son John. The other John came to Maryland, married Mary, the widow of John Mills, and stayed in Maryland to at least the early 1670's. Records of land and business transactions exist for him in Maryland Archives. However, he is not identified here to my knowledge, nor was he likely the second John above. We have determined that there were a number of Helmes in the Caribbean in colonial times, but have not successfully attached any of them here. We have the extensive genealogies of the Tilghmans by Col. Stephen Tillman, and others, and see Elizabeth, born 1694 in the Christopher/Gideon line, as a possible mother, on a date basis. She would be distantly to Richard [Tilghman.] Their ancestral lines come together in England some generations back. Col. Tillman did not have a disposition for Elizabeth. She was an aunt of a John Tilman who was known to be in North Carolina on a timely basis, before he went to Ohio with his son Tobias. Some of the descendants of Gideon changed the spelling to Tillman."

[Ref: Information in quotes compiled in 1998 by Ira Helms, 26705 Haney Avenue, Damascus, MD 20872 (or E-Mail: Irahelms@aol.com). She has been searching for the parents of the North Carolina Helms brothers or cousins for several years, together with Gerald Helms, the principal author of "Helms Descendants, 1720-1991." Some of the information was gleaned by me (Peden) from *Abstracts of Charles County, Maryland Court and Land Records, Volume 1, 1658-1666*, by Elise Greenup Jourdan (1993), pp. 160, 175.]

HENRY

John Henry died at Pocomoke, Somerset County, Maryland and left a will dated October 1, 1715 and proved on June 20, 1717. He mentioned his wife Mary, minor sons John Henry and Robert Jenkins Henry, and also his brother Hugh Henry in Dublin, Ireland. John Henry, the testator, owned a lot of land, and to his son Robert Jenkins Henry he left "two tracts of land on the Morattock River in North Carolina, one containing 930 acres and the other 640 acres." It is not known whether or not Robert moved to North Carolina or sold the land. Additional research will be necessary before drawing conclusions. [Ref: *Maryland Calendar of Wills, Volume IV, 1713-1720*, pp. 114-115.]

HERMAN

The following is recorded in the land records in Rowan County, North Carolina: "George Herman, of Frederick County, Maryland, received Sacrament of Lords Supper on Protestant Congregation in Maryland with 2 witnesses in pursuance of Act of Parliament for naturalizing foreign protestants in the Colonies, having been in America 7 years, and took the oath of allegiance 14 Sept 1763. Reverdy Ghiselon. Reg 28 May 1770." [Ref: *Rowan County, North Carolina, Deed Abstracts, Vol. II, 1762-1772*, by Jo White Linn (Salisbury, N. C.: Privately published, 1972), p. 138.]

Similar information appears in the records of Maryland for Georg Michael Doorn, John Hahn, and George Herman, of Frederick County (Germans), members of Silber Runte (Silver Run) Lutheran Church. Their date of communion by Rev. Beck was August 7, 1763 and the date of naturalization or denization was September 14, 1763 (as recorded in Rowan County, North Carolina on May 28, 1770). The witnesses were John Lewis, Daniel Stern, Jacob Bencker, and Leinhard Zug. [Ref: *Colonial Maryland Naturalizations*, by Jeffrey A. Wyand and Florence L. Wyand (Baltimore: Genealogical Publishing Co., 1975), p. 47.]

On August 20, 1765, George Hermann, of Frederick County, Maryland, sold 27 acres to Bartell Cesar for £27, part of a tract called *Whiterbark* on a small branch descending into Bair Branch, a draught of Great Pipe Creek. He signed his named Georg Harman in German Script, and his wife Mary Herman released her dower. It is interesting to note that the name was spelled three different ways in the same record. [Ref: *Frederick County, Maryland, Land Records, Liber J Abstracts, 1763-1767*, by Patricia Abelard Andersen (Gaithersburg, MD: GenLaw Resources, 1996), p. 95.]

HOLDMAN

Isaac Holdman removed from Anne Arundel County, Maryland and settled on the Yadkin River in Rowan County, North Carolina circa 1750. [Ref: *Carolina Cradle*, by Robert W. Ramsey (1964), p. 83, citing North Carolina Land Grants VI:162, and Harry Wright Newman's *Anne Arundel Gentry*, p. 437.]

HORAH

"Henry Horah, originally from Cecil County, Maryland, asked to keep a tavern at his dwelling where Deacon formerly lived. The reference to James Deacon indicates that the inn may have been located on Second Creek, twelve miles west of Salisbury [North Carolina], for both Deacon and Horah possessed land along the creek. On the other hand, Horah's inn (and Deacon's home) might have been in the town, for the former obtained title to four lots in 1757 and 1762. Horah operated a weaver's shop on one of his lots, probably one of the three which he obtained in the southwest square in 1762. He also bought lot number nine in the north square from a tailor named Bostian Boise." During the French and Indian War, Henry Horah provided a service and was paid (public claim) in the amount of £27 for "waggoning the expedition" on May 1, 1760. [Ref: *Carolina Cradle*, by Robert W. Ramsey (1964), pp. 162, 198, citing North Carolina Land Grants XI:8, Rowan County Deeds III:17, and the Horah file in the McCubbins Collection at the Salisbury Public Library in Salisbury, North Carolina.]

HOWARD

Philip Howard, Sr., Philip Howard, Jr., Benjamin Howard, and Cornelius Howard migrated from Anne Arundel County, Maryland to Frederick County, Maryland sometime between 1749 and 1754. They then moved to the forks of the Yadkin River and settled in the Trading Camp settlement in Rowan County, North Carolina. [Ref: *Carolina Cradle*, by Robert W. Ramsey (1964), pp. 76-77, 107, and citing Harry Wright Newman's *Anne Arundel Gentry*, pp. 295-299.]

On November 20, 1764, in Frederick County, Maryland, Mathew Howard recorded a bill of sale from John Howard, of the County of Rockwell, Province of North Carolina, for valuable consideration paid by said Mathew Howard, of Frederick County, Maryland, for one negro man named Toby that said John Howard had left in the hand of Lydia Howard, of Anne Arundel County, Maryland. [Ref: *Frederick County, Maryland, Land Records Liber J Abstracts, 1763-1767*, by Patricia Abelard Andersen (1996), p. 28.]

HOWELL

On "10 May 1769, Daniel Howell, planter, of Aramascoot, Hyde Co., North Carolina, power of attorney to Jacob Giles, of Baltimore Co., Maryland. Signed: Daniel Howell. Wit: Elizabeth Giles and Amos Garrett." And, on "7 Apr 1769, Thomas Wilkins, laborer, of Hyde Co., North Carolina, power of attorney to Daniel Howell, of same. Signed: Thomas (x) Wilkins. Wit: John Clarkson and David Sweeny, Jr." [Ref: *Baltimore County, Maryland, Deed Records, Book Four: 1767-1775*, by John Davis (1997), p. 47.]

Samuel Howell was in Baltimore County, Maryland by December, 1720, when he married Priscilla Freeborne. Their children were: Daniel (born September 15, 1721); Samuel (born January 11, 1723 or 1732?); Mordecai (born June 10, 1725); Phebe (born November 3, 1726); Aquila (born September 3, 1728); Frenella (no date of birth was given); and, Job (born March 10, 1733). [Ref: *Baltimore County Families, 1659-1759*, by Robert W. Barnes (1989), p. 344.]

HUFFMAN-HUFMAN

Martin Huffman or Hufman was living in Maryland at least from 1772 to after 1777. He and his family appear in the 1776 Census of Maryland in North West Hundred of Frederick County:
    Martain Hufman, age 41;
    Barbara Hufman, age 35;

John Hufman, age 14;
Elizabeth Hufman, age 12;
Joseph Hufman, age 10;
Hannah Hufman, age 8; and,
Mary Hufman, age 4.

"It is fairly conclusive that this was the Catawba County, North Carolina family of Martin Huffman [for these reasons]:

"First, Martin's age corresponds with the birth date on his tombstone, April 10, 1735.

"Second, the wife's name, Barbara, is the same.

"Finally, the names of the five children in the census are the same as those in the estate settlements (Polly in the estate settlements is a nick name for Mary)."

"The birth and baptism of Mary is recorded in the records of Evangelical Lutheran Church in Frederick, Maryland: Anna Maria, daughter of Martin and Anna Barbara Hoffman, born May 12, 1772, baptized July 22, 1772. Sponsors: Theodorous and Dorothea Kraus. Three of the children, Martin Jr., George, and Henry, were apparently born after 1776."

"As pointed out by Mrs. Eaker [referring to Lorena Shell Eaker's book in 1994 entitled *German Speaking People West of the Catawba River in North Carolina, 1750-1800*] the 1850 U. S. Census for Catawba County gives the birth date of Martin Jr. as about 1777 in Maryland. According to the dates on George's tombstone, he was born about 1780. The age of Martin's oldest child, John, suggests that Martin had married by at least 1761. There is a discrepancy between this date and the date of 1765 given for the marriage of Martin Huffman to Barbara Aker in Orange County, North Carolina (See, for example, the Naugle genealogy in Anne W. McAllister's *Through Four Generations*, p. 798). If this date is correct, then Martin must have had a prior marriage.

"Of possible interest here is a marriage of a Martin Hoffmann to Barbara Weiner at St. Michael's and Zion Lutheran Church, Philadelphia, Pennsylvania, dated August 11, 1759. I can't be sure this is the Catawba County Martin Huffman, though, since there were other Martin Hoffmans in Pennsylvania during the same general time period. I have not done a thorough investigation, but of sources I have checked (church records for Berks, Bucks, and Adams Counties), none had a wife Barbara. It would be reasonable, though, for someone marrying in later 1759 to have a first child in 1762."

[Ref: Information gleaned from an article in *Catawba Cousins* (Journal of the Catawba County Genealogical Society), Vol. 12, No. 1 (June, 1997), pp. 5-8, by Ray A. Yount, entitled "Some Pre-1800 Emigrants from Frederick County, Maryland to Old Lincoln County" which was contributed by Ray A. Yount, 10031 Shortest Day Road NW, La Vale, MD 21502-0611, or E-Mail: alby6@juno.com.]

HUSBAND

Herman Husband was a trustee of the Bush River Meeting, Society of Friends, circa 1750. [Ref: *Baltimore County Families, 1659-1759*, by Robert W. Barnes (1989), p. 349.]

Harman Husbands appears in the Baltimore County Debt Book in 1754 on a tract called *Harman's Addition*. [Ref: *Inhabitants of Baltimore County, 1692-1763*, by F. Edward Wright (1987), p. 68.]

Harman Husband is listed among the unpatented certificates and leased in Cecil County in 1750. Herman Husband patented a 30-acre tract called *Herman's Ramble* by 1756 and appears in the debt books in 1755 and 1757. William Husbands owned several tracts between 1734 and 1766, and the heirs of James Husbands owned a tract called *Hog Pen Neck* in 1739. [Ref: *Inhabitants of Cecil County, Maryland, 1649-1774*, by Henry C. Peden (1993), pp. 122, 30, 103.]

On "16 Mar 1758, Herman Husband, of Orange Co., North Carolina, power of attorney to his brother William Husband, of Baltimore Co., Maryland. Signed: Herman Husband. Wit: Thomas Ragh and John Woods." [Ref: *Baltimore County, Maryland, Deed Records, Volume Three: 1755-1767*, by John Davis (1996), p. 75.]

HYNDS-HINDS

James Hynds of Queen Anne's County, Maryland acquired land in the Irish Settlement of Rowan County, North Carolina sometime between 1752 and 1762. [Ref: *Carolina Cradle*, by Robert W. Ramsey (1964), p. 125, citing Rowan County Deeds IV:373.]

Thomas Hinds died in Queen Anne's County in July, 1720 and in his will he mentioned his wife Mary, daughter Mary, and sons James, Thomas, John, Vincent, Charles and Nathaniel. [Ref: *Maryland Calendar of Wills, Volume V, 1720-1726*, p. 20.]

IRELAND

"John and William Ireland originated in Calvert County, Maryland, where the family settled in 1725." They migrated westward before 1750 and settled in Rowan County, North Carolina. [Ref: *Carolina Cradle*, by Robert W. Ramsey (1964), p. 96.]

Actually, John Ireland was in St. Mary's County before October 22, 1722, at which time he witnessed the will of William Hoskins (Haskins). Thomas Ireland, Jr. was in Calvert County before February 3, 1736/7, at which time he witnessed the will of William Hickman, who bequeathed land on the Gunpowder River in Baltimore County called *Clarkson's Hope* to his daughter Mary Ireland, and also £12 to William Ireland. [Ref: *Maryland Calendar of Wills, Volume V, 1720-1726*, p. 122; *Maryland Calendar of Wills, Volume VII, 1732-1738*, p. 206.]

It should also be noted that a William Ireland was married in Talbot County in 1704 and Samuel Ireland was married there in 1715. [Ref: *Maryland Marriages, 1634-1777*, by Robert W. Barnes (1975), p. 95.]

JETTON

Abraham Jetton migrated to western North Carolina from Cecil County, Maryland and settled in the Davidson's Creek Settlement in Rowan County by 1762, when he purchased land from John Gullick. [Ref: *Carolina Cradle*, by Robert W. Ramsey (1964), pp. 103, 105, citing Rowan County Deeds IV:247, IV:297, and North Carolina Land Grants VI:201.]

JOHNSON

Amos Johnson, of Baltimore County, died by February 17, 1761 when administration bond was posted by Lydia Johnson with Peter Miles. The estate was administered on November 8, 1762 by Lydia, now wife of William Bain, and Peter Miles. Amos Johnson left six children, of whom William was in Colleton County, South Carolina by January, 1773, when he sold a tract called *Robinson's Outlet* to William Bull. [Ref: *Baltimore County Families, 1659-1759*, by Robert W. Barnes (1989), p. 367.]

On "4 Jan 1773, William Johnson, (son and heir of Amos Johnson), late of Baltimore Co., Maryland, but now of Colleton Co., South Carolina, to William Bull, planter, of Baltimore Co., Maryland, £294.6, 170 acres. Signed: William Johnson. Wit: John Howard and Thomas Franklin." [Ref: *Baltimore County, Maryland, Deed Records, Book Four: 1767-1775*, by John Davis (1997), p. 221.]

JONES

On November 3, 1742, the following indenture was recorded in Prince George's County, Maryland at the request of Henry Wright: "Indenture between John Courts, of Charles County, gentleman, and Henry Wright, gentleman; for 5s.; part of a greater tract which Griffith Jones, late of North Carolina, sold John Courts for 80 acres. Signed: John Courts. Wit: Wm. Ragen and Josh. Hopkinson." [Ref: *The Land Records of Prince George's County, Maryland, 1739-1743*, by Elise Greenup Jourdan (1996), p. 93.]

"Henry Jones, from Philadelphia County, Pennsylvania or from Kent County, Maryland, was an inhabitant of the Carolina frontier by March, 1753. Six years later he witnessed a deed from Jonathan Boone to John Frohock on the east side of Hunting Creek. Henry Jones may have been related to David Jones (first sheriff of Rowan County, North Carolina)." [Ref: *Carolina Cradle*, by Robert W. Ramsey (1964), p. 81, citing Philadelphia Wills I:25-26; Maryland Wills 1635-1777, XXVIII:41; Rowan County Deeds IV:92.]

"Ralph Jones and Mary (Harrison) his wife, grandparents of Lucretia Jones, wife of Joseph Alexander Wylie. From *South Carolina Baptist, 1670-1800*, by

Leah Townsend, published in recent years and a copy is now in the Library at the University of South Carolina, page 140: 'Sandy River Church originated from a group of Virginia and North Carolina Baptists who settled on Sandy River and invited ministers from Buffalo, Little River, Fairforest, and Congaree churches to preach for them. They built Flat Rock Meeting House somewhere near Turkey Creek and had members living in Pacolet, Turkey Creek, and Little River. This group requested the 1776 meeting of Congaree, also at Fairforest, to constitute them a church. The Rev. Messrs. Ralph Jones, Joseph Camp and Joseph Logan met with them at Flat Rock Meeting House, December 23, 1778 and organized a church."

"A footnote in the above book mentioned Mary, wife of Ralph Jones. This Jones family, along with several of the same name, settled in Fairfield County, South Carolina in 1769. The Ralph Jones "Meeting House" (M. H.) is plainly marked on Mill's Atlas of Fairfield County, published in 1825. The name of Ralph Jones does not appear on any of the ship lists of that period, that I have seen, so he and Mary must have come down by way of Maryland or Pennsylvania."

"Ralph Jones wrote his will in 1811 and died in 1817, naming his wife Mary Jones, sons John Jones, Elijah Jones, William Jones, Elisha Jones, and daughters Sarah Pearsons, Mary Willingham, Phebe McGraw, and Catherine Merideth." [Ref: *The Bulletin* of the Chester District Genealogical Society, Volume X, No. 1 (March, 1987), pp. 21-22.]

On October 16, 1780, William Jones, of Cabin Creek in Dorchester County, Maryland, planter, conveyed to Benjamin Collison, of the same county, planter, part of *Goodridge's Choice*, containing 209 acres, on Cabin Creek. Acknowledged by William Jones and Delitha his wife before witnesses Joseph Richardson and Thomas Jones, Justices. On October 22, 1791, William Jones, of Rockingham County, North Carolina, planter, conveyed to Benjamin Collison, of Dorchester County, planter, 209 acres of *Goodridge's Choice* on Cabin Creek. Henry Waggaman and Nicholas Hammond, Esquires, were named as attorneys for William Jones to acknowledge this deed in court. Witnesses: Timothy Corkran, Edward Collinson, and Jonathan Bird. Proved by witnesses and acknowledged by attorneys in Dorchester County Court on March 22, 1792. H. Dickinson, Clerk. [Ref: *Abstracts of the Land Records of Dorchester County, Maryland, Volume 30 (Liber HD#3)*, by James A. McAllister, Jr. (1967), p. 51.]

JORDAN

On August 14, 1723, John Jordan, son of John Jordan, late of North Carolina, conveyed to Richard Tilghman, in consideration of £50 current money, 935 acres called *Forlorn Hope*, granted to Robert Smith and sold to John Jordan, Sr. and John Jordan, Jr. and their heirs (refer to the records of Kent County, Maryland), lying at the head of Chester River on the east side of Shewell Branch near one mile from Ducke Creeke road. Witnesses were Thomas Hynson Wright, James Earle, and Benjamin Hallowell. Acknowledged before Arthur Emory and Solomon Clayton.

Benjamin Hallowell, of North Carolina, made oath that for about twelve years last past he has been acquainted with John Jordan, Sr. and Charity his wife and that they did acknowledge John Jordan, Jr. who is almost blind and had been for some time, to be their lawful son. John Jordan, Sr. has been dead about three years. [Ref: *Queen Anne's County Land Records, Book One, 1701-1725*, by R. Bernice Leonard (1992), p. 88.]

John Jordan and Jane Jordan were both buried on February 8, 1708 in St. Paul's Parish, Kent County, Maryland. Mary Ann Jordan married Samuel Day on February 17, 1723 in St. Peter's Parish, Talbot County, Maryland. [Ref: *Maryland Eastern Shore Vital Records, 1648-1725*, by F. Edward Wright (1982), p. 26.]

John Jordine, planter, of Kent County, Maryland, died leaving a will dated February 19, 1708/9 (proved March 29, 1709) and left his entire estate to wife Mary, executrix, and heirs (unnamed). [Ref: *Maryland Calendar of Wills, Volume III, 1703-1713*, p. 125.]

Mary Hutchison (Huchison) died in Kent County, Maryland and left a will dated February 19, 1721 (proved June 30, 1722). She left to her husband Robert Hutchison, 100 acres called *Have Att All* on a branch of Worton Creek, which had been bequeathed to her by her former husband John Jordine. [Ref: *Maryland Calendar of Wills, Volume V, 1720-1726*, p. 111.]

KISER-KIZER

Lawrence Kiser (Kizer, Keiser, Kyser) was probably born circa 1709 in Grossgratch, Neckar, Wurttemburg, Germany and may be the Lorentz Kayser who arrived at Philadelphia on the ship *St. Andrew Galley* on September 26, 1737. Johan Adam Kayser, son of Lorentz Kayser, was born in February, 1750 and baptized on July 29, 1750 at Monocacy Congregation and Evangelical Lutheran Church in Frederick County, Maryland. On May 17, 1754 Lawrence Skycer entered a land entry for 200 acres on the south side of Beaverdam Creek "including the place he now lives on" in Anson County, North Carolina. On April 10, 1761 Lawrence Kysar acquired 300 acres on both sides of Beaverdam Creek "including his own improvements." On October 2, 1787 Adam and George Kiser divided the 300 acres granted to their father Lawrence Kiser on April 10, 1761. Adam signed his name in German as Hans Adam Keiser.

Lorance Kiser wrote his will on January 25, 1786 and it was proved in July, 1786 in Lincoln County, North Carolina and probated in September, 1786. His wife was Sarah --- and their children were as follows:

(1) Laurence or Lorentz Kiser, Jr. (born in Maryland or Pennsylvania circa 1740, married ----, had 7 children, and died in North Carolina after 1820);

(2) Joseph Kiser or Kizer (born circa 1745 in Maryland or Pennsylvania, married ----, had 12 children, and died before 1810 in North Carolina);

(3) George Kiser (born circa 1748 in Maryland or Pennsylvania, married ----, had 9 children, and died in 1819 in Lincoln County, North Carolina);

(4) Adam Kiser or Kyser (born in February, 1750 in Frederick County, Maryland, married Sarah Best (1759-1834, daughter of Sebastian Best and Catharine Hoyle), had 10 children (four of whom died in the typhoid fever epidemic of 1809), and died in April, 1833 in Lincoln County, North Carolina);

(5) Ca---- Kiser or Kizer (believed to be Catherine, wife of Valentine Mauney, but no proof);

(6) Mary Kiser (possibly married William Fronebarger, but no proof);

(7) Christina Kiser (born circa 1755 in North Carolina, married Jacob Plonk (born 1747 or 1748 in Lancaster County, Pennsylvania), and died July 30, 1823 in Lincoln County, North Carolina); and,

(8) Elizabeth Kiser (born circa 1765, married Peter Plonk, and died after 1824 (year of Peter's death) in Lincoln County, North Carolina.

[Ref: *German Speaking People West of the Catawba River in North Carolina, 1750-1800*, by Lorena Shell Eaker (1994), pp. 262-266.]

KENNEDY-CANADAY

"Felix and John Kennedy (or Canaday), probably from Kent County, Maryland, entered the Shendandoah Valley [of Virginia] prior to 1744. Eleven years later, both were living in the Waxhaw Settlement on the border between North and South Carolina, where they served in Andrew Pickens' company of militia. However, Felix evidently resided for several years after 1748 in the Irish Settlement [in North Carolina], where he had a small tract on the west bank of Sill's Creek, three miles above John Holmes." [Ref: *Carolina Cradle*, by Robert W. Ramsey (1964), pp. 43-44, citing Kent County Deeds IV:550; North Carolina Land Grants VI:235; Robert N. McNeely's "Union County and the Old Waxhaw Settlement" in *The North Carolina Booklet* (Salisbury, N. C.: Daughters of the American Revolution), Volume XII, No. 1, pp. 8-9.]

The name of John Kennedy appears on a list of petit jurors in Union County, South Carolina in 1786. [Ref: *Union County, South Carolina, Minutes of the County Court, 1785-1799*, by Brent H. Holcomb (1979), p. 53.]

In Maryland, the debt books of Kent County record that a John Canaday owned a tract called *Heritage* on which he paid taxes between 1736 and 1741. [Ref: *Inhabitants of Kent County, Maryland, 1637-1787*, by Henry C. Peden, Jr. (1994), p. 6.]

The register of St. Paul's Parish in Kent County indicates that John Canaday and Elizabeth Douge were married on May 31, 1701. A later entry indicates that John Cannaday and Elizabeth his wife were "buried December 29, ----" (appears to be 1704). [Ref: *Maryland Eastern Shore Vital Records, 1648-1725*, by F. Edward Wright (1982), pp. 16-17.]

Also, the register of St. Peter's Parish in Talbot County, Maryland records the marriage of John Canaday and Margaret Summers [Marget Sumers] on August 17, 1727, and the register of St. Paul's Parish records the birth of their five children between 1728 and 1735, the oldest of whom was John Cannaday, born on July 22,

1728. [Ref: *Maryland Eastern Shore Vital Records, 1726-1750*, by F. Edward Wright (1983), pp. 20, 64.]

KILPATRICK-KILLPATRICK

John Kilpatrick originated in Cecil County, Maryland and migrated to Rowan County, North Carolina sometime between 1752 and 1762, settling in the Irish Settlement. [Ref: *Carolina Cradle*, by Robert W. Ramsey (1964), p. 128, citing Rowan County Deeds IV:802 and Cecil County Deeds X:302.]

John Killpatrick was a private in Capt. Peter Bayard's Company of Foot in Cecil County, Maryland in 1740. John Kilpatrick also appeared on a list of taxables in 1752. [Ref: *Inhabitants of Cecil County, Maryland, 1649-1774*, by Henry C. Peden, Jr. (1993), pp. 52, 129.]

KIRKMAN

James Kirkman died in Guilford County, North Carolina in 1791, leaving a will dated March 25, 1790 and probated in May, 1791. His named heirs were his wife Mary, sons George, William, Elijah, Elisha, Thomas Sherwood, and Rodger, and grandson James Hendrick (son of Mary Hendricks). His executors were Mary Kirkman, Hendnay Henricks [Henry Hendricks] and Robert Hanna. [Ref: *Guilford County, North Carolina, Will Abstracts, 1771-1841*, compiled, indexed and published by Irene B. Webster, p. 34, citing wills liber A, folio 208.]

Peter Kirkman died in Guilford County, North Carolina in 1801, leaving a will dated November 20, 1800 and probated in February, 1801. His named heirs were his wife Eleanor, daughter Sarah, eldest sons John and George, and sons William and Peter. His executors were his wife Eleanor Kirkman and brother William Kirkman. [Ref: Webster, *Ibid.*, citing wills liber A, folio 209.]

"The move of Kirkmans from England, sailing from London to Maryland, began with a George Kirkman in 1649, followed by two or more brothers within a few years and several others later. They appear to all have settled in Dorchester County, Maryland. In 1785 the Second Migration started to Guilford County, North Carolina and was fairly complete by the time of the first U. S. census in 1790. It appears from the records that at least one Kirkman family continued in Dorchester County; also that at least one family moved to Baltimore. And there were probably others. When Kentucky and Tennessee opened up in the later 1700's and early 1800's as extensions of Virginia and North Carolina, they attracted some children of the Guilford County, North Carolina Kirkmans. In Todd County, Kentucky is Kirkmansville, a mountain village and still home of several Kirkman families. Soon after 1810 settlement north of the Ohio River was begun and several young Kirkmans and their families moved from Guilford County to Wayne County, Indiana. Several families still reside in Richmond, the county seat, but many have moved to the cities and further west. Likewise, several families from Guilford moved to Harrison County, Indiana. When Illinois and Iowa were opened some children of the second and third generations at Greensboro, North Carolina were ready to start west. One group settled near Moravia in south-central Iowa [and at Kirkman, Iowa.] The chief group of the Kirkman family in America continued to be in Guilford County, North Carolina, just as it was at the time of the first United States Census in 1790." [Ref: Information compiled before 1995 by Donna Kirkman, 6878 77 Terr. N., Pinellas Park, Florida 34665 and Dora W. Mitchell, Box 35, Preston, Maryland 21655. Their research material is on file at the Maryland Historical Society Library, 201 W. Monument Street, Baltimore, Maryland 21201.]

Kirkman, sometimes spelled Kirkmon and Kirkham, is an early family name on the Eastern Shore of Maryland, as noted in Gust Skordas' *The Early Settlers of Maryland* and Peter Wilson Coldham's *Early Settlers of Maryland*, and the following from the Maryland Historical Society Library:

"*Maryland Genealogies and Historical Recorder, Vol. XI*, p. 40, Section 69: Thomas Walker: Patt: 500 acres for transporting Mary Sewell, Elizabeth Hide, Thomas and Mary Coates, George Kirkman, Benj. Cooke, William Horne ... and others ... to habitate province. Land laid out called *Courtisie* on Delaware Bay in Dorchester County in neck called Prime Hooke. Record nearing date at London July 2, 1649. Witness: Charles Calvert."

"Folio 529, Section 56, Year 1664: Resurvey asked for John Rawlings, which land was formerly surveyed for Anthony Rawlings, father of the aforesaid John Rawlings; Samuel Groom enters rights, viz: Ann Fisher, Matthew Smith, Christopher Cambridge, Roger Kirkman, Samuel Barnes ... and others ... rights which he assigned to Jerome Smith and Nicholas Goodridge."

"Folio 462, Book 7, Section 40: Warrant to Anthony Delaney, John Singleton and Richard Jones, and desire warrant for 460 acres, Year 1662; Came Oeter [Peter?] Mills, John Davies, Year 1663; Came William Boutell, William Kirkman, John Richman, Year 1664."

"George Kirkman died in Dorchester County, Maryland, leaving a will dated January 13, 1749 and probated on January 30, 1749. His named heirs were his wife Elizabeth, sons George Jr. and Roger, and daughters Comfort Reding, Rosannah Hackett [wife of Oliver] and Ann Twyford [wife of John, who died in 1768.]"

"James Kirkman, son of George, moved to Guilford County, North Carolina after 1774. His wife was Mary Sherwood (who had married first to ---- White) and their children were: George Kirkman, Jr. (born c1735 in Maryland, married Elizabeth ----, and died October 32, 1820 in North Carolina); William Kirkman (married Rhoda Sullivan); Elisha Kirkman; Elijah Kirkman; Mary Kirkman (married Henry Hendricks); Thomas Sherwood Kirkman (born October 1, 1771, married Tabitha Fields, and died March 6, 1850); and, Roger Kirkman (born March 30, 1774, married Sarah Wood, and died April 22, 1862)."

"Roger Kirkman, son of James, was born in Dorchester County (the part that became Caroline County in 1774), Maryland on March 30, 1774 and married Sarah Wood (born November 9, 1778 in Randolph County, North Carolina), daughter of

Zebedee and Mary Wood [who were from Anne Arundel County, Maryland.] Their children were: Isabell Kirkman (married 1st Nehemiah Causey and 2nd Kivett Meredith); James Kirkman (born May 16, 1798, married Ruhamah Fields, daughter of Peter Fields and Charlottey Vickrey, on August 22, 1818; he died on January 17, 1876, buried in Pin Hook Cemetery, Vandalia Township, Fayette County, Illinois; she died on October 30, 1867, buried in Simmons Cemetery, Jackson Township, Hancock County, Indiana); Zebedee Kirkman (born 1800/1, married Sarah Windly on April 27, 1824, and died in 1838); Thomas Kirkman (born 1802, married 1st Rebecca Dobson on September 6, 1824 and 2nd Elizabeth Dobson on November 2, 1833, and died in 1889 in Buchanan County, Missouri); Joseph Kirkman (married Elizabeth Pool on July 8, 1834); William Kirkman (born November 2, 1808, married Lucinda McCain on June 4, 1836, and died on September 27, 1880 in Buchanan County, Missouri); Roddy D. Kirkman (born October 10, 1813, married 1st Nancy Ann Doak on November 7, 1838 and 2nd Nancy Elliott on July 20, 1852, and died July 1, 1862 in Guilford County, North Carolina); Nancy Letitia Kirkman (married William Smith on September 24, 1836); Mary Molly Kirkman (born March 21, 1819, married John Milton Fentress on May 8, 1844, and died July 10, 1886); Samuel Edward Kirkman (born September 7, 1821, married Elizabeth McCulloch on April 20, 1843, and died October 25, 1896); and, Robert Kirkman (born September 19, 1830, married Letitia Plunkett on October 10, 1849, and died June 19, 1912). Roger Kirkman, the father, died in Guilford County, North Carolina on April 22, 1862 and Sarah Wood Kirkman died on July 17, 1866. They are buried in Tabernacle Church Cemetery in Greensboro." [Ref: Information compiled by Donna Kirkman and Dora W. Mitchell before 1995, *loc. cit.*, with additional information in brackets.]

KNOX

"John Knox may have migrated north and west from Somerset County, Maryland, or he may have removed from Colerain, Ireland to Pennsylvania. The name appears but seldom in the records. In either event, he settled on Third Creek (where his descendants still reside) in 1757 or 1758" in the Irish Settlement of Rowan County, North Carolina. [Ref: *Carolina Cradle*, by Robert W. Ramsey (1964), p. 127, citing *The Knox Family*, by Hattie S. Goodman (Richmond, Virginia: Whittet and Shepperson, 1905), pp. 30-31.]

John Knox died testate in Somerset County, Maryland in June, 1723, leaving a wife Ann, sons John, William, Mark, and Samuel, and three daughters (unnamed). [Ref: *Maryland Calendar of Wills, Volume V, 1720-1726*, p. 142.]

LAWSON

Roger Lawson originated in Cecil County, Maryland and migrated to western North Carolina circa 1760, settling in the Fourth Creek Settlement. Hugh Lawson was in Milford Hundred, Cecil County, in 1724. Nine years later he obtained land there from Roger Lawson, whose name appears in the Cecil County judgment records as early as 1712. [Ref: *Carolina Cradle*, by Robert W. Ramsey (1964), pp. 94, 103.]

Roger Lawson was one of the first purchasers of part of the tract *Society* in 1718 or 1719, west of New Munster in Cecil County. This manor was just west of Little Elk and extended some miles northward. The deed from James Carroll to Roger Lawson warranted to defend his title "against all persons claiming title, under ye government of Pennsylvania or ye territories thereunto belonging." This was due to the raging controversy between the Penns and Lord Baltimore about the boundaries of their respective provinces. [Ref: *History of Cecil County, Maryland*, by George Johnston (1881), p. 137.]

The debt books of Cecil County indicate that Roger Lawson owned the tract *Society* on which he paid taxes between 1734 and 1760. [Ref: *Inhabitants of Cecil County, Maryland 1649-1774*, by Henry C. Peden, Jr. (1993), p. 105.]

LAZENBY

Members of this family migrated to Iredell County, North Carolina from Montgomery County, Maryland after 1777. The following family members are buried in the Lewis Graveyard in Iredell County: Joshua Lazenby, a Revolutionary War soldier, died in 1841 in his 81st year; his wife Keziah died in 1826 in her 73rd year; and, their children: Robert (1785-1828), Joshua (1789-1793), Rezin (1792-1856), Henry (1797 - October 8, 1870). Also buried there are: Robert Lewis Lazenby, son of Robert and Margaret, who died in 1838 in his 14th year; Keziah Lazenby, daughter of James and Polly, who died on November 17, 1823, aged 13 years and 28 days; and, two children of Henry Lazenby and Elizabeth Fitzgerald, Talitha C. Lazenby (1830-1833) and Susan Lazenby (1831-1833). [Ref: Information gleaned from "Lewis Graveyard With Mention of Some Early Settlers Along Fifth Creek, Iredell County, North Carolina" written in 1944 by Mary Elinor Lazenby (born 1875) in a booklet maintained in the Michigan Microfilm Collection (LH110) and published in the *Maryland Genealogical Society Bulletin*, Vol. 39, No. 1 (Winter, 1998), p. 94.]

One Robert Lazenby served on a jury in Frederick County, Maryland in 1753 and 1755. [Ref: *This Was The Life: Excerpts from the Judgment Records of Frederick County, Maryland, 1748-1765*, by Millard Milburn Rice (1979), pp. 129, 169.]

LEMASTER-LAMASTER

Joseph Lemaster or Lamaster was a son of Isaac Lemaster. He lived in Maryland when he enlisted at Morgantown, [West] Virginia for service in the Virginia Line during the Revolutionary War. After the war he moved to Abbeville District, South Carolina and married Mary Waddell, daughter of John and Mary Waddell, in 1791 or 1792. They afterwards moved to Tennessee where Joseph applied for a pension in Maury County on June 21, 1819, aged 61. In 1823 he was living in Williamson County, Tennessee, where he died in August, 1828 while visiting relatives. His widow applied for a pension (W797) in Maury County on May 23, 1839, aged 81, and died there on April 16, 1842. They had 7 children (5 daughters and 2 sons), but the only ones named were son John Waddell Lemaster (born October 21, 1793, married Nancy Lee Almond on October 11, 1821, and their children were Mary Elizabeth Lemaster who was born August 6, 1822, Marcus Lafayett Lemaster who was born December 10, 1824 and died July 25, 1825, Saphrona Ann Lemaster who was born August 5, 1827, Charlott Rebakah Lemaster who was born March 9, 1830, John Brown Lemaster who died August 29, 1833, and James Knox Polk Lemaster who died May 28, 1835), and daughters Mary Lemaster (aged 24 in 1823) and Elizabeth Lemaster (aged 16 in 1823).

Also mentioned in Joseph Lemaster's pension were his brothers Isaac, Richard, Benjamin and Thomas Lemaster and sisters Mary, Charity and Cathryne (no last names were given). Joseph's wife Mary Waddell had brothers John, William, George and James Waddell and sisters Jane and Elizabeth (no last names were given). Joseph's daughter Rebecca McKay was aged about 55 when she made affidavit on May 15, 1839 in Maury County, Tennessee and stated she was a daughter by Joseph's first wife and was 8 years old when her father married Mary Waddell. [Ref: *Genealogical Abstracts of Revolutionary War Pension Files, Volume II: F-M*, by Virgil D. White (1990), p. 2053.]

Joseph Lemaster or Lamasters was a sergeant in the 9th Virginia Continental Line who subsequently applied for bounty land. [Ref: *Historical Register of Virginians in the Revolution, 1775-1783*, by John H. Gwathmey (1938), pp. 454, 468.]

LEWIS

"Among the very early settlers from Montgomery County, Maryland to Iredell County, North Carolina was Daniel Lewis and his eighteen year old wife Margery Waters, arriving in 1777. Daniel had already served with the Maryland Flying Camp in the Battle of Long Island [August 27, 1776] and had some service ahead of him in his new home. It is likely that he and Margery lived on Prior Smallwood Robey's land, for the latter is not found again in any local records, until ten years later he transferred to Daniel Lewis the two tracts in his father's will, amounting to 170 acres. Here Daniel Lewis lived until his death in 1836, meantime adding to his holdings by small purchases. Prior Smallwood Robey was back in Maryland after his stepmother's death."

"In 1789 Daniel Lewis' first wife Margery died. She was buried in the plot known as the Lewis Graveyard. Here is the earliest marked grave, and for this there is an obvious reason. One of their old neighbors, Zachariah Summers, had come from Maryland and settled among them, and he was a skilled stone-cutter. He carved most of the inscriptions in the graveyard, where his headstone stands today, though

Ninean Steele (1815-1858) carved some of them, as his name appears on them."

"The Lewis Graveyard continued to be the burying ground of those Maryland people who came to the section in early years, until other burying grounds developed around churches. Interments continued to be made there as late as 1878, when some living in 1944 recall that of Margaret Fitzgerald, wife of Henry Fitzgerald, who was a daughter of Daniel Lewis. It was natural that members of families should be buried by those long resting there, even though the old graveyard was getting a little out of date."

Daniel Lewis died in 1836 in his 81st year. Margery (Waters) Lewis, his first wife, died in 1789, age 30. Elizabeth (Belt) Lewis, his second wife, died in 1838 in herd 80th year. Also buried in the Lewis Graveyard is Samuel Green (husband of Venelia Lazenby, daughter of Robert and Margery Lazenby) who died in 1849.

[Ref: Information gleaned from "Lewis Graveyard With Mention of Some Early Settlers Along Fifth Creek, Iredell County, North Carolina" written in 1944 by Mary Elinor Lazenby (born 1875) in a booklet maintained in the Michigan Microfilm Collection (LH110) and published in the *Maryland Genealogical Society Bulletin*, Vol. 39, No. 1 (Winter, 1998), pp. 93, 95.]

Richard Lewis resided in Cecil County, Maryland in 1740 at which time he was a private in the militia. Sometime before 1762 he migrated to western North Carolina and resided in the Fourth Creek Settlement. Ann Lewis, daughter of Richard Lewis and his wife Amey, married Nathaniel Sympers (Simpers) in St. Mary Anne's Parish (North Elk Parish) in Cecil County on October 10, 1759. The debt books of Cecil County indicate that Richard Lewis owned part of "St. John's Manor" on which he paid taxes between 1734 and 1760. Richard Lewis (Lowis), Sr. died testate in Cecil County and his will was probated on August 4, 1720, naming his wife Anne Lewis, son John Lewis, eldest son Richard Lewis, son-in-law Thomas Simper (Simpers), and Kesia Clark.

[Ref: *Carolina Cradle*, by Robert W. Ramsey (1964), p. 94; *Early Anglican Church Records of Cecil County*, by Henry C. Peden, Jr. (1990), p. 72; *Inhabitants of Cecil County, Maryland, 1649-1774*, by Henry C. Peden, Jr. (1993), pp. 51, 106; *Maryland Calendar of Wills, Volume V, 1720-1726*, p. 21.]

LINDSAY

Little is known of the origin of Walter Lindsay who settled in the Fourth Creek Settlement of Rowan County, North Carolina circa 1752. "Lindsay, who removed to Rowan from the Shenandoah Valley, was made a major in the militia in 1764 and qualified as a justice of the peace the same year. He may have originated in Prince George's County, Maryland." Anthony and Alice Lindsay, and son Samuel, were mentioned in the will of Francis Tolson in Prince George's County in 1730. [Ref: *Carolina Cradle*, by Robert W. Ramsey (1964), p. 101; *Maryland Calendar of Wills, Volume VI, 1726-1732*, p. 181.]

LOYD

On October 28, 1765, in Frederick County, Maryland, Dickinson Lenkin recorded a deed between himself and John Loyd, of Roan [Rowan] County, North Carolina, for £22, title to a tract called *Elder's Spring* on the south side of a bottom descending into a branch of Linganore, containing 49 1/2 acres. John Loyd signed before J. Dickson and Thomas Price. Receipt acknowledged. No dower release. [Ref: *Frederick County, Maryland Land Records Liber K Abstracts, 1765-1768*, by Patricia Abelard Andersen (1997), p. 19.]

LOMAX

William Lomax was born in Charles County, Maryland on January 12, 1764 and at the age of 16 he moved to Guilford County, North Carolina. He lived there at the time of his enlistment in the North Carolina Line. A few years after the war he moved to Montgomery County, North Carolina and then moved to Rowan County, North Carolina where he applied for a pension on the 3rd Monday in May, 1819. In 1829 he lived in that part of Rowan County that became Davidson County and died there on November 5, 1835. His widow Tabitha applied for a pension (W5028) on October 19, 1838 and stated she was born on November 4, 1769, a daughter of Alexander Gooden or Goodin, and she married William Lomax at her father's home in Montgomery County, North Carolina on December 26, 1793. She also received bounty land warrant #34833-160-55. Tabitha Lomax died on February 15, 1856, leaving 5 children whose names were not given in her file. In 1857 the oldest son John A. Lomax was administrator of Tabitha's estate. He lived in Davidson County and died there "some years prior to 1877."

In 1857 Wesley Lomax lived at Troy, Montgomery County, North Carolina and he named the children of William Lomax (the soldier) as follows:

John Lomax (born November 6, 1794);
Amy Lomax (born October 16, 1796);
Nancy Lomax (born January 20, 1799);
Polly Lomax (born June 19, 1801);
William Lomax (born June 20, 1803);
Cornelius Lomax (born March 8, 1806);
West Lomax (born May 31, 1809).

[Ref: *Genealogical Abstracts of Revolutionary War Pension Files, Volume II: F-M*, by Virgil D. White (1990), pp. 2107-2108.]

William Lomax enlisted as a private in Capt. Blount's Company on May 10, 1779 and served 18 months. He apparently enlisted again on May 9, 1781 in Capt. McRee's Company and served as a private for another 12 months. There appears to have been more then one soldier named William Lomax or Lomack in North Carolina. Additional research may be necessary before drawing conclusions. [Ref: *Roster of Soldiers from North Carolina in the American Revolution*, published by the North Carolina Daughters of the American Revolution (Durham, 1932), pp. 141, 180, 205, 218, 219, 247, 579, 580.]

The Lomax family was in Maryland in 1668 at which time Cleborne Lomax and wife Blanch immigrated to Charles County. By July 5, 1687 Cleborne Lomax owned a 98-acre tract called *Lomax's Addition*. [Ref: *The Early Settlers of Maryland*, by Gust Skordas (1968), p. 293; *Settlers of Maryland, 1679-1700*, by Peter Wilson Coldham (1995), p. 106.]

One Clayborn Lomax died intestate in Charles County and distribution of his estate was made to his 7 children (names not given) by Benjamin Lomax, administrator, on February 1, 1776. It is probable that William Lomax, who went to North Carolina in 1780, was of this family. [Ref: *Abstracts of the Balance Books of the Prerogative Court of Maryland, 1770-1777*, by Vernon L. Skinner, Jr. (1995), p. 83.]

LOVELACE

"In the forefront of those who came from Maryland [to Iredell County, North Carolina] was Isaac Lovelace, who bought into the William Archibald tract in 1772, from William Archibald, Jr. and Martha Archibald. Again Isaac Lovelace bought into an old grant when he purchased from Margaret Rosebrough on December 26, 1772, one-half of the Rosebrough land, or 320 acres which had been transferred to her by her son John on March 22, 1768, shortly after his father's death. Two days after buying the land from Margaret Rosebrough, Isaac and Catherine Lovelace transferred it to his step-father Thomas Robey. The writer can not definitely fix an earlier date to the arrival of any Marylanders among those who came in numbers to Fifth Creek, and northward to South Yadkin River, than that of the Lovelace-Robey group. Montgomery County, Maryland, from which most of the Maryland settlers in Iredell of the immediate Revolutionary period came, was a part of Frederick County until 1776, and so it is at Frederick that we find the will of John Baptist Lovelace, dated July 13, 1765. He left his land, part of the well-known tract called *The Hermitage* and now covered by Washington suburbs, to his widow Eleanor during her life, after which it was to go to William, Luke and Elias. His son Charles was to have the remainder of the survey and his son Isaac a tract in Charles County known as *Job's Comfort* after the quaint way of naming Maryland land grants. One-third of the personal estate was to go to the widow and the rest to Vachel (sometimes spelled Vechtel), Archibald, Mary Ann and Millicent, minors."

"Incidently, the two Lovelace brothers, Charles and William, married sisters, Catherine and Margaret Beall, respectively, daughters of James and Margaret Edmonston Beall. The widow, Eleanor Lovelace, married the widower Thomas Robey, and with him and their families they came to the Fifth Creek property. Their wills show them to have been slave owners, and Thomas Robey mentions an indentured servant with freedom dues to be paid. Perhaps no other indentured servant came to Fifth Creek, but in Maryland they were not unusual. Eleanor

Robey's will at Salisbury, October 8, 1776, mentions the same children that John Baptist Lovelace named in his will. Mary Ann had become Shaw and Archibald and Millicent were still minors. Descendants of these children held on to the old place along Fifth Creek, and made entries on Hunting Creek and Dutchman Creek, but the name has long since disappeared from the locality. Elias and Vachel, sons of John and Eleanor Lovelace, moved to Kentucky after the Revolution, in which both served." Among those buried in the Lewis Graveyard in Iredell County, North Carolina are Thomas Lovelace (1772-1829) and his wife Amelia.

[Ref: Information gleaned from "Lewis Graveyard With Mention of Some Early Settlers Along Fifth Creek, Iredell County, North Carolina" written in 1944 by Mary Elinor Lazenby (born 1875) in a booklet maintained in the Michigan Microform Collection (LH110) and published in the *Maryland Genealogical Society Bulletin*, Vol. 39, No. 1 (Winter, 1998), pp. 90-91.]

LOWE

On October 6, 1783, in Dorchester County, Maryland, a deed was recorded between Isaac Lowe, of Guilford County, North Carolina, planter, and John Payne, of Dorchester County, Maryland, planter, for part of *Taylor's Promise* or *Loockermans Mannor* on the road from Cabin Creek Mill to Northwest Fork Bridge, containing 100 acres more or less. Witnesses: John Dickinson and Joseph Richardson, Justices. [Ref: *Abstracts of the Land Records of Dorchester County, Maryland, Volume 26 (Liber NH#2)*, by James A. McAllister, Jr. (1965), p. 29.]

LYNN-LINN

"John, Andrew, and James Lynn (Linn) were originally inhabitants of Talbot or Queen Anne's County, Maryland. John Lynn (probably a relative) was in the Shenandoah Valley before August, 1746, on a tract of land located between the Augusta County courthouse and Tinkling Spring Presbyterian Church. James Lynn (designed as 'architectus') appears on record there in August, 1747, and Andrew Lynn three years later. John Lynn went to North Carolina in 1751 and bought 312 acres from George Cathey in February of the following year. This transaction was a rather significant one because Lynn sold twelve of these acres early in 1753 to a 'Congregation known by the Congregation belonging to ye Lower Meeting House between the Yadkin River and the Catawba River adhering to a Minister licensed from a Presbytery belonging to the old Synod of Philadelphia.' This was the origin of Thyatira Presbyterian Church. It is possible that James and Andrew accompanied John Lynn to Carolina in 1751, for both obtained land there in the spring of 1753. In any event, both John and Andrew Lynn proceeded to the 'Waxhaw settlement' where Andrew died before the spring of 1762." [Ref: *Carolina Cradle*, by Robert W. Ramsey (1964), p. 60, citing Anson County Deeds B-1:179; Rowan County Deeds I:29, 39, 46; Robert N. McNeely's "Union County and the Old Waxhaw Settlement" in *The North Carolina Booklet* (Salisbury, N. C.: Daughters of the American Revolution, Volume XII (No. 1), pp. 8-9.]

Land records in Queen Anne's County, Maryland indicate that Andrew Linn, son and heir of James Linn of Talbot County, sold land to George Cubbage on April 7, 1721 which was the same land that James and Elizabeth Linn had purchased on September 20, 1698. [Ref: *Queen Anne's County, Maryland Land Records, Book One, 1701-1725*, by R. Bernice Leonard (1992), p. 72.]

David Linn served on a jury in Frederick County in 1753 and Joseph Linn was overseer of roads in Kinnoloway [Tonoloway] Hundred. [Ref: *This Was The Life: Excerpts of the Judgment Records of Frederick County, Maryland, 1748-1765*, by Millard Milburn Rice (1979), pp. 128-129.]

MACE

On May 11, 1793, Ezekiel Mace and Angell Mace, of Orange County, North Carolina, granted to Edmund Brannock, of Dorchester County, Maryland, power of attorney to convey to Alexander Robbs, of Orange County, North Carolina, a tract called *Grass Reading* on St. Stephen's Creek in Dorchester County, "belonging to use by the last will and testament of our father Josias Mace," containing 60 acres more or less. Witnesses were Hardy Hurdle and John, Justices of the Peace. Acknowledged before Abner B. Bruce, Clerk of the Court, Orange County, North Carolina. [Ref: *Abstracts of the Land Records of Dorchester County, Maryland, Volume 32 (Liber HD#6)*, by James A. McAllister, Jr. (1967), p. 61.]

On June 20, 1794, Edmund Brannock, of Dorchester County, attorney for Ezekiel Mace and Angell Mace, of Orange County, North Carolina, conveyed to Alexander Robbs, of Orange County, part of *Grass Reading* on the south side of Little Choptank River on St. Stephen's Creek, formerly purchased by Josias Mace from Levin Woolford, containing 60 acres more or less. Witnesses were Richard Pattison and Thomas Jones, Justices. [Ref: McAllister, *Ibid.*.]

On May 24, 1794, Ezekiel Mace, John Dorris and Angell his wife, all of Orange County, North Carolina (the said Ezekiel and Angell being the only surviving children and heirs of Josias Mace late of Dorchester County, Maryland, deceased), granted to "our uncle" Alexander Robbs, of Orange County, planter, power of attorney regarding land on Blackwater called *Button's Intent* and *Addition to Button's Intent*. Witnesses were Hardy Hurdle, Stephen Mureign, and Jacob Morton. Acknowledged before William McCauley, Esq., one of the Justices of the County Court of Pleas and Quarter Sessions of Orange County, North Carolina, A. B. Bruce, Clerk. [Ref: *Abstracts of the Land Records of Dorchester County, Maryland, Volume 33 (Liber HD#8)*, by James A. McAllister, Jr. (1967), p. 12.]

On June 28, 1794, Alexander Robbs, of Orange County, North Carolina, planter, attorney for Ezekiel Mace, John Dorris and Angel his wife, conveyed to John King, of Dorchester County, Maryland, planter, a tract called *Button's Intent*, adjoining *Cow Pasture*, and containing 163 acres more or less. Witnesses were

Thomas Jones and John Keene, Justices of Dorchester County. [Ref: McAllister, *Ibid..*]

MACKEY

William Mackey of Cecil County, Maryland acquired land in the Irish Settlement of Rowan County, North Carolina sometime between 1752 and 1762. [Ref: *Carolina Cradle*, by Robert W. Ramsey (1964), p. 125, citing Rowan County Deeds III:19, Anson County Deeds 1:312, Cecil County Deed VI:218.]

There was a William Mackey who recorded his cattle mark in Kent County court in May, 1703. William Mackey (or McKey) and wife Mary had the following children born in St. Paul's Parish, Kent County, Maryland:

    Elinor Mackey (baptized in 1704);
    Mary Mackey (born in 1706);
    William Mackey (born and died in 1712);
    Ezabella Mackey (born in 1713);
    Lylius Mackey (born in 1714, died in 1716);
    Martha Mackey (born in 1717).

One William Mackey was buried in St. Paul's Parish, Kent County, on July 11, 1714. [Ref: *Maryland Eastern Shore Vital Records, 1648-1725*, by F. Edward Wright (1982), pp. 6, 28, 29.]

There was also a William Mackey who lived in South Milford Hundred of Cecil County in 1761 and 1766. [Ref: *Inhabitants of Cecil County, Maryland, 1649-1774*, by Henry C. Peden, Jr. (1993), pp. 44, 76.]

William Mackey, son of William and Mary, was born in St. Paul's Parish, Kent County, on May 25, 1728. Another William Mackey was buried there in February, 1728. Hezekiah Mackey (born in 1731) and Philip Mackey (born in 1734) were sons of William and Sarah Mackey of St. Peter's Parish, Talbot County, Maryland. Robert Mackey, son of William and Rachel, was born there in 1745. [Ref: *Maryland Eastern Shore Vital Records, 1726-1750*, by F. Edward Wright (1983), pp. 26, 90, 91.]

MANLEY

On May 16, 1767 a number of inhabitants of Baltimore Town presented a petition in support of the German inhabitants who had complained about the justices who took advantage of their inability to understand English. Two of the petitioners were Robert Manley and Joseph Burgess. [Ref: *Archives of Maryland*, Volume 32, pp. 203-204.]

In 1768 a vote was taken in Baltimore County to determine whether or not the county seat should be moved from Joppa to Baltimore Town (which resulted in the relocation of the seat and the eventual creation of Harford County in 1773). Two of the voters in favor of the move were Robert Manley and Joseph Burgess. [Ref: *Inhabitants of Baltimore County, 1763-1774*, by Henry C. Peden, Jr. (1989), p. 34.]

On "6 Apr 1774, Robert Manley, now of Carolina, by Joseph Burgess, of Baltimore Co., Maryland, to Samuel Worthington, of Baltimore Co., Maryland, £92, lot #31 in town of Baltimore. Signed: Joseph Burgess. Wit: William Spencer and David Shields. [Ref: *Baltimore County, Maryland, Deed Records, Book Four: 1767-1775*, by John Davis (1997), p. 275.]

MARDERS

On September 16, 1741, Edward Marders, of North Carolina, conveyed to John Smith, of Dorchester County, Maryland, planter, a tract called *Hobb's Kindness* located on a small branch on the north side of the northeast branch of Wattses Creek, adjoining *Jameses Park* and containing 100 acres more or less. Signed by Thomas Maid, attorney in fact for said Edward Marders. Witness: John Leverton. Acknowledged on November 11, 1741 before Henry Hooper, Justice of the Provincial Court of Maryland. [Ref: *Abstracts from Land Records of Dorchester County, Maryland, Volume C, 1732-1745*, by James A. McAllister, Jr. (1962), p. 52.]

MARLIN-MARLING

"A James Marlin was in St. Mary's County, Maryland in 1707 and the family may have originated there." Some of the Marlin family may have moved northward into Chester County, Pennsylvania since an Alexander and John Marlin obtained land warrants there in 1736 and 1738. It appears the Marlins proceeded westward from there and then south into North Carolina. A James Marlin was in Rowan County by 1755, hence the name Marlin's Creek, a stream west of the Yadkin River. [Ref: *Carolina Cradle*, by Robert W. Ramsey (1964), pp. 42-43, citing Testamentary Proceedings of Maryland, 1657-1777, XIX.C:215; *Pennsylvania Archives*, Third Series, XXIV:86-87; North Carolina Land Grants XI:5.]

It is also interesting to note that a Francis Marling was transported to Maryland in 1665, according to Mr. Skordas, but Dr. Gibb states a Francis Marling or Marley had immigrated by 1663. Talbot County land records indicate that a Francis Marling owned three tracts of land (200 acres) in 1679. Isaac and Jacob Marling owned a different 60-acre tract in 1713. [Ref: *The Early Settlers of Maryland*, by Gust Skordas (1968), p. 304; *A Supplement to the Early Settlers of Maryland*, by Carson Gibb, Ph.D. (1887), p. 144; *Settlers of Maryland, 1679-1700*, by Peter Wilson Coldham (1995), p. 112; *Settlers of Maryland, 1701-1730*, by Peter Wilson Coldham (1996), p. 105.]

MARSHALL

Benjamin Marshall applied for a pension (S7176) for his service in the Revolutionary War on December 13, 1832 in Stokes County, North Carolina, stating that he was born in 1760 in Calvert County, Maryland and lived in Albemarle County, Virginia at the time of his enlistment in the Virginia militia.

Benjamin died on October 26, 1834? [record abstract mistakenly stated 1804], leaving children, but no names were given in the record. [Ref: *Genealogical Abstracts of Revolutionary War Pension Files, Volume II: F-M*, by Virgil D. White (1990), p. 2196.]

Both "Benjamin Marshall, of Albemarle" and "Benjamin Marshall, of Stokes County, N. C." are listed, among other soldiers named Benjamin Marshall, in Virginia records during the revolution. [Ref: *Historical Register of Virginians in the Revolution, 1775-1783*, by John H. Gwathmey (1938), p. 501.]

It should be noted that there were several men named Marshall who served from Calvert County during the Revolutionary War, but none were named Benjamin. There was also a Benjamin Marshall who was born in 1755 in Prince George's County, Maryland and died in 1834 in Hardy County, Virginia. He should not be confused with the above mentioned Benjamin Marshall. For additional information about him, see Revolutionary War Pension File W4279. [Ref: For other patriots named Marshall in southern Maryland, see Henry C. Peden, Jr.'s *Revolutionary Patriots of Calvert & St. Mary's Counties, Maryland, 1775-1783* (1996), *Revolutionary Patriots of Prince George's County, Maryland, 1775-1783* (1997), *Revolutionary Patriots of Charles County, Maryland, 1775-1783* (1997), and *Revolutionary Patriots of Anne Arundel County, Maryland* (1992), all of which are available from Family Line Publications, 65 East Main Street, Westminster, MD 21157.

MARTIN

John Peter Martin served with the German Fusiliers in the South Carolina Continental Line in 1775 and was captured by the British in 1777. He was taken to New York and after five months in prison was exchanged at Newport. He walked back to Charleston and in 1779 was in the assault on Savannah and the expedition against Fort Royal under General Moultrie. John was also in the siege of Charleston, but escaped when it fell. He married Isabella Innes on June 21, 1814 at Philadelphia, Pennsylvania and she applied for a pension (R6956) on October 10, 1853 in New Haven, Connecticut, aged 73. She stated that John was born in North Carolina and lived most of his early years at Charleston, South Carolina where his father was a Lutheran clergyman who had come to America from Germany. After the war John lived many years in Lumberton, North Carolina and then moved to Mount Holly, New Jersey. He later moved to Trenton, New Jersey where he resided at the time of his death on June 2, 1832, aged 72, but he died in Baltimore, Maryland. [Ref: *Genealogical Abstracts of Revolutionary War Pension Files, Volume II: F-M*, by Virgil D. White (1990), p. 2206; *Roster of South Carolina Patriots in the American Revolution*, by Bobby Gilmer Ross (1985), p. 66.]

Samuel Martin lived in Guilford County, North Carolina at the time of his enlistment in the Revolutionary War and died on August 2, 1826. His widow Jennet applied for a pension (R15990) in Davidson County, North Carolina on June 19, 1843, aged 80, stating she had married Samuel on September 4, 1779 in Montgomery

County, Maryland and he died on August 2, 1826. [Ref: *Genealogical Abstracts of Revolutionary War Pension Files, Volume II: F-M*, by Virgil D. White (1990), p. 2210.]

Two men named Samuel Martin lived in the Upper Part of Potomac Hundred in Montgomery County, Maryland in 1777 (one with one taxable, and one with two taxables, in their respective households). One Samuel Martin was a private in the militia, 3rd Company, Middle Battalion, in September, 1777. One Samuel Martin was a private in the Maryland Line, Capt. Thomas Beall's Company, in 1780. One Samuel Martin took the Oath of Allegiance in 1778. Additional research may be necessary before drawing conclusions. One Samuel Martin married Jane Walker in Montgomery County on September 5, 1779, and he appears to have been the soldier in North Carolina as mentioned above. [Ref: *Revolutionary Patriots of Montgomery County, Maryland, 17750-1783*, by Henry C. Peden, Jr. (1996), p. 221; *Maryland Records: Colonial, Revolutionary, County and Church From Original Sources, Volume II*, by Gaius M. Brumbaugh (1928), p. 519.]

MAYNARD

On October 31, 1764 John Howard, of Rowan County, North Carolina, conveyed to Nathan Maynard, of Frederick County, Maryland, for £100, 500 acres on the east side of the Yadkin River, part of a 700-acre tract granted on December 21, 1761. [Ref: *Rowan County, North Carolina, Deed Abstracts, Vol. II, 1762-1772*, by Jo Linn White (Salisbury, N. C.: Privately published, 1972), p. 57, citing Deed Book 6, pp. 93-95.]

In Frederick County, Maryland on December 20, 1758 (bill of sale): "I Robert Lamar, for and in consideration of Simon Nichols, William Cummings, and Nathan Maynard, being special bail for me in Frederick County Court ... sell negro Sambo." [Ref: *Frederick County, Maryland, Land Records, Liber F Abstracts, 1756-1761*, by Patricia Abelard Andersen (Gaithersburg, MD: GenLaw Resources, 1995), p. 65.]

One Nathan Maynard, who married Susanna Beatty in Frederick County, Maryland, served on jury duty, 1777-1785, was a captain in the militia in the Revolutionary War (Linganore Battalion, 1777), and had children, one of whom was named Nathan (born 1783). His relationship to the Nathan Maynard in the aforementioned deed in North Carolina is not yet determined. Also, the Maynard name has been spelled Manard, Manyard, and Mainyard in various records. [Ref: *Genealogical Index to Frederick County, Maryland*, by John Stanwood Martin (Malvern, PA: Conlin's Copy Center (1992), p. 146; *Revolutionary Patriots of Frederick County, Maryland, 1775-1783*, by Henry C. Peden, Jr. (1995), p. 241.]

McALLISTER-McCALLISTER

William McAllister or McCallister applied for a pension for his Revolutionary War services on September 7, 1832 in McMinn County, Tennessee, stating that he was born in Dorchester County, Maryland on March 23, 1762 and moved to North Carolina after the war (name of county was not stated). From there he moved to Blount County, Tennessee and married Henrietta Shipley on May 6, 1828 in Hamilton County, Tennessee. They were in McMinn County by 1832 and he died on October 3, 1842 in Bradley or McMinn County. His widow applied for a pension (W801) in Hamilton County on May 2, 1853, aged 75, but when she applied for bounty land warrant #35722-160-55 on October 4, 1855 she gave her age as 67. Henrietta McAllister or McCallister died on November 15, 1857. [Ref: *Genealogical Abstracts of Revolutionary War Pension Files, Volume II: F-M*, by Virgil D. White (1990), p. 2239.]

He was probably related to the McCollister family of Dorchester County, where Jeremiah McCollister owned land by 1774 and Vachel McCollister died testate in 1776. [Ref: *Maryland Calendar of Wills, Volume 16, 1774-1777*, p. 181; Land Records of Dorchester County, 1773-1775, Liber 27, folio 333.]

McDOWELL

"John McDowell acquired a square mile of land on McDowell's (later Lambert's) Creek and his father, Charles McDowell, a planter in Cecil County, Maryland before 1731, died in Anson County [North Carolina] in 1754. Less than a year after his father's death, McDowell sold the tract on Lambert's Creek and departed from the region. He was a leader in the westward movement following the French and Indian War, settling in 1768 as far west as Pleasant Gardens in present-day McDowell County. John McDowell's cousin Joseph McDowell lived near the Waxhaws in 1750. It is probable that John was in the Davidson Creek settlement at that time." [Ref: *Carolina Cradle*, by Robert W. Ramsey (1964), p. 72, citing North Carolina Land Grants XI:16; Cecil County Judgments SK#4 (1730-111732), p., 65; Rowan County Deeds II:278; and, "Anson County, North Carolina, Abstracts of Early Records," *The May Wilson McBee Collection*, edited by May Wilson McBee (Greenwood, Mississippi, 1950), p. 114.]

McGARITY

William McGarity applied for a pension (R67813) on March 13, 1835 in Chester District, South Carolina, stating that he was born in Cecil County, Maryland on February 14, 1756 and served in the South Carolina Line during the Revolutionary War. He stated that he enlisted during December, 1775, while residing in Craven County (Chester District) under Capt. Robert Patton, Col. Joseph Kershaw and Col. William Thomson. During the fall of 1778 he served under Capt. John Nixon, Col. John Winn, Capt. John McClure and Col. Richard Winn, and was in the battles of Kettle Creek, Stono, Rocky Mount, William's Old Place, Hanging Rock,

Fishing Creek, Fish Dam Ford, and Blackstock's Plantation. In August, 1781, he served under Capt. Robert Hanna and Col. Stratton and was in the battle of Monck's Corner. During the fall of 1781 he was elected lieutenant under Capt. James Crawford and Col. Lacey. He served three months as a lieutenant, eighteen months as a private, and the rest of the war as a scout. [Ref: *Genealogical Abstracts of Revolutionary War Pension Files, Volume II: F-M*, by Virgil D. White (1990), p. 2275; *Roster of South Carolina Patriots in the American Revolution*, by Bobby Gilmor Ross (1985), p. 622.]

He was probably related to James McGarity and Patrick McGarity who appeared on a list of taxables in North Susquehanna Hundred in Cecil County, Maryland in 1766, at which time Patrick McGarity was a constable. [Ref: *Inhabitants of Cecil County, Maryland, 1649-1774*, by Henry C. Peden, Jr. (1993), pp. 69, 81.]

McGEE

On August 20, 1773, John McGee, of Guilford County, North Carolina, granted to William Edmondson, of Dorchester County, Maryland, power of attorney to manage lands in Dorchester County or elsewhere in Maryland left by the will of Andrew McGee, brother of the said John McGee, to the said John McGee's two sons Samuel and John McGee. Witnesses: McKeel Bonwell and Peter Richardson. Proved on March 10, 1774 by the oath of Peter Richardson, one of the witnesses, before John Dickinson, Justice of Dorchester County. [Ref: *Abstracts from Land Records of Dorchester County, Maryland, Volume H, 1772-1775*, by James A. McAllister, Jr. (1964), p. 56.]

Andrew McGhee, merchant, of Dorchester County, Maryland, left a will dated February 25, 1773 and proved on March 12, 1773. He left all his lands to his two nephews Samuel and John McGhee (sons of John McGhee) who lived in Guilford County, North Carolina. He also left money to Isabell and Mary McGhee (daughters of John McGhee), of Ireland, as well as his brothers William, Alexander and Joseph McGhee, of Ireland, and John McGhee, of North Carolina. [Ref: *Maryland Calendar of Wills, Volume 16, 1774-1777*, p. 112.]

On November 23, 1797, John McGee, of Randolph County, North Carolina, manumitted his negro girl named Rose. Witnesses were Jacob Wright and Elisha Wright. Acknowledged before John Eccleston, Justice of Dorchester County, Maryland. [Ref: *Abstracts of the Land Records of Dorchester County, Maryland, Volume 28 (Liber NH#9)*, by James A. McAllister, Jr. (1967), p. 51.]

McPHERSON

"The name Robert McPherson is closely associated with the origins of no less than four different frontier settlements [in western North Carolina]: the Shenandoah Valley, where Robert McPherson proved his importation in 1741; the Monocacy Valley in Maryland, where Robert McPherson signed a petition in 1739 requesting the creation of Frederick County; the Marsh Creek settlement of western Lancaster County [Pennsylvania], where Robert McPherson was among the initial settlers in 1743; and the northwest Catawba frontier [in North Carolina], where Robert McPherson petitioned for a land warrant in 1751. It would appear that the Robert McPherson with whom this study is concerned [growth of the western settlement of North Carolina] migrated from the Monocacy Marsh Creek region, where he was associated with Hugh McWhorter." [Ref: *Carolina Cradle*, by Robert W. Ramsey (1964), pp. 59-60, citing *The Tinkling Spring, Headwaters of Freedom: A Study of the Church and Her People*, by Howard M. Wilson (Richmond, VA: Garrett and Massie, Inc., 1954), p. 427; *The German Element of the Shenandoah Valley of Virginia*, by John W. Wayland (Charlottesville, VA: Published by the author, 1907), p. 58.]

The Robert McPherson who settled in North Carolina may have been the son of Robert McPherson who was born in Northern Ireland in 1687, settled in the Marsh Creek area of Adams County, Pennsylvania, and died there on September 23, 1767. [Ref: *Genealogical Index to Frederick County, Maryland: The First Hundred Years, Volume III*, by John Stanwood Martin (1992), p. 178, citing *History of Frederick County, Maryland*, by T. J. C. Williams (1910), p. 765.]

MEEK

Among those listed as holding unpatented certificates and leases in Cecil County, Maryland were Adam Meek in 1747 and William Meek in 1753. Adam Meek, Sr. and Adam Meek, Jr. were listed together as taxables in 1752. Adam Meek and his slave Bett were listed among the taxables in North Susquehanna Hundred in 1761 and Adam Meek and one slave were listed in 1766. [Ref: *Inhabitants of Cecil County, Maryland, 1649-1774*, by Henry C. Peden, Jr. (1993), pp. 30, 42, 81, 128.]

"John Barron and his wife Margaret, with their family, moved from Maryland to New Acquisition (York County, South Carolina after 1785) and bought a 200-acre plantation on Broad River near Tate's Ferry and the mouth of Buffaloe Creek in 1778, a few days after Jane Meek, widow of Adam Meek of Cecil County, Maryland, bought a plantation on Bullock's Creek from Daniel and Mary (Stephenson) McClaron. The Barrons and Meeks were related, according to James Madison Hope, youngest son of Jane Barron (1767-1841) by her second husband James Hope, Jr., and this suggests that they may have come together from Cecil or a nearby county." [Ref: *The Bulletin* of the Chester District Genealogical Society, Volume IX, No. II (June, 1988), p. 35, featuring an article entitled "The Barrons of Western York County, South Carolina" by Elmer Oris Parker.]

MEREDITH

Henry Meredith applied for a pension (S9402) on October 19, 1832 in Lauren District, South Carolina, stating that he was born in 1757 in Baltimore County,

Maryland and lived in Orange County, North Carolina during the Revolutionary War. He served in the North Carolina Continental Line and in 1784 he moved to South Carolina. [Ref: *Genealogical Abstracts of Revolutionary War Pension Files, Volume II: F-M*, by Virgil D. White (1990), p. 2327. However, he is not listed in the *Roster of Soldiers from North Carolina in the American Revolution*, compiled by the North Carolina Daughters of the American Revolution in 1932, nor is he listed in the *Roster of South Carolina Patriots in the American Revolution*, compiled by Bobby Gilmor Ross in 1985.]

Thomas Meredith and Susanna Cox were married on May 22, 1755 in St. John's Protestant Episcopal Parish in Baltimore County, Maryland, Their daughter Ann Meredith was born on March 7, 1756 and their son Henry Meredith was born on August 4, 1757. [Ref: *Baltimore County Families, 1659-1759*, by Robert W. Barnes (1989), p. 443.]

It is interesting to note that a Henry Meredith owned a 22-acre tract called *Henry's Luck* in Queen Anne's County, Maryland in 1775. [Ref: *Settlers of Maryland, 1766-1783*, by Peter Wilson Coldham (1996), p. 103.]

Also, John Meredith died testate in Queen Anne's County, Maryland in 1764 (distribution made in 1768) and he had a son Thomas Meredith (among others), and a Thomas Meredith died testate in Queen Anne's County in 1772 and he had a son Thomas Meredith (among others). It is possible that they were related to Henry Meredith of Baltimore County, Maryland and Orange County, North Carolina. [Ref: *Maryland Calendar of Wills, Volume 13, 1764-1767*, p. 51; *Maryland Calendar of Wills, Volume 14, 1767-1772*, p. 216; *Abstracts of the Balance Books of the Prerogative Court of Maryland, 1763-1770*, by Vernon L. Skinner, Jr. (1995), p. 45.]

MERINE-MARINE

William Merine was born in June, 1744, married in Somerset County, Maryland (wife's name not known), and died in North Carolina (date and county not stated). He was a son of William Merine (1698-1767) and Mary ----, of "Buck's Lodge" in Somerset County, Maryland, and a grandson of Jonathan Maren or Marien (died 1736) and Kezia ----, of Sewell Creek, Maryland. William Merine's siblings were John Merine (1733-1808), Matthew Merine (removed to Philadelphia), Zorobabel Merine or Marine (1736-1821, an influential citizen and Quaker on the lower Eastern Shore of Maryland and Sussex County, Delaware), Charles Merine (1738-1823), James Merine (died young), David Merine (died young), Janet or Jenett Merine (no further record after 1767), and Esther Merine (no further record after 1767). [Ref: *Colonial Families of the United States of America, Volume VII*, by Nelson Osgood Rhoades, ed. (1920), p. 352, and *Maryland Calendar of Wills, Volume 14, 1767-1772*, p. 22.]

MERRYMAN

On "27 Sep 1773, Charles Merryman, of Carolina, formerly of Baltimore Co., Maryland, to Darby Lux, of Baltimore Co., Maryland, and Thomas Johnson, Jr., of Annapolis, Anne Arundel Co., Maryland, of the third part, £40, 246 acres. Signed: Charles Merryman, Darby Lux and Thomas Johnson, Jr. Wit: Robert Alexander and Samuel Chase." [Ref: *Baltimore County, Maryland, Deed Records, Book Four: 1767-1775*, by John Davis (1997), p. 241.]

The Merryman family was prominent in colonial Maryland and they are included in Robert W. Barnes' *Baltimore County Families, 1659-1759*, which notes that "The Merryman Family" was an article by Francis B. Culver published in the *Maryland Historical Magazine*, Volume X (pp. 176-185, 286-299, 398) and Volume XI (p. 85), and reprinted in *Maryland Genealogies*, Volume 2 (pp. 208-232).

MICHAEL-MICHEL

Bennett Michael, son of George Baltsher Michael or Michel and his second wife Ann Osborn, and grandson of Johann Jacob Michel and his second wife Mary Philippina Stab, "was born circa 1767 presumably in Susquehanna Hundred, Baltimore (now Harford) County, Maryland, and died probably in the 1840's in Shelby County, Indiana. By 1800 he had left Harford County and was living in Abbeville District, South Carolina, with three females in the household. He and Thomas Osborn [Ozburn] and Jeremiah McWhorter prepared the estate inventory of Zelpha Lacey in Abbeville on January 31, 1805. About 1808 he removed to Scott County, Kentucky, again in the company of persons of the Osborn name, and was listed there in the 1810 census. He next went to Fairfield, Franklin County, Indiana, where his sister Elizabeth lived, and carried on the trade of shoemaking, reportedly without much success. He was asked by the first settler of the area which became Shelby County, Indiana, to join him, and he is recorded there in 1820 in Flat Rock Parish, then part of the unorganized area known as Delaware County. He got into some skirmishes in his early years but soon settled in as a good member of the community. The 1830 census has him in Shelby Township, and the 1840 in Marion. In all communities in which he lived, Bennett was associated with Osborns, likely relatives of his mother."

The name of his wife is unknown, but their children were as follows:
(1) Daniel Michael;
(2) William Michael (married Delilah Endsley);
(3) Betsy Michael (married Henry Selward);
(4) Bennett Michael (married first to Margaret Wright and second to Catherine (Ellis) Monroney, widow of Sylvester Monroney);
(5) Sarah Michael (unmarried); and,
(6) George W. Michael (married Sally Ann Curry).

[Ref: "Baltsher Michael of Harford County, Maryland: Probable German Origins and Immediate Posterity," by Jon Harlan Livezey, published in the *Maryland Genealogical Society Bulletin*, Vol. 39, No. 1 (Winter, 1998), pp. 96-115.]

MILLER

"Abraham, James, and Michael Miller (evidently close kin of James Miller of Fourth Creek) migrated southward from Cecil County, Maryland or New Castle County, Delaware." They settled in the Trading Camp Settlement in Rowan County, North Carolina sometime between 1750 and 1762. [Ref: *Carolina Cradle*, by Robert W. Ramsey (1964), p. 110, citing New Castle County Court of Common Pleas, 1793-1717, 1727-1740; Cecil County Deeds VIII:198, IX:389; Rowan County Deeds III:309, IV:750; Rowan County Wills A:91, B:32, B:124; North Carolina Land Grants VI:164.]

The Miller or Millar family was in Cecil County during the colonial and revolutionary periods. For additional information see *Inhabitants of Cecil County, Maryland, 1649-1774*, by Henry C. Peden, Jr. (Westminster, MD: Family Line Publications, 1993), and *Maryland Eastern Shore Vital Records, 1726-1750*, by F. Edward Wright (Westminster, MD: Family Line Publications, 1983).

On February 5, 1744, in Craven County, North Carolina, the deposition of Thomas Browne, aged about 50, of Craven County, mentioned that he was the executor to the will of Robert Miller, deceased, who lived near Dividing Creek in Great Choptank in [Talbot County] Maryland. "Robert Miller left unto his care and charge one son named William Miller, now about 28 years of age and living in Craven County, aforesaid, who is identical legatee of Robert Miller who devised a small plantation on which he dwelled until he dyed near Dividing Creek to his son." [Ref: *Talbot County, Maryland, Land Records, Book Eight*, by R. Bernice Leonard (1988), p. 72.]

Robert Miller died testate in Talbot County, Maryland and left a will dated April 4, 1718 (date of probate not stated). To his son William he left all his real estate and to his two other children (unnamed) he left the residue of his estate. All three children were left in the care of his executor, Thomas Brown. Witnesses were Terrence Connolly and William Goforth. Earlier, in Talbot County, the will of John Preston was probated on January 13, 1713 (written on December 9, 1712). Among his heirs were "To two grandsons, viz., Willoby Goforth and eldest son of daughter Elizabeth and Robert Miller, her husband, equally, residue of lands, and to Mary, daughter of said Robert, personalty." The eldest son referred to in this will was apparently William Miller who went to Craven County, North Carolina with Thomas Brown (Browne). [Ref: *Maryland Calendar of Wills, Volume IV, 1713-1720*, pp. 7, 158.]

The aforementioned Robert Miller, of Talbot County, may have been the son of Robert and Elizabeth Miller, of Somerset County, Maryland, who had at least four children as follows: Susanna Miller, born February 8, 1676; Mary Miller, born

February 19, 1678; Robert Miller, born August 23, 1682; and, Elizabeth Miller, born December 19, 1693. Robert Miller died in Talbot County, St. Peter's Parish, on April 5, 1718. [Ref: *Maryland Eastern Shore Vital Records, 1648-1725*, by F. Edward Wright (1982), pp. 84, 133.]

MINOR-MINNER

William Minor, Sr. was born in 1739 and lived at Centreville (heretofore Chester Mill) in Queen Anne's County, Maryland. He moved to South Carolina (county not stated) in 1786 and died at Mount Vernon Plantation on November 23, 1804, in his 66th year. [Ref: Notice in the *Republican Star* newspaper in Talbot County, Maryland on January 5, 1805, as published in F. Edward Wright's *Maryland Eastern Shore Newspaper Abstracts, 1790-1805, Volume 1* (1981), page 101.]

William Minor and Elijah Minor took the Oath of Allegiance and Fidelity to the State of Maryland in 1778. William Minor served on the Grand Jury on August 25, 1778 and took an oath to prevent the growth of Toryism in Queen Anne's County. [Ref: Henry C. Peden, Jr.'s *Revolutionary Patriots of Kent and Queen Anne's Counties, Maryland, 1775-1783* (1995), pp. 183-184, citing Queen Anne's County Court Minutes and Maryland Historical Society Manuscript Collection MS.1814.]

The 1778 census in Caroline County lists William Minner, Elisha Minner, and Edwd. Minner (in Sussex). The 1778 census in Queen Anne's County lists William Minor living in Worrel Hundred and Elija Minor living in Wye Hundred. [Ref: Bettie Stirling Carothers' *1778 Census of Maryland* (1972), pp. 4, 5, 34, 35.]

On October 4, 1781, William Minor wrote from the Talbot County Courthouse to Matthew Tilghman regarding the state of the prisoners being held there. [Ref: Edward C. Papenfuse, et al., *An Inventory of Maryland State Papers, Volume I, 1775-1789*, p. 443, citing Accession No. MdHR4591-17 at the Maryland State Archives.]

MITCHELL

"John Mitchell, probably from Cecil County, Maryland, was a merchant who bought land in Salisbury from William Williams in July, 1760. On November 30, 1767, he received from Hugh Forster lot number thirty-seven in the north square 'to be appropriated to no other use than for the residence of a schoolmaster and the place for a school house, for the public use and benefit of the inhabitants now and hereafter of the town of Salisbury.' [North Carolina.] This is the first reference to any kind of educational institution in the township, indicating that there was no school in Salisbury during the period covered by this study [1747 to 1762.] Mitchell left Rowan County in 1770 or 1771 and established himself in St. John's Parish, Colleton County, South Carolina." [Ref: *Carolina Cradle*, by Robert W. Ramsey (1964), p. 168, citing the *Maryland Historical Magazine* VI:47, Rowan County Deeds IV:251,

VI:559, VII:312, and the Mitchell file in the McCubbins Collection at the Salisbury Public Library in Salisbury, North Carolina.]

Solomon Mitchell applied for a pension (S4222) on November 12, 1832 in Sumner County, Tennessee, stating that he was born in 1769 [sic] in Dorchester County, Maryland and lived there at the time of his enlistment in the Revolutionary War. He later moved to Guilford County, North Carolina and enlisted there in 1781. He moved to Sumner County, Tennessee in 1804. To support his application, an Abraham Martin, Sr., clergyman, aged 58, of Sumner County, made an affidavit. [Ref: *Genealogical Abstracts of Revolutionary War Pension Files, Volume II: F-M*, by Virgil D. White (1990), p. 2382.]

It is interesting to note, however, that Solomon Mitchell does not appear in *Archives of Maryland, Volume 18*, "Muster Rolls of Maryland Troops in the American Revolution, 1775-1783," nor does he appear in *The Maryland Militia in the Revolutionary War*, by S. Eugene Clements and F. Edward Wright (1987). In fact, there must be a mistake in his year of birth (1769) for he would only have been 12 years old when he enlisted in 1781 for the second time. He apparently was born in 1759 or 1760. It is even more interesting to note that there was a Solomon Mitchell who was born in 1759 in Granville County, North Carolina, served in the South Carolina Line, died in 1832, and his widow received a pension (W181). Additional research will be necessary before drawing conclusions.

MOORE

In November, 1763, in Frederick County, Maryland, Robert Wood recorded the power of attorney granted to him by William Moore, of Cumberland County, Province of North Carolina, "to recover such cattle as may be hereafter mentioned." Signed by Robert Wood before Joseph Wood and John Harlan on October 22, 1763. [Ref: *Frederick County, Maryland, Land Records Liber J, 1763-1767*, by Patricia Abelard Andersen (1996), p. 1.]

On November 25, 1786, in Dorchester County, Maryland, Thomas Moore and his wife Sarah of Dorchester County, but now residing in North Carolina, conveyed to John Eccleston, of Dorchester County, part of a tract called *Connawhy* not included in a deed given to Isaac Lowe dated November 22, 1786, containing 24 3/4 acres more or less, on the south side of the said tract. Witnesses: Levin Kirkman and R. Stevens, Justices. [Ref: *Abstracts of the Land Records of Dorchester County, Maryland, Volume 28 (Liber NH#9)*, by James A. McAllister, Jr. (1967), p. 20.]

MOSER

Francis Moser, son of Leonard and Sarah Moser, was born in 1763 in Frederick County, Maryland. He enlisted in the Revolutionary War in Surry County, North Carolina and afterwards returned to Maryland. Francis also served as a militia substitute from May to December, 1781 in Frederick County, as did his brother

Michael. Their father, Leonard, was an Associator in 1775 and took the Oath of Allegiance and Fidelity to the State of Maryland in Frederick County in 1778. Francis remained there for 3 years and then went to Surry County for 2 years before moving to Lincoln County. He lived there for 30 years and then moved to Greene County, Tennessee for 1 year, to Jefferson County for 10 years, and then to Monroe County in 1830. There he applied for a pension on September 20, 1832 and died on November 22, 1836 in Monroe County, Tennessee. His widow Mary Moser applied for pension on November 24, 1853, aged 56, in McNairy County, Tennessee. William and Mary Sipe made affidavit that Mary Moser, widow, was their sister. [Ref: *German Speaking People West of the Catawba River in North Carolina, 1750-1800*, by Lorena Shell Eaker (1994), p. 307, and *Revolutionary Patriots of Frederick County, Maryland, 1775-1783*, by Henry C. Peden, Jr. (1995), p. 262.]

The Mosers appear in German church records in Pennsylvania and Maryland and later in the records of the Graceham Moravian Church in Frederick County. There is a discussion of Leonard Moser in Calvin E. Schildknecht's *Monocacy and Catoctin, Volume III* (1994), as follows:

"In 1735 the youth Leonard Moser was with leader Thomas Cresap supporting Maryland in the so-called 'War Between Maryland and Pennsylvania' over the boundary dispute. At Conojohela, south of later Wrightsville, Pennsylvania, where Cresap and others had settled west of the Susquehannah River in defiance of Pennsylvania authorities, Moser was captured by the Lancaster County sheriff and about 30 Pennsylvania supporters, and he was in prison briefly. Along with several other followers of Cresap who retreated from Pennsylvania territory about 1736, Leonard Moser came to the German Monocacy Settlement [Frederick County, Maryland] ... In 1744 Leonard married Maria Kocher. Several records indicate that Leonard was a weaver ... In 1758, when the Moravian Congregation of Graceham was formally organized, Leonard and second wife (Maria) Sarah were members ... Rev. Jacob Lischy [Reformed] recorded baptisms of Samuel Moser (1751) and Elizabeth Moser (1755), children of Leonard by his first wife. The following children of Leonard and Sarah are recorded in the Moravian Archives of Graceham: John Michael (born 1759; first son, John, born 1784), Samuel (born 1761), Frances [Francis] (born 1763), Christian (born 1765), Ann Elizabeth (born 1767), Henry (born 1769), and, Joseph (1772-1773). Numerous Moser descendants were named after Leonard the immigrant ..."

Additional information on the Leonard Moser family is in the book entitled *The Ancestors of Claude Rankin Moser, Pioneers of Catawba County, North Carolina*, by James Decatur Beddingfield and Mary Carolyn Moser Beddingfield (4714 Shady Waters Lane, Birmingham, Alabama 35243-2634).

"Leonard Moser's second wife is given as Maria Sarah Binkley. Additional children mentioned are Leonard Jr. and Jacob. (Leonard Moser, Jr. does appear in the Graceham Church records). In later years, Leonard Moser, Sr. was stated to have came to the Bethania (Moravian) Settlement in North Carolina. Several years later, his son Jacob came to Lincoln County."

[Ref: Information gleaned from an article in *Catawba Cousins* (Journal of the Catawba County Genealogical Society), Vol. 12, No. 1 (June, 1997), pp. 5-8, by Ray A. Yount, entitled "Some Pre-1800 Emigrants from Frederick County, Maryland to Old Lincoln County" which was contributed by Ray A. Yount, 10031 Shortest Day Road NW, La Vale, MD 21502-6011, or E-Mail: alby6@juno.com.]

MUSGROVE

"The first found of this family was Cuthbert Musgrove who held a grant of land in Prince George's County, Maryland and died there in 1687. His one known child was John Musgrove who settled across the Potomac River in Fairfax County, Virginia. John Musgrove wrote his will in 1744 and it was filed in 1746, naming seven children: Edward Musgrove, John Musgrove, William Musgrove, Cuthbert Musgrove, Mary Musgrove, Ann Moxley (wife of Daniel Moxley), and Margaret Musgrove. To them he left ten plantations in Fairfax and Frederick Counties, Virginia, and the land in Prince George's County, Maryland."

"William Musgrove died in Loudoun County, Virginia in 1777, leaving a wife Linney, a daughter Margaret Tyler (wife of John Tyler), and sons John Musgrove, Gilbert Musgrove and Cuthbert Musgrove under the guardianship of Nathaniel Smith. William Musgrove also appeared in the will of Daniel Moxley written in 1761."

"By 1750 Edward and John Musgrove had taken up residence on the Frederick County land located on the Shenandoah River near Winchester, Virginia. They appear in the survey papers of George Washington of that year. In 1750 Edward Musgrove purchased two additional tracts of land in Frederick County from Joist Hite, who had settled that part of the valley in 1732. Edward Musgrove again appears in the records there in 1752. During this time, John Musgrove disposed of his land in Fairfax County. In 1755 John applied for a grant of land in South Carolina, stating he was unmarried, had one slave and an indentured servant. This grant consisted of 150 acres on the Santee River in Berkeley County, presently the Saluda River in Newberry County where the Bush River empties into the Saluda. This tract was surveyed by Edward Musgrove, establishing the fact that the brothers came to South Carolina together. John Musgrove late acquired two more tracts for a total of 500 acres. Sometime after arriving in South Carolina, he married Arramenta Gordon and had one known child, John William Musgrove."

"Other researchers assign additional children to them, but can offer no proof. Colonel John Musgrove held a commission in the State Militia and participated in the Cherokee Indian War, also supplied provisions to Brook's Fort on the Saluda River during that time. He opposed the Backcountry Regulator movement as lawless, was twice pulled from his home and whipped for his opposition. He formed the Moderator movement in an attempt to bring order to the area, but made the great mistake of employing Joseph Coffell to head his army. Coffell immediately hired every bandit and renegade in the area, made them soldiers and this led to a final confrontation in 1769 that ended both parties. This occurred on the plantation of Col. John Musgrove. In 1770 the two brothers entered into a dispute, resulting in John Musgrove suing Edward Musgrove for a debt of £1150 and winning the suit. There can be no doubt that brotherly love vanished after this."

"John Musgrove was a Loyalist Colonel during the Revolution, holding a King's Commission. In 1782 his property was confiscated by the Jacksonborough Legislature, although it is suspected he died in 1781. In 1783 his widow, Minty Musgrove, sued for the return of the property. His remaining property was sold in 1784, with Minty Wilson and John Musgrove appointed as administrators, thus indicating his widow had remarried. His estate was sold to four persons: Minty Wilson (the widow), John Musgrove (the son), Thomas Waters (son of Col. Philemon Waters), and William Musgrove. John William Musgrove married Nancy Tate. By 1796 they were living in Georgia. In 1797 they moved back to South Carolina and then to Cocke County, Tennessee in 1807. Their known children were as follows:

(1) Larkin Cuthbert Musgrove, who was recorded in Jackson County, Florida in 1850 as aged 63, born in South Carolina; on that same census was Larkin C. Musgrove II, aged 28, born in Georgia, and Larkin C. Musgrove III, aged six months, born in Georgia;

(2) Edward Gordon Musgrove, who married Rachel Hycklyn and they were living in Saluda District, South Carolina prior to their removal to Blount County, Alabama in 1822, then to Walker County of that state; their one known child was Francis Asbury Musgrove, born August 22, 1827, married Elizabeth Cain on January 6, 1853, and died July 22, 1865 (his children were Missouri Musgrove, Lycurgus Musgrove, Coleman Musgrove, and Calpernia Musgrove);

(3) John Tate Musgrove married and had one known child, Philip M. Musgrove, born March 12, 1817 in Edgefield, South Carolina, married Louisa White of Tennessee on December 8, 1836, was a physician, lawyer, Baptist minister, and Confederate soldier (his children were John W. Musgrove, who died in the Civil War, William H. Musgrove, Jr. Edward G. Musgrove, and Joseph Musgrove); and,

(4) William Henry Musgrove, born January 15, 1796 in Georgia, died March 6, 1862 in Pensacola, Florida, a captain in the Confederate Army; he was a teacher, Baptist minister, served six terms in the Alabama Legislature, married a Miss Fowler, and had no known children.

"In 1756, Edward Musgrove received a land grant of 150 acres on the Tyger River in present Union County, South Carolina. Soon after this, he established residence at Horseshoe Bend on the Enoree River, the later site of the Revolutionary War battle on August 18, 1780. Edward Musgrove was the Commander of Fort William Henry Lyttleton on the Enoree River during the Cherokee War of 1760, a Deputy Surveyor, Justice of the Peace, Tax Collector, Road Commissioner, and neighbourhood lawyer, all before the Revolution.

His letter to William Henry Drayton on October 14, 1775 seems to dispute the fact that he was a Tory. The DAR lists him as a Patriot, based on that letter. His will was written in 1790, named ten children, and corrects the misbelief that Mary Musgrove died in 1784, for she is named as Mary Berry. From other information, he died in 1792 at the age of 76. He was married three times. The name of his first wife is yet unknown, but their child was Edward Beaks Musgrove. His second wife was Hannah Fincher, a daughter of the Quakers Francis and Hannah Fincher. Their two children were Rebecca Musgrove Cannon and Mary Musgrove Berry. His third wife was Ann Crosby of Fish Dam Ford on the Broad River, a daughter of Dennis and Hannah Crosby (not proven). This late marriage produced seven children: Margaret, Ann, Hannah, Leah, Rachel, Liney, and William. After the death of Edward Musgrove his widow married David Smith of Laurens County."

[Ref: *The Bulletin* of the Chester District Genealogical Society, Volume VII, No. III (September, 1984), pp. 70-74, featuring an article entitled "The Musgrove's of Upper South Carolina" by Robert J. Stevens, which should be consulted as it is documented and contains additional information on Musgrove family descendants spread throughout the Southern states.]

As for early Musgroves in Maryland, Jane Musgrove was transported to Maryland in 1665, Charles Musgrove was transported in 1674, and Anthony Musgrove was transported in 1675. [Ref: *The Early Settlers of Maryland*, by Gust Skordas (1968), p. 330.]

"Dorothy Musgrove, widow" married Charles Charleson in Charles County on November 14, 1689, "Anthony Musgroves" married Margaret Deaver in Anne Arundel County on November 25, 1707, "Mary Mushgrove" married Thomas Kelly in Baltimore County on June 4, 1736, and "Lydia Musgrove" married Robert Gill, Jr. in Charles County on November 19, 1749. [Ref: *Maryland Marriages, 1634-1777*, by Robert W. Barnes (1975), pp. 32, 69, 102, 128.]

In 1682 "Cuthbert Musgrove (late of Charles County) and his wife Dorothy" appeared in court on August 9th to answer the complaint of Roger Dickinson regarding his plea of trespass, noting "Roger is now and from ye times of his nativity --- hath hither to both of Kingdom of England and in this Province." Dorothy called Roger "a hogg stealing rogue" and promised to prove it. She said Roger stole her husband's hogs and Roger, of course, denied it; disposition of case not stated. [Ref: *Early Charles County, Maryland Settlers, 1758-1745*, by Marlene Strawser Bates and F. Edward Wright (1995), p. 200.]

In Charles County, "Cuthbert Musgrave" witnessed a deed conveyance (made his mark) on January 11, 1674, was party to land indentures from Robert Wheeler on March 8, 1678 and March 8, 1681 for a parcel of land called *Shrewsbury* on the north side of the Piscataway River and Chingamuxen Creek, and he registered his cattle mark in 1678. [Ref: *Abstracts of Charles County, Maryland Court and Land Records, Volume 2, 1665-1695*, by Elise Greenup Jourdan (1993), pp. 40, 60, 67, 88.]

NEILL

James, Andrew, and William Neill were in the Davidson's Creek Settlement of Rowan County, North Carolina by 1754 when William purchased land from John McDowell. They seem to have originated in Charles County or Anne Arundel County, Maryland, and were residents of New London Township, Chester County, Pennsylvania in 1750 before migrating southward. [Ref: *Carolina Cradle*, by Robert W. Ramsey (1964), p. 103, citing *The Black Books: Calendar of Maryland State Papers, No. 1*, p. 27; Chester County Tavern License Papers, 1749-1750, VIII:67; Rowan County Deeds II:278, II:299; North Carolina Land Grants VI:200-201; Neill family data in the Curry Collection of the Southern Historical Collection at the University of North Carolina in Chapel Hill, North Carolina.]

NEVITT

William Miles Nevitt married Priscilla Miles in Prince George's County, Maryland by license dated January 1, 1779, and moved to Fairfield County, South Carolina by 1790. Their children were Cornelius Nevitt, William Nevitt, Benjamin Nevitt, Kellis Nevitt, and Elizabeth Nevitt. The children of Cornelius Nevitt were as follows:

(1) Frances P. Nevitt (born 1822, married Stephen Crosby of Chester County);

(2) Precious Anne Nevitt (born 1823, married Francis H. Ederington, moved to Florida, and had ten children);

(3) Joseph K. Nevitt (born 1831, married Margarett ----, possibly a Crosby);

(4) John M. Nevitt (killed in Civil War); and,

(5) Cornelius Q. Nevitt (married first to Elizabeth Smith of Anderson County and had a daughter Sallie, and married second to Christian McCoy Arick, moved to Florida to be with Edringtons).

[Ref: Information contained in a query from Mrs. Christian Nevitt Gregory, 308 Seward Road, Brentwood, Tennessee 37027, in *The Bulletin* of the Chester District Genealogical Society, Volume VII, No. IV (December, 1984), p. 135; *Index to Marriage Licenses, Prince George's County, Maryland, 1777-1886*, by Helen W. Brown (1973), p. 160.]

Mary Macatee wrote her will on November 8, 1774 and died testate in Charles County, Maryland. Her will was probated on December 21, 1774 and among her heirs was a grandson William Miles Nevitt, son of Richard Nevitt; also, her son John Nevitt was named executor and if he died then her grandson William Miles Nevitt would be the executor. [Ref: *Maryland Calendar of Wills, Volume 16, 1774-1777*, page 35.]

NIBLET

From the *Republican Star* newspaper at Easton in Talbot County, Maryland on November 14, 1815: "Died 15th ultimate in Laurens District, South Carolina,

Solomon Niblet aged 143, born in England, where he lived til 19 years old and then emigrated to this country; remained in Maryland until about 55 years ago; he then removed to South Carolina; he never lost his teeth nor his eyesight." [Ref: *Maryland Eastern Shore Newspaper Abstracts, Volume 3, 1813-1818*, by F. Edward Wright (1982), p. 37.]

NICHOLS

On March 12, 1792, in Dorchester County, Maryland, Isaac Nichols and Dolly his wife, of Guilford County, North Carolina, granted to Abraham Lewis, of Dorchester County, power of attorney concerning a tract called *Cole's Venture* or *Cole's Regulation*. "(Dolley is the daughter of George Cole)." [See "John Breeden," q.v.] Witnessed by Aaron Lewis and acknowledged before William Gray, Justice for Guilford County, North Carolina. John Hamilton, clerk. [Ref: *Abstracts of the Land Records of Dorchester County, Maryland, Volume 39 (Liber HD#3)*, by James A. McAllister, Jr. (1967), p. 63.]

NULL-NOLL

John Null or Noll was born November 10, 1754 and married Elizabeth Eckert, daughter of Adam and Anna Maria Eckert, who was born on November 27, 1766 in Frederick County, Maryland and died on May 11, 1852 in Lincoln County, North Carolina. In July, 1788, in the case of the State of North Carolina versus John Null (no details were given), it was ordered that John Null "to receive ten lashes on his bare back well laid on." His will which was probated in Lincoln County in January, 1832 (John had died on December 30, 1831), leaving wife, Elizabeth; youngest son Jacob Noll; son Peter Noll; daughters Catharina, Magdalena, Barbara, Elizabeth, Mary, Sarah, Margaret (wife of Solomon Hedrick), and Christina.

Marriage bonds in Lincoln County, North Carolina:
Christine Null and Jacob Wineberger, December 16, 1827;
Elizabeth Null and David "Foote" Bolick, November 30, 1820;
Margaret Null and Solomon Hedrick, May 23, 1821;
Mary Null and William Winebarger, November 28, 1822;
Sarah Null and Elias Hefner, October 26, 1824; and,
Jacob Null and Magdalena Hedrick, May 26, 1825.

In July, 1832, the heirs of John Null, deceased, divided the real estate agreeable to his last will and testament: Jacob and Christina Winnebarger, 46 acres; Michael and Barbara Hefner, 47 acres; William and Mary Winebarger, 48 acres; and Elias and Sarah Hefner, 45 acres. [Ref: *German Speaking People West of the Catawba River in North Carolina, 1750-1800*, by Lorena Shell Eaker (1994), p. 322.]

PARSONS

"A Peter Parsons died in Somerset County, Maryland, in 1686, leaving sons Peter and John. Peter, Joshua, John, and George Parsons were there in 1762, whence Peter Parsons removed to Carolina." [Ref: *Carolina Cradle*, by Robert W. Ramsey (1964), p. 83, citing Rowan County Deeds VI:194, and Probate Records 4:246, 31:807.]

Actually, Peter Parsons wrote his will in Somerset County on November 5, 1686, and it was probated on March 28, 1687, naming his wife Mary and sons Peter and John, leaving each son 200 acres. [Ref: *Maryland Calendar of Wills, Volume II, 1685-1702*, p. 13.]

Peter Parsons immigrated to Somerset County in 1672. [Ref: *The Early Settlers of Maryland*, by Gust Skordas (168), p. 350.]

Peter Parsons patented 200 acres in Somerset County on November 13, 1685. [Ref: *Old Somerset on the Eastern Shore of Maryland*, by Clayton Torrence (1935), p. 470, which gave the date as [1665?], and *Settlers of Maryland, 1679-1700*, by Peter Wilson Coldham (1995), p. 129, which gave the date as "1685".]

The Parsons were subsequently in Worcester County, Maryland, where Peter Parsons owned 15 acres on March 20, 1759, and 45 acres on August 24, 1762, George Parsons owned 25 acres on October 8, 1761, George Parsons, Jr. owned 850 acres on September 29, 1763, Joseph Parsons owned 130 acres on September 11, 1759, and William Parsons owned 50 acres on October 5, 1758. [Ref: *Settlers of Maryland, 1751-1765*, by Peter Wilson Coldham (1996), p. 209.]

Peter Parsons, son of Peter and Mary, was born on January 10, 1681 or March 17, 1682 (both dates were given) and John Parsons, son of Peter and Mary, was born on December 1, 1685. Peter Parsons and Ursulla Jenkins were married on May 2, 1703 in Stepney Parish (now in Wicomico County, Maryland) and they had three sons:

John Parsons (born February 7, 1705);
Peter Parsons (born March 10, 1707); and,
George Parsons (born August 5, 1708).
[Ref: *Maryland Eastern Shore Vital Records, 1648-1725*, by F. Edward Wright (1982), pp. 137, 165.]

John Parsons married Mary Smith on April 3, 1729 in Stepney Parish and they had four children:

Peter Parsons (born May 14, 1730);
Nelly Parsons (born December 24, 1733);
John Parsons (born September 11, 1736); and,
George Parsons (born April 14, 1738).
[Ref: *Maryland Eastern Shore Vital Records, 1726-1750*, by F. Edward Wright (1983), p. 120.]

PERKINS

In Rowan County, North Carolina on November 28, 1769, Richard Perkins gave power of attorney to his son William to recover from Rubin Perkins and Jacob Giles, of Baltimore County, Maryland, regarding tracts of 32 acres and 75 acres. Also mentioned in other deed conveyances in Rowan County were Charles Perkins (1767), Benjamin Perkins (1769), and Moses Perkins and wife Sebert (1769). [Ref: *Rowan County, North Carolina, Deed Abstracts, Vol. II, 1762-1772*, by Jo White Linn (Salisbury, N. C.: Privately published, 1972), p. 117, citing Deed Book 7, pp. 187-188, 192-193, 194-196.]

"In 1700 Richard Perkins, who owned *Paradise* on Swan Creek in Baltimore [now Harford] County, came into possession of 300 acres on the Susquehanna River near Lapidum. He added about 180 acres to this tract by purchase, and all of his holdings descended to his three sons, Richard, William and Elisha. This land was the tract known as *Eitrop* or *Eightrupp*. Richard Perkins, Jr. and William Perkins settled near Lapidum about the year 1732 and the latter operated the ferry at that place which was known as Perkins' Ferry. Reuben Perkins, son of William, became the operator of the ferry in 1737. About 1760 Reuben Perkins erected a stone grist mill on Herring Run, and after ten years sold it to Nathaniel Giles, who resided at Lapidum until his death in 1775. Nathaniel's father, Jacob Giles, built a large stone warehouse in 1772, north of Herring Run, for storing supplies for Cumberland Forge and his mills. This warehouse was purchased by John Stump, Jr. in 1794. Perkins Ferry became known as Smith's Ferry in 1772 and as Bell's Ferry in 1791." [Ref: *Our Harford Heritage*, by C. Milton Wright (Glen Burnie, Maryland: The French-Bray Printing Company, 1967), pp. 348-349.]

PHELPS

On "20 Apr 1762, Avinton Phelps, farmer, of Roan Co., North Carolina, and David McTwain, of Baltimore Co., Maryland, to Edward Morgan, planter, of Baltimore Co., Maryland, £30, 50 acres ... north side of Deer Creek. Signed: Vinton Phelps and David McTwain. Wit: William Husband and Gerard Hopkins Jr." [Ref: *Baltimore County, Maryland, Deed Records, Volume Three: 1755-1767*, by John Davis (1996), p. 158.]

Regarding the foregoing, please note the following:

In August, 1738, Thomas Phelps told the vestry of St. George's Parish in Baltimore County [now Harford County] that he had married Rose ---- on May 28, 1710 and "his wife had formerly eloped from one ---- Swift." On September 26, 1741 Elizabeth McShaine bound her son David McShaine to Thomas and Rose Phelps. Thomas Phelps died leaving a will dated April 2, 1758 in which he named his wife Rosanna and son Avinton (who was to be a ward of Edward Morgan), and friends David and Hannah McSwain. Avinton Phelps, son of Thomas, in April, 1762, was in Rowan Co., N. C., when he and David McSwain conveyed 50 a. *Jones' Venture* to Edward Morgan. Avinton Phelps married Rachel Muckeldory on 23 April 1730.

[Ref: *Baltimore County Families, 1659-1759*, by Robert W. Barnes (1989), p. 503.]

On April 17, 1723, "Avanto Phelps" registered his cattle and hog marks in Baltimore County Court at the request of his father Thomas Phelps. [Ref: *Inhabitants of Baltimore County, 1692-1763*, by F. Edward Wright (1987), p. 34.]

PIPPEN-PIPPIN-PIPEN

Joseph Pippen applied for a pension for his Revolutionary War service as an ensign in Edgecombe County, North Carolina on August 29, 1832, aged 80. He stated that he was born in Talbot County, Maryland and at age 11 moved with his father (not named) to Halifax County, North Carolina where he lived at the time of his enlistment in the North Carolina militia. Joseph married Mrs. Temperance Lee on February 10, 1827 in Edgecombe County; also, in 1827, a Henry Austin was referred to, but no relationship was given. Joseph died on April 10, 1833, and his widow Temperance applied for a pension (W5546) on May 23, 1853 in Edgecombe County. In 1833 the daughters referred to were Lydia Austin, Martha Porter, and Nancy Ward. In 1853 a Robert H. Austin, aged 43, was mentioned in Edgecombe County. Temperance Pippen died on June 7, 1754. Joseph appears to have been a brother of Robert Pippen who served in North Carolina (pension file S8960) and Richard Pippen (pension file W8519) who served in Maryland. Additional research may be necessary before drawing conclusions. [Ref: *Genealogical Abstracts of Revolutionary War Pension Files, Volume III: N-Z*, by Virgil D. White (1990), p. 2707; *Roster of the Soldiers from North Carolina in the American Revolution*, published by the North Carolina Daughters of the American Revolution (Durham, 1932), pp. 432, 582, 583.]

In Queen Anne's County, a Joseph Pippen married Margaret Maccoy on January 22, 1746, a John Pippin married Elisabeth Mounticue on April 11, 1751, and a Benjamin Pippin married Charity Montague on December 16, 1756. [Ref: *Maryland Marriages, 1634-1777*, by Robert W. Barnes (1975), p. 140.]

It is interesting to note that some time between November 11, 1753 and March 29, 1754, a John Pipen, planter, and wife Rebecca, leased a tract called *Bee Tree Ridge* from John Johnston for seven years, the rent being 500 pounds of tobacco per annum. Pipen agreed to build a twenty-feet log house, eighteen-feet high with "hued" logs, provided Johnston found a hand to "hue" them. Pipen further agreed not to allow any other person to use the land or to cut timber except for necessary repairs. [Ref: *Queen Anne's County, Maryland Land Records, Book Four, 1743-1755*, by R. Bernice Leonard (1994), p. 81.]

John Pipen died testate in Queen Anne's County in March, 1763, leaving a wife Rebecca, sons Joseph, John Jr., Robert, Solomon, and Benjamin Pipen, and daughter Rebecca Emory. [Ref: *Maryland Calendar of Wills, Volume 12, 1759-1764*, p. 179.]

There were also Pippens in Caroline County, Maryland subsequent to the war as noted in the land commission records in 1814, at which time Solomon Pippin, aged 51, mentioned Joseph Pippin and John Pippin, both deceased. Derias Pippin was also mentioned as a chain carrier. [Ref: *Heirs and Legatees of Caroline County*, by Irma Harper (1989), p. 28.]

POTTS

Henry Potts applied for a land warrant in Anson County, North Carolina in the fall of 1750. James Potts and John Potts were in the Fourth Creek Settlement in the 1750's. It appears that they came from the Eastern Shore of Maryland. The land records of Dorchester County contain the depositions on September 7, 1725 of Henry Potts, aged about 56, and Daniel Rutty, aged about 67, who stated that they were servants to Walter Dickson of Talbot County, Maryland, about 40 years ago. [Ref: *Carolina Cradle*, by Robert W. Ramsey (1964), pp. 54, 96, 103, citing Rowan County Deeds IV:351, Rowan County Wills A:197; North Carolina Land Grants VI:205, XV:3; *Abstracts from Land Records of Dorchester County, Maryland, Volume B, 1689-1733*, by James A. McAllister, Jr. (1960), p. 108.]

One James Potts witnessed the will of Laurence Everett, Sr. in Queen Anne's County on January 14, 1720/1. [Ref: *Maryland Calendar of Wills, Volume 5, 1720-1726*, p. 125.]

One John Potts owned a 60-acre tract in Talbot County in 1744. [Ref: *Settlers of Maryland, 1731-1750*, by Peter Wilson Coldham (1996), p. 178.]

On October 8, 1832, at Sneedesborough in Anson County, North Carolina, Thomas Potts, aged 71, applied for a pension (S7326) for his Revolutionary War service, stating he was born and raised in Talbot County, Maryland and he served in the 4th Maryland Line in 1778. [Ref: *Genealogical Abstracts of Revolutionary War Pension Files, Volume III: N-Z*, by Virgil D. White (1990), p. 2746, and *Archives of Maryland, Volume 18*, "Muster Rolls of Maryland Troops in the American Revolution, 1775-1783," p. 153.]

PRITCHETT

On August 27, 1794, Edward Pritchett, of Craven County, North Carolina, conveyed to Thomas Kallender, of Dorchester County, Maryland, parts of tracts *Hereford* and *Pritchett's Regulation Regulated* not heretofore conveyed to James Moore and Moses Barns, on Hodson Branch, containing 10 acres more or less. Witnesses were Levin Woolford and Richard Pattison, Justices. [Ref: *Abstracts of the Land Records of Dorchester County, Maryland, Volume 33 (Liber HD#8)*, by James A. McAllister, Jr. (1967), p. 7.]

REED-REID

Richard Reed (Reid) applied for a pension for Revolutionary War service on March 6, 1833 in Anderson District, South Carolina, stating that he was born about 1763 in Baltimore County, Maryland and lived in Burke County, North Carolina at the time of his enlistment. The pension application (S32471) of his brother

Robert Reed stated that he (Robert) was born in Ireland and was brought to America when he was an infant. He also stated his brother Richard lived in Anderson District, South Carolina and also provided an affidavit in 1835 as to his service. Their father (not named) died when they were young. Robert Reed lived in Lincoln County, North Carolina at the time of his enlistment and he also served as a substitute for his brother-in-law George Cather (or Garner?, name illegible). He subsequently moved to Missouri and then to St. Clair County, Alabama, where he died on January 16, 1862. Richard Reed, brother of Robert, married Jane Craven in February, 1788 in Abbeville District, South Carolina at the home of John Miller. Richard died on May 25, 1835 and his widow applied for pension (W22054) on April 15, 1848, aged 82. Leut Hall and wife Polly (relationship not stated) made affidavit at that time. [Ref: *Genealogical Abstracts of Revolutionary War Pension Files, Volume III: N-Z*, by Virgil D. White (1990), p. 2840.]

It is interesting to note that a Robert Reid was born circa 1760 in Ireland, served in the revolution in South Carolina under Capt. Field Farrar, and married Joanna Garner Miles. [Ref: *Roster of South Carolina Patriots in the American Revolution*, by Bobby Gilmer Ross (1985), p. 808.] It is even more interesting that no one named Richard Reed, Reid, or Read appears in the *Roster of Soldiers from North Carolina in the American Revolution* compiled by the North Carolina Daughters of the American Revolution at Durham in 1932.

REID-REED-READ

"One of the older settlers in the Davidson's Creek district was Joseph Reid, who died on the Catawba [in western North Carolina] in 1750, the probable year of his arrival. Reid evidently originated in Kent County, Maryland, whence he removed to the Shenandoah Valley as early as 1738." [Ref: *Carolina Cradle*, by Robert W. Ramsey (1964), p. 54.]

The records of St. Paul's Parish in Kent County, Maryland indicate the marriage of a Joseph Reed and Mary ---- before July 2, 1720, the date of birth of their first child Jane. Their second child was a son Joseph, born December 9, 1722. [Ref: *Maryland Eastern Shore Vital Records, 1648-1725*, by F. Edward Wright (1982), p. 33.]

The debt books of Kent County record that a Joseph Read owned a tract called *Subbards* or *Suburbs* on which he paid taxes from 1736 to 1747. However, a Joseph Reed was listed as owning tracts *Providence* and *Suburbs* after 1753. [Ref: *Inhabitants of Kent County, Maryland, 1637-1787*, by Henry C. Peden, Jr. (1994), p. 30.]

RIDDLE-RUDDLE

Stephen Riddle or Ruddle originated in the Nottingham area of the Chester County, Pennsylvania and Cecil County, Maryland border, five miles east of where the Susquehanna River flows across the Maryland-Pennsylvania boundary line. A

Margaret Riddle was in Frederick County, Maryland sometime between 1749 and 1754. Stephen Riddle migrated to western North Carolina and settled in the forks of the Yadkin River. On October 20, 1768, the Rowan County court minutes state that "John Riddle, aged 5 years, presented testimony at the request of his father Stephen Riddle that part of John's ear was lost through mortification and not from a court punishment." [Ref: *Carolina Cradle*, by Robert W. Ramsey (1964), p. 80, citing Rowan County Court Minutes I:10 and Rowan County Deeds II:194, IV:740.]

ROBERTS

Edward Roberts and William Roberts migrated from Philadelphia County, Pennsylvania to Frederick County, Maryland by 1749 (at which time William was charged with "stealing a hog with force of arms." In 1761, Edward Roberts was granted 200 acres of land in the forks of the Yadkin River on Bear Creek in western North Carolina, where he was close neighbors to the Boones. [Ref: *Carolina Cradle*, by Robert W. Ramsey (1964), pp. 76-77, citing North Carolina Land Grants VI:212; Frederick County Judgments, 1748-1750, p. 386; and, *Publications of the Genealogical Society of Pennsylvania*, Volume I (No. 4), pp. 171, 180, 183.]

ROBEY

"Thomas Robey, who died [in Iredell County, North Carolina] three years before his wife Eleanor [widow of John Baptist Lovelace of Frederick County, Maryland] mentions some of the Lovelace children in his will. Obviously, two daughters married Lovelaces, since he refers in his will to his daughter Sarah Lovelace. His daughter Ann married Elias Lovelace on January 11, 1775, he being her step-brother. The will mentions Nathan Robey, who was to have 150 acres on both sides of Fifth Creek, and Prior Smallwood Robey, who was to have 79 acres at the north of Robey's tract and eventually the 91 acres left as a life estate to the widow Eleanor. The witnesses to Thomas Robey's will were John Rosebrough, Robert Shaw, and Isaac Lovelace. Among the descendants of Thomas Robey who kept the name alive into the next century were John Robey, whose will is at Statesville, 1804, with wife Rachel and children Berry, Elizabeth, Basil, Leonard, Milly Barker, Esther Tucker, deceased, Mary Tucker, Ede Smith, and Tobias Robey, who had seven daughters. Then we have John Boswell Robey, whose will at Statesville, 1820, mentions wife Patta (Martha) and children Betsey, who married Ebenezer Holman, Anne, Polly, Cynthia, Matilda, Patta and sons Greenberry, James, Barton, Absalom and John Randolph. The name was on the map for a time as old deeds refer to Robey's Branch, which ran into Fifth Creek."

"Let us take a glance over the neighborhood say as of the day that Thomas Robey lay dead in his home on the north fork of Fifth Creek, late in 1773. Where should a man, stranger in a strange land, be interred? So far as appears, he was the first of the Marylanders to die in the neighborhood. The only burying ground was six or seven miles away, by rough road, at what came to be known as Fourth Creek Cemetery. There had been an interments [sic] there as early as 1764 when William Archibald died. It is said that Rev. John Thompson had held religious services there, or near by, and that the beginnings of a congregation were in existence. There they buried Rev. James Rosebrough, when he died in 1767. There was no Bethany until 1775, no New Hope until around 1802, and no Providence until considerably later. However, the Fourth Creek burying ground had been used, apparently, only, by the Pennsylvanians who held to Presbyterian tenets. Maryland people were of a different strain and custom. It is very likely that the Robey family was not invited to mingle its dust with the dust of the Covenanters. However that may be, there is no record of the interment of Thomas Robey, or any of his family, at Fourth Creek. It must be, then, after the Maryland custom, they rest on lands that were once their own. May it not be on that spot of higher ground, somewhat above the creek, which had been willed to Prior Smallwood Robey, and which is known as the Lewis Graveyard?"

[Ref: Information gleaned from "Lewis Graveyard With Mention of Some Early Settlers Along Fifth Creek, Iredell County, North Carolina" written in 1944 by Mary Elinor Lazenby (born 1875) in a booklet maintained by the Michigan Microform Collection (LH110) and published in the *Maryland Genealogical Society Bulletin*, Vol. 39, No. 1 (Winter, 1998), pp. 91-93.]

ROBINSON-ROBISON

Charity Spencer was born in 1744, daughter of Zachariah Spencer, and she married Job Robinson "somewhere in Maryland about 1760-1765. By family tradition they had five children upon arrival in North Carolina. Job applied for a land grant there in 1773. It seems likely that the Spencer and Robinson families came together to North Carolina. Children of Job and Charity Robinson were, in approximate order of birth: Ezekiel, Zachariah, Job Jr., Mary, Martha, James A., John, William, Charity, Amos, and Samuel Robinson. Earliest information as to Charity's husband Job Robinson is his land record in North Carolina." [Ref: Information compiled in 1998 by Ray A. Yount, 10031 Shortest Day Road NW, La Vale, MD 21502-6011, or E-Mail: alby6@juno.com.]

Henry Robinson, George Robinson, John Robinson, William Robinson, and Richard Robinson (or Robison) were in Calvert, Charles, and St. Mary's Counties, Maryland, before 1680. All but Henry were in the Irish Settlement in western North Carolina prior to 1763. "There is no will, deed, or land grant for John Robinson, but he was appointed constable 'on the south side of Grant's Creek to the Forks of said Creek' in 1753. He evidently died very soon thereafter. William Robinson, who died in 1757, was probably the brother of John Robinson and uncle of George and Richard Robinson." [Ref: *Carolina Cradle*, by Robert W. Ramsey (1964), pp. 124-125, citing Rowan County Deeds VI:248, North Carolina Land Grants VI:209, and Rowan County Wills C:198, D:91.]

ROSS

On August 21, 1765, Charles Ross, of Craven County, North Carolina, conveyed to Thomas Baynard, of Dorchester County, Maryland, part of a tract called *Rosses Venture*, being all that part of the aforesaid tract of land that remains unsold and clear of an elder survey called *Chittle's Lott*, containing 30 acres more or less. Witnessed and acknowledged by Thomas White and John Campbell, Justices of Dorchester County. [Ref: *Abstracts from Land Records of Dorchester County, Maryland, Volume F, 1763-1767*, by James A. McAllister (1964), p. 42.]

RYALL-RYLE

William Ryall applied for a pension (R9118) in Davidson County, Tennessee on January 5, 1839, aged 72, stating that he was born in Maryland in 1747 and lived in Craven County, North Carolina at the time of his enlistment at Kingston during the Revolutionary War. He also served as a substitute for his brother Daniel Ryall. [Ref: *Genealogical Abstracts of Revolutionary War Pension Files, Volume III: N-Z*, by Virgil D. White (1990), p. 2990.]

It should be noted that the *Roster of Soldiers from North Carolina in the American Revolution* (published by the North Carolina Daughters of the American Revolution in 1932) lists the following: David Ryal (p. 214), William Ryal (pp. 18, 19, 252, 310), Young Ryal (p. 358), William Ryall (p. 159), Joseph Ryals (p. 307), David Ryles (p. 157), and William Ryles (pp. 198, 215, 230, 358). There was also a John Ryalls who served as a matross in the Fourth Regiment of Artillery under Capt. James Mitchell in South Carolina during 1779. [Ref: *Roster of South Carolina Patriots in the American Revolution*, by Bobby Gilmer Ross (1985), p. 839.]

One John Ryall was a private in the 5th Maryland Continental Line who enlisted on June 6, 1778 and was discharged on March 20, 1779. [Ref: *Archives of Maryland, Volume 18*, "Muster Rolls of Maryland Troops in the American Revolution, 1775-1783," p. 241.]

It should be noted that the 5th Maryland Line was organized in 1777 and was comprised of soldiers from Queen Anne's, Kent, Caroline, and Dorchester Counties. There were families named "Ryle" in Kent County, Maryland in the 1700's. One "John Ryall" was a private in Capt. Henry Downes' Company, Caroline County Militia, 28th Battalion, on August 13, 1777. [Ref: *The Maryland Militia in the Revolutionary War*, by S. Eugene Clements and F. Edward Wright (1987), p. 152.]

SANDERS

"The earliest Sanders of whom we have knowledge is one Phillip Sanders, the possible emigrant to Virginia in 1768 [this appears to be a typographical error, which most likely should be 1708] and probably the same Philip who signed his will in Westmoreland County, Virginia in 1722. The legatees mentioned in this will are:

son, William; daughter, Ursulee Taylor; grandsons, Philip and John; grand daughter, Mary Sanders. He does name his wife Elizabeth ... [but she] ... is not named executrix. Next, we have the will of William Sanders [son of Philip, above] signed in Westmoreland County in 1727 and he is married, at this time to Elizabeth, who may not have been his first wife, or the mother of his children, as her writes [in his will]: 'Item - It is my will that all the rest of my estate of any kind whatever be equally divided between my wife Elizabeth and her children.' Throughout the rest of this will he strictly identifies other legatees. They are: sons, John, Phillip, William and James; daughters, Mary, Ursula and Sarah. No grandchildren are mentioned. Mary Elizabeth Sanders, of Baton Rouge, Louisiana first called this subtle wording in this will to my attention and since then we have found that there was a William Sanders of Westmoreland County who married one Mary Remy in 1709 in Adingdon Parish: June 19, 1709."

"It will be noticed from the above list that William did have a daughter named Mary and did not have a daughter named Elizabeth. He may have, of course, and she may have died before the will in 1727. However, more important, then, becomes the will of William's father Phillip Sanders. He seems to have included everyone, since there were few legatees --- only two children, and he appears to have named all grandchildren. No grand daughter named Elizabeth is mentioned in his will. I am well aware of the conjecture inserted here, but is must be addressed and considered for future research. Bear with me, with each paragraph, we move closer to Chester District, and the years 1768-1791. As noted in the 1727 will of William Sanders of Westmoreland County, Virginia, two of his sons are William and James. It is a possibility that they may have been twins. Descendants of this line have stated that twins have been repeated throughout the generations. It appears that they remained close during their adult life and both of these men married Gunnell sisters, the daughters of William Gunnell of (first) Westmoreland County, Virginia, then Stafford, and finally Fairfax County, Virginia."

"William also asks in his will that his young son Hendry be raised by his brother James. William Sanders married Elizabeth Gunnell and James Sanders married Sarah Gunnell. Both women received substantial Fairfax County, Virginia land from their father, William Gunnell. When William Sanders signed his will in the year 1768 he was living in Frederick County, Maryland. He was a resident of Fairfax County, Virginia for most of his adult life, and he may have gone to live with a son, possibly William Sanders, after the death of his wife, Elizabeth (Gunnell) Sanders." [A copy of his will was included in the article, but has not included here. See Frederick County, Maryland Wills Liber AL, folio 304, for the will written on January 2, 1768 and probated in February, 1768, or *Maryland Calendar of Wills, Volume 14, 1767-1772*, p. 25.]

"William Sanders of the above 1768 Frederick County, Maryland will had a brother named James [who] left his will in 1778 in Loudoun County, Virginia. We must be careful not to confuse the brother James Sanders with the son of William: James Sanders I. A horizontal comparison of the names of their children will be interesting as well as informative [n/f = nothing further]: James Sanders married Sarah Gunnell; will signed April 10, 1778, Loudoun County, Virginia; children: James (n/f), John (executor of will), Presly (n/f), Henry (n/f), Aaron (executor of will), Lynus (n/f), Barbara (n/f), and Henry (nephew, - son of William) [sic.] William Sanders married Elizabeth Gunnell; will signed January 1, 1768 [Ed. Note: An error in the date; it was actually signed on January 2, 1768], Frederick County, Maryland; children: Hardy (n/f), William (married Easter Gore), Elias (n/f), Lewis (n/f), Robert (n/f), Hendrey (raised by uncle James), John (n/f), Elizabeth (daughter) [sic], Mary, and James I (married Mary Gore)."

"It was probably William Sanders [son] with whom William Sanders [father] was living when he signed his 1768 Frederick County, Maryland will. A William Sanders was being taxed for land in Sugarland Hundred, Frederick County, Maryland in 1761. [This could have been, of course, father or son, but William Sanders, father, it is thought, was a life-long resident of Fairfax County, Virginia.] In this same tax list for Sugarland, we find Gores, also: James Gore, Sr. [listed on tax roll as senior!] [sic], Michael Gore, Clemsias Gore, Thos. Gore -- either the son of James Gore, Sr. or his brother who later went to South Carolina. James Sanders I of Frederick County, Maryland, and of Fairfax County, Virginia, married Mary Gore around the year 1768 and this marriage probably took place in Maryland or Virginia. No marriage record has yet been found. We can place this marriage with some certainty because of a notation found by Mary Elizabeth Sanders of Baton Rouge, Louisiana in the Vestry Book of Shelburne Parish, Loudoun County, Virginia, 1771-1805. For the date of May 10, 1785 she found the following: 'The CW [Church Warden] of S. P. [Shelburne Parish] bind Wm. Gunnell Sanders, aged 16 years the 16th of Feby. last to Edward Stephens to learn the trade of blacksmith accg. to law.' This places his date of birth as February 16, 1769."

"William Gunnell Sanders was a son of Mary Sanders Gore and James Sanders I. This is the direct line of Mary Elizabeth Sanders of Baton Rouge, Louisiana, and from this line would come a Governor of Louisiana: Jared Young Sanders III, b. January 29, 1869, d. March 23, 1944. From the book *Records of Attakapas District, Louisiana, Vol. II, St. Mary Parish, 1811-1860*, compiled by Mary Elizabeth Sanders, 1963, we find that William Gunnell Sanders bought property in Chester County, South Carolina in 1799 and that he married circa 1790, Mary Young, known to be a resident of Chester County, South Carolina. It has been thought that William Gunnell Sanders was, perhaps, the oldest, but this has not thoroughly been established. Both William Gunnell Sanders and James Sanders II [perhaps, for James II] [sic] are found in records of Chester District, South Carolina and it was from here that they continued their westward migration, finally settling in Adams County and Wilkinson Counties, Mississippi [William Gunnell Sanders] and for James Sanders II, first, Natchez District, circa 1797-1798, and in 1808, permanently in St. Mary Parish, Louisiana [Refer again to the above book by Mary Elizabeth Sanders, p. 87.]"

[Ref: *The Bulletin* of the Chester District Genealogical Society, Vol. XVI, No. 3, September, 1992, featuring the article entitled "The Gore-Sanders Connection of Chester District, South Carolina" by Ann Lynch Boyer, pp. 81-84.]

In Frederick County, Maryland, August Court, 1765, is this entry: "Ann Dempsey sues John Hyde Sanders for her freedom, and the Court orders that Sanders discharge Ann from his service." [Ref: *This Was The Life: Excerpts from the Judgment Records of Frederick County, Maryland, 1748-1765*, by Millard Milburn Rice (1979), p. 271. It should be noted that this is the only entry for anyone named Sanders in these records for that time period.]

SEGO-SEAGO

Robert Sego or Seago served in the South Carolina Line during the Revolutionary War and married Elender Whorton on September 15, 1788 in Greenville District, South Carolina. She was born on January 5, 1764 in Granville County, North Carolina. He died on June 17, 1810 in Pendleton District, South Carolina. Elender Sego applied for a pension (R9368) on May 16, 1855 in Cherokee County, Alabama at which time she was living with a son Robert Sego. She stated she had lived at one time with her son Benjamin Sego in Cherokee County, Georgia [sic.] The following family data was given, but the exact relationships were not stated: John Sego or Segore was of Queen Anne's County, Maryland in 1762; Seago births were as follows:

William Seago (born August 23, 1744);
Ann Seago (born December 13, 1746);
John Seago (born February 19, 17??);
Robert Seago (born September 12, 1754);
Abraham Seago (born February 6, 1757);
Margaret Seago (born in August, 175?);
James Seago (born January 18, 1762);
Elizabeth Seago (born January 2, 1765);
Benjamin Horton Seago or Sego (born Feb. 20, 178?);
Sarah Seago (born February, 1786);
--?-- Seago (born September 24, 1789); and,
James Seago (born February 10, 1796).

[Ref: *Genealogical Abstracts of Revolutionary War Pension Files, Volume III: N-Z*, by Virgil D. White (1990), p. 3065.]

John Sego was a private in the Queen Anne's County, Maryland militia in 1776 and is the only Sego or Seago listed in Henry C. Peden, Jr.'s *Revolutionary Patriots of Kent & Queen Anne's Counties, Maryland, 1775-1783* (1995), p. 352.

Thomas Seego (Scego, Sergo) was a private in the Maryland Line and served under Capt. Edward Spurrier and Capt. Walker Muse from July 22, 1782 to November 15, 1783. [Ref: *Archives of Maryland, Volume 18*, "Muster Rolls of Maryland Troops in the American Revolution, 1775-1783," pp. 467, 503, 557.]

Benjamin Sego was a private in Capt. Henry Clarkson's Company of Militia, 12th Battalion, in 1777 in Charles County, Maryland, and is the only Sego or Seago listed in S. Eugene Clements & F. Edward Wright's *The Maryland Militia in the Revolutionary War* (1987), p. 159.

John Seago (c1715-c1784) married Margaret Birmingham or Burmingham (1719-c1780), daughter of John Birmingham and Elizabeth (Brown?), at St. Luke's Parish in Queen Anne's County, Maryland on April 17, 1740, and their children were as follows:

(1) William Crain Seago (born August 23, 1744, married first to Mary Dunham and second to Sarah Key, and died November 6, 1828);

(2) Ann Seago (born December 13, 1746);

(3) John O. Seago (born in Queen Anne's County, Maryland on February 19, 1750 or 1751, married about 1773 in Anson County, North Carolina to Lucretia (Lucresey) Dunham who was born in 1752, and died on December 6, 1784); John and Lucretia had these children born in Anson County, North Carolina:

    (31) Joseph Seago (b. 1774, married Martha Gulledge);

    (32) Lucretia Seago (b. 1776);

    (33) Nancy Seago (b. 1778, died before 1846);

    (34) John Seago (b. 1781, married Hannah Low);

    (35) Sarah Seago (b. c1783, married Jessie McLendon);

    (36) Mary Seago (b. c1785, married Jessie Smith).

(4) Robert Seago (born September 12, 1754, married Ellender Wharton on September 12, 1788 in Greenville County, South Carolina, and died on June 17, 1810 in Pendleton District, South Carolina); Abraham Seago (born February 6, 1757 and died before 1784);

(5) Margaret Seago (born in August, 1759 and died before 1784);

(6) James Seago (born January 18, 1762 and died before 1784); and,

(7) Elizabeth Seago (born January 2, 1765).

[Ref: Information compiled in 1998 by Andrea K. Juricic, 1557 W. 2320 S., West Valley, Utah 84119; *Maryland Eastern Shore Vital Records, 1726-1750*, by F. Edward Wright (1983), pp. 44, 53.]

It must be noted that the Seegar family also lived in Queen Anne's County. Since "Seegar" and "Seago" sound alike, additional research will require caution as the families may or may not be the same and they may or may not have the same origins.

SHELBY

On June 17, 1761, in Frederick County, Maryland, David Brown recorded a deed made to him from Moses Shelby, of Caravan [Craven?] County, South Carolina, for £285 current money of Maryland, for a 310-acre tract called *Hunts Cabbin* in Frederick County, Maryland, on the west side of Licking Creek. Signed by Moses Shelby before Thomas Prather and Thomas Norris. [Ref: *Frederick*

County, Maryland Land Records, Liber G & H Abstracts, 1761-1763, by Patricia Abelard Andersen (1996), p. 6.]

On August 26, 1762, Jonathon Hunt, of Rowan County, North Carolina, conveyed to Evan Shelby, of Frederick County, Maryland, for £53, 10s. Virginia money, 700 acres on Swearing Creek. The witnesses were James Craige, John Shelby, and John Braly. [Ref: *Rowan County, North Carolina, Deed Abstracts, Vol. II, 1762-1772*, by Jo White Linn (Salisbury, N. C.: Privately published, 1972), p. 94, citing Deed Book 6, pp. 545-547.]

On August 30, 1763 in Frederick County, Maryland, Evan Shelby sold 254 acres, part of *Rangers Venture*, for £72 current money, to Elias Stilwell; recorded September 3, 1763. Letitia Shelby, wife of Evan, released her dower. [Ref: *Frederick County, Maryland, Land Records, Liber G & H Abstracts, 1761-1763*, by Patricia Abelard Andersen (Gaithersbury, MD: GenLaw Resources, 1996), p. 91.]

Evan Shelby, who came to Maryland from Wales, settled in the Antietam Valley at an early date. His sons were Isaac Shelby (who became the first governor of Kentucky) and Evan Shelby. Local history books are replete with information about this prominent family. [Ref: *Genealogical Index to Frederick County, Maryland*, by John Stanwood Martin (Malvern, PA: Colin's Copy Center, 1992), p. 84; *History of Frederick County, Maryland*, by T. J. C. Williams (1910); also see Peden's first volume of *Marylanders to Carolina*.]

SHELL-SCHELL

Johannes Casper Shell or Schell was born in Germany circa 1720 and may be the Johanna Caspar Schell who arrived in Philadelphia on the ship *Robert and Alice* on September 24, 1742. He married Anna Catharine Gertrude Bott circa 1748, probably in Berks County, Pennsylvania, and resided in Lancaster County. Caspar Schell appears there on the 1757 tax list in Donegal Township. Between June 22 1768 and June 29, 1770 Caspar moved to Hampden Township in what is now Cumberland County (then in Lancaster County). By May, 1772 he was in Hagerstown, Maryland and in 1778 he appears in the land records of Burke County, North Carolina.

Caspar Shell died in Lincoln County, North Carolina by June 2, 1804, but there is no list of heirs in his estate file. His will only mentions Mary Conrad "to fall an equal share with my children" and Charles Frederick Shell "to have an equal share with the brothers and sisters." Henry Shell and Christian Hawn were his executors. It appears that the children of Johannes Casper Shell were as follows:

[1] Johannes Schell (born January 8, 1749, Hempfield Township, Lancaster County, Pennsylvania, baptized at Trinity Lutheran Church on August 7, 1753, married Anna Catherine Feigley, daughter of Johannes Feigley and Anna Ursula Schneckenberger, in Hagerstown, Maryland circa 1770-1772 (he was probably the John Shell who was a first sergeant in the militia of Washington County, Maryland, 1776/1777), and their children were:

(11) Christian Shell, born March 21, 1773 in Hagerstown, Maryland and married Rachel Martin;

(12) Charles Shell, born circa 1775 in Hagerstown, Maryland, married Hannah Martin in Lincoln County, North Carolina, and moved to Tennessee after 1830;

(13) ---- Shell, born circa 1777 in Maryland or North Carolina and married Isaac Martin;

(14) John Shell, Jr., born April 17, 1779 in Burke County, North Carolina, married Margaret McCall in 1801, and died in Hawkins County, Tennessee on March 25, 1861;

(15) Daniel L. Shell, born circa 1780 in North Carolina, married Mary Miller, and died in Carter County, Tennessee after 1860);

[2] Anna Maria Schell (born April 30, 1753, baptized at Trinity Lutheran Church in Lancaster County, Pennsylvania on August 7, 1753);

[3] Henry Schell (born circa 1755, Lancaster County, Pennsylvania, married with six children by 1790, and was over age 45 in 1800 census);

[4] Michael Schell (born circa 1757, Lancaster County, Pennsylvania, date of birth unknown but he was old enough to serve in the Revolutionary War; confirmed at South Fork in 1779);

[5] Elizabeth Schell (born circa 1759, Lancaster County, Pennsylvania, and was confirmed at South Fork in 1779);

[6] Sarah Schell (born circa 1761-1762, Lancaster County, Pennsylvania, but no proof found);

[7] Catherina Schell (born circa 1764, Lancaster County, Pennsylvania, but no proof found);

[8] Gertrude Schell (born November 14, 1766, baptized at Reformed Congregation Church in Hagerstown, Washington County, Maryland on June 5, 1773 and confirmed at South Fork in 1783);

[9] Anna Magdalena Schell (born June 29, 1770, baptized at Reformed Congregation Church in Hagerstown, Washington County, Maryland on June 5, 1773);

[10] Caspar Schell, Jr. (born May 27, 1772, baptized at Reformed Congregation Church in Hagerstown, Washington County, Maryland on June 5, 1773, married Frances Mull, daughter of John Mull and Anna Maria Anthony, on June 3, 1794 in Lincoln County, North Carolina, and died in Cape Girardeau County, Missouri before November 10, 1846);

[11] Charles Frederick Schell, also known as Carl Frederich Schell (born November 25, 1774, baptized at Zion Reformed Church in Hagerstown, Washington County, Maryland on February 4, 1775, married Elizabeth Hahn (1789-1867) on July 16, 1808 in Lincoln County, North Carolina, and died in Weston Township, Platte County, Missouri on October 9, 1851); and,

[12] Henry Schell (born December 25, 1780, Lincoln County, North Carolina).

[Ref: *German Speaking People West of the Catawba River in North Carolina, 1750-1800*, by Lorena Shell Eaker (1994), pp. 385-405, and *Revolutionary Patriots of Washington County, Maryland, 1776-1783*, by Henry C. Peden, Jr. (1998), p. 337.]

SEWELL

Samuel Sewall appears in the Baltimore County Debt Book in 1754 as owner of tract called *Samuel's Delight*. [Ref: *Inhabitants of Baltimore County, 1692-1763*, by F. Edward Wright (1987), p. 70.]

Samuel Sewell, Christopher Sewell, Comfort Sewell, and Joshua Sewell all appear in Aquila Hall's tax assessment ledger between 1762 and 1765 in Baltimore County. [Ref: *Inhabitants of Baltimore County, 1763-1774*, by Henry C. Peden, Jr. (1989), p. 22.]

On "30 Jul 1770, Samuel Sewell, planter, of Rowan Co., North Carolina, to John Elder, of Baltimore Co., Maryland, £300, 191 acres and 20 acres ... Morgan's Run. Signed: Samuel (x) Sewell. Wit: Jonathan Plowman, William Ottey and John Barney." [Ref: *Baltimore County, Maryland, Deed Records, 1767-1775*, by John Davis (1997), p. 91.]

SHERRILL

"The most picturesque, and probably the most significant, of the early settlers on the Catawba was the Sherrill family. Not only were the Sherrills trail-blazers in the settlement of western North Carolina, but they also played a key role in opening up the Susquehanna Valley. William Sherrill was among the earliest of the so-called Conestoga traders, and he was joined in 1720 by Adam, Rudil, and Samuel Sherrill as residents in Conestoga Township [in Lancaster County, Pennsylvania.] Soon after 1730 the Sherrills moved into western Maryland where, in 1738, Adam Sherrill obtained a tract of land in the back parts of Prince George's County on the Potomac River immediately opposite the modern village of Falling Waters, in Berkeley County, West Virginia. Several of the Sherrills were in the Shendandoah Valley in 1747, whence William, Adam, Ute, and Yont moved on to the Catawba. There they established themselves on both sides of the river at a shallow, island-studded crossing to which they gave their name." [Ref: *Carolina Cradle*, by Robert W. Ramsey (1964), pp. 47-48, citing Chester County Tax Lists, 1737-1738; *The Black Books: Calendar of Maryland State Papers, No. 1*, pp. 60-61; North Carolina Land Grants XI:19; Rowan County Deeds IV:77-78, 659.]

Robert Ramsey also noted that "descendants of these Sherrills have erected a marker two miles southwest of Sherrill's Ford which carries an inscription to the effect that Adam Sherrill and eight sons crossed the Catawba there in 1747." He also noted that "the family is of French (probably Huguenot) origin. The anglicized name "Sherrill" is derived from the French "Chérel".]

It must be noted also that, although there was a William Sherrill in Monocacy Hundred in 1733, there were no deeds found for anyone named Sherrill in *The Land Records of Prince George's County, 1702-1743* (6 volumes), abstracted and published by Elise Greenup Jourdan between 1990 and 1996; nor were there any Sherrills mentioned in *The History of Western Maryland*, by J. Thomas Scharf (1882).

Nevertheless, Adam Shirrell did make his mark on a petition in 1739 as an inhabitant of the back parts of Prince George's County, requesting the Maryland Assembly to divide the county and create a courthouse at Salisbury Plain because, among other reasons, "the court of judicature is from 120 to 200 miles away." [Ref: *Calendar of Maryland State Papers, No. 1, The Black Books*, Hall of Records Commission (1943), p. 60.]

SIGLEY

On June 9, 1718, William Sigley, of Bath County, North Carolina, planter, granted to John Whittington, of Chester, power of attorney to sell *Fresh Runn*, 160 acres in Queen Anne's County, Maryland. Witnesses were Daniel and David Pearkins (Parkins). On July 9, 1718, William Sigley, late of Kent County, Maryland, but now of North Carolina, and Johanna his wife, conveyed to James Smyth, of Kent County, in consideration of £20 current money of North Carolina, 160 acres, a tract taken up by Robert Smyth and by him sold to one Richard Dawson and by Dawson to William Sigley, called the *Fresh Runn*. Corners at Richard Turbutt's (being the plantation where William Sigley formerly lived on). Witnesses were Daniell Pearkins and David Parkins. [Ref: *Queen Anne's County Land Records, Book One, 1701-1725*, by R. Bernice Leonard (1992), p. 60.]

SILL

"The Sill family was in Kent County, Maryland as early as 1711 and in Chester County, Pennsylvania by 1723. John Sill appears to have left Edgmont Township, Chester County, in 1747 and to have proceeded directly to North Carolina." John Sill was in Rowan County by 1748 and settled west of the Yadkin River on a stream known as Sill's Creek. [Ref: *Carolina Cradle*, by Robert W. Ramsey (1964), p. 42.]

Joseph Sill, son of Joseph and Elizabeth Sill, was born in St. Paul's Parish in Kent County, Maryland on March 19, 1711. [Ref: *Maryland Eastern Shore Vital Records, 1648-1725*, by F. Edward Wright (1982), p. 34.]

Thomas Sill was a church official in 1729 at Holy Trinity (Old Swedes) Church in Wilmington, Delaware. [Ref: *Early Church Records of New Castle County, Delaware, Volume 2* (1994), a reprint of the original register, 1713-1799, as translated by Horace Burr circa 1890.]

Joseph Sill witnessed the will of George Wetherell in Kent County, Maryland in 1743. [Ref: *Maryland Calendar of Wills, Volume VIII, 1738-1743*, p. 228.]

SIPE-SEIP-SEIB

Johann Paul Seib (or Seip) was born on May 16, 1726 in Zweibrücken, Germany, a son of Johann Paul Seib and Maria Margaretha Schmid. On October 4, 1752 Paulus Seip and Philip Seip arrived in Philadelphia on the ship *Neptune* and settled in Lampeter Township, Lancaster County, Pennsylvania. Paul Sipe married Mary ---- and subsequently moved to Frederick County, Maryland. Their oldest son Daniel Sipe was born circa 1761 in Lancaster County, Pennsylvania and lived in Frederick County, Maryland at the time of his enlistment in the Revolutionary War in 1776. He is believed to have had three marriages and left two sons, Jacob and Henry, in Lincoln County, North Carolina before moving to Haywood County, North Carolina and then Harrison County, Indiana before 1830. On October 1, 1832 Daniel Sipes, aged 71, applied for a pension (S17092) and Paul Sipes, aged 61, gave his supporting affidavit. Daniel died on February 14, 1834. The children of Johann Paul Seip (Sipe, Sipes) were as follows:

(1) Daniel Sipe (born c1761);

(2) Abraham Sipe (born circa 1763 in Lancaster County, Pennsylvania, married first to Nancy Plunk and second to Mary Plunk, both daughters of Peter and Barbara Plunk or Plonk of Lincoln County, North Carolina, and died in Jefferson County, Tennessee circa 1825);

(3) Susannah Sipe (born circa 1766 in Pennsylvania or Maryland, married Daniel Woodring in Frederick County, Maryland on May 7, 1786, had 7 children, and died in Lincoln County, North Carolina after 1825 (her husband died on February 3, 1825); and,

(4) Paul Sipe, Jr. (born circa 1771, married Sarah Edward on July 1, 1798 in Lincoln County, North Carolina, and moved to Harrison County, Indiana.

[Ref: *German Speaking People West of the Catawba River in North Carolina, 1750-1800*, by Lorena Shell Eaker (1994), pp. 420-421.]

SOLLERS

On June 19, 1767, Sabret Sollers, of Chowan County, North Carolina, sold to Josias Bowen, of Baltimore County, Maryland, for £93.25, negroes Ben and Joe in the possession of Francis Phillips and negro Will in the possession of Joseph Taylor. Signed: Sabret Sollers. Wit: John Ensor, Jr. and Charles Ridgely, Jr. On that same day, Sabret Sollers, of Chowan County, North Carolina, heir of James Sollers, of Baltimore County, Maryland, granted power of attorney to Josias Bowen, of Baltimore County, Maryland. Signed: Sabret Sollers. Wit: John Ensor, Jr., Benjamin Bowen and Solomon Bowen. [Ref: *Baltimore County, Maryland, Deed Records, Volume Three: 1755-1767*, by John Davis (1996), p. 193.]

It should be noted that Sollers Point is located in the Dundalk area of southeastern Baltimore County. The Sollers family is included in Robert W. Barnes' *Baltimore County Families, 1659-1759* (1989), noting that the family is discussed more fully in *Taney and Allied Families* (New York: American Historical Society, 1935).

SPARKS-SPARKES

Solomon Sparks, Matthew Sparks, and Jonas Sparks from Kent County or Queen Anne's County, Maryland, moved westward to Frederick County, Maryland sometime between 1749 and 1754. They then migrated to the forks of the Yadkin River in Rowan County, North Carolina. [Ref: *Carolina Cradle*, by Robert W. Ramsey (1964), pp. 76-77, citing Kent County Deeds I:426, I:507; Maryland Land Warrants Y&S:131; Rowan County Wills C:114; Frederick County Judgments, 1750, p. 282; Rowan County Deeds IV:738, V:326, VI:455, VI:484.]

Edward Sparkes patented a 50-acre tract called *Sparkes Point* in 1668 in Kent County. [Ref: *Inhabitants of Kent County, Maryland, 1637-1787*, by Henry C. Peden, Jr. (1994), p. 67.]

William Sparkes, planter, owned *Sparkes Outlet* (114 acres) in 1687 and *Sparkes Own* (100 acres) in 1683, both tracts lying in Talbot County. [Ref: *Settlers of Maryland, 1679-1700*, by Peter Wilson Coldham (1995), p. 160.]

William Sparks patented *Sparks Delight* (50 acres) in Frederick County on November 4, 1749. [Ref: *Settlers of Maryland, 1731-1750*, by Peter Wilson Coldham (1996), p. 210.]

SPARROW

Thomas Sparrows, of Road [Rhode] River, Anne Arundel County, Maryland, died leaving a will dated June 10, 1713 and proved on May 12, 1719. To his sons Solomon and John he left a tract called *Crany Island* in North Carolina. To his son Kensey he left part of tract called *Sparrow's Rest* in Anne Arundel County and land on Dereham's Creek in Pamplicoe, North Carolina. To daughters Elizabeth and Matilda he left land on Dividing Creek in Pamplicoe, North Carolina. To son Solomon he left "ground in Rathtown, Pamplicoe, being front of Simond Alderson's and boundary of him" and to sons John and Kensey he left each "a lot adjoining said front." One should consult the actual will because inheritances would change based on the gender of the testator's unborn child. [Ref: *Maryland Calendar of Wills, Volume IV, 1713-1720*, pp. 202-203.]

SPENCER

James Wyatt and wife Bethlehem of Tryon County, North Carolina, conveyed to Zechariah Spencer of "Delaware County, Maryland" (probably Delaware Hundred in Baltimore County), for 26 pounds proclamation money, land on the south side of the South Fork of the Catawba, 193 acres adjacent to Hugh Berry, granted to said James Wyatt on October 26, 1765. One of the witnesses was William Spencer. The conveyance was recorded in January, 1773. [Ref: *Deed Abstracts of Tryon, Lincoln, and Rutherford Counties, North Carolina, 1769-1786*, by Brent Holcomb, p. 50.]

"The Zachariah Spencer of the above deed was the son of Zachariah Spencer who left a Harford County, Maryland will dated August 13, 1782 and probated December 16, 1783 (Liber AJ#2). This will named wife Charity Spencer (daughter of James Cobb and wife Rebecca, the widow of James Emson) and eight children including Zachariah Spencer, Charity Robinson, and William Spencer who removed to North Carolina. The 1826 estate settlement of the bachelor William Spencer who died in Burke County, North Carolina named the children of Zachariah Spencer who died in Lincoln County, North Carolina in 1789 with a will, and the children of Job and Charity Robinson, also deceased by 1826. In the estate settlement Elisha Jones gives a deposition as to the children of the first Zachariah Spencer of Baltimore/Harford County, Maryland." [Ref: Information gleaned from Burke County Estate Papers, 1776-1934, North Carolina Archives C.R.014.508.50, in 1998 by Ray A. Yount, 10031 Shortest Day Road NW, La Vale, MD 21502-6011, or E-Mail: alby6@juno.com.]

SPURRIER

"A considerable number of Spurriers in America today are descended from men who lived in North Carolina in 1790 and 1800. We don't know whether this North Carolina Family is related to the Maryland Family, but we think it appropriate to state what we know of the North Carolina line.

"The earliest member of the North Carolina family of whom we have a definite record is Theophilus Spurrier, thought to have been born about 1730 ... [and] ... this date approximates that of Green Spurrier of the Maryland family ... The sole datum we have on this man is his listing as head of family in the 1790 Census of North Carolina in the Salisbury District of Rockingham County. The tally for his family is 1-0-1-0-0, indicating one male over 16 years of age and one female. We infer from this datum that Theophilus was probable a man of advanced years in 1790; his name does not appear in the census of 1800. The tally indicates that in 1790 he probably did not have any children in his household."

"Thomas Spurrier, born c1750 [of Theophilus.] The only datum we have on this man is his listing in the 1800 census of Rockingham County, North Carolina, with a tally of 00001/00001. The count indicates that Thomas was born before 1755 as was the female in the household, who is probable his wife. The couple had no children in the household in 1800."

"John Spurrier, born c1756 [of Theophilus], married Frankie Roach c1795. This man is also recorded in the 1800 census of Rockingham County (p. 669). His tally is 30010/00001. The implications of this tally are that he was born after 1755, but that the female, probably his wife, was born before. They have in the household three young males born in the ten year period 1790-1800. We have a record of the children of this couple from one J. M. Spurrier, formerly of Overton County, Tennessee:

(1) Thomas Spurrier, born February 24, 1797 in North Carolina and married c1830 to Elizabeth ----, born in Tennessee c1800;
(2) John Spurrier, born July 15, 1798 in North Carolina and married c1820 to Rachel Cawood, born in Tennessee c1800;
(3) Elizabeth Spurrier, born July 23, 1800;
(4) William Spurrier, born March 8, 1802;
(5) Daniel Spurrier, born March 20, 1804;
(6) Martha Spurrier, born August 20, 1806;
(7) Mary Spurrier, born May 8, 1808; and,
(8) Samuel Spurrier, born April 5, 1810, married Jane McCollum.

"The memorandum covering the birth dates of the above children is in the possession [1974] of Mrs. Ellis Baird (Lorine Spurrier) of Charlestown, Indiana, niece of the late Harry Thomas Spurrier of Louisville [Kentucky.] It is part of the collection of Spurrier records which she received from her uncle's estate after his death. This John [Spurrier] took up land in Sullivan County, Tennessee about 1810."

"Thomas Spurrier [of John] was born in North Carolina on February 24, 1797 and married c1830 to Elizabeth ---- [who was] born c1800 in Tennessee. Their children were as follows:
(1) Frances Spurrier, born 1831 in Tennessee;
(2) Theophilus Spurrier, born 1833 in Tennessee;
(3) James Laid Spurrier, born 1840 in Virginia;
(4) Frances D. Spurrier, born 1844 in Virginia;
(5) Elbert Spurrier, born 1846 in Virginia.

"The information on this family comes from the 1850 Census of Scott County, Virginia. We can reconstruct the movements of this family to some extent from the places of birth. Thomas was born in North Carolina where John resided in 1800, no doubt in Rockingham County. As a young man he went with his family to Sullivan County, Tennessee, where his father took up land (records in the Tennessee State Archives). By 1830 Thomas had married, doubtless a Tennessee girl in Tennessee, and he is recorded in the 1830 census in Sullivan County; which is reflected in the birth of son Theophilus in the State of Tennessee in 1833. By 1840 the family had removed to Virginia, probably to Scott County where he is counted in the census of 1850. Although we did not find him in Scott County in 1860 he is recorded there in 1870 at age 74. Elizabeth, 78, and Theophilus and his wife and family are in the household. The fact that Thomas named a son Theophilus, a rare given name, is additional evidence that Thomas is indeed the grandson of Theophilus."

"John Spurrier [of John] was born in North Carolina on July 15, 1798, married c1827 [1821?] to Rachel Cawood (born in Tennessee in 1801), and died in Overton County, Tennessee in October 15, 1879. Their children were as follows:
(1) Mary Jane Spurrier, born 1829 [sic];

(2) John Spurrier, born April 22, 1821 [sic], married Elizabeth Bright (1821-1912), and died January 11, 1900;

(3) William G. Spurrier, born January 24, 1823 [sic], married first to Elizabeth Wallace and second to M. Gobble;

(4) Margaret Spurrier, born 1833;

(5) Thomas W. Spurrier, born July 10, 1835;

(6) Nancy Spurrier, born October 13, 1837;

(7) Sarah E. Spurrier, born April 16, 1840 and unmarried in the 1880 census; and,

(8) Anna Amanda Spurrier, born August 23, 1844."

"This man [John] and his family appear with precise birth dates (for the children above who show them) in the J. M. Spurrier memorandum of the Overton County, Tennessee Spurriers. He and part of his family also appear in the 1850 census of Scott County, Virginia. Hence he provides firm evidence that the Overton County Spurriers are descendants of the North Carolina family. Rachel Cawood Spurrier was still living in 1880 and appears with her spinster daughter, Sarah E., in the 1880 census of Scott County, Virginia."

[Ref: *Spurriers in America*, by John and Gertrude Hamlin (1974), pp. 104-106. In the foreword to their book is the following: "Three families of Spurriers are covered in this compilation. The largest, by far, is the Maryland Family, descendants of William Spurrier. He married Elizabeth Turner in 1702 in Talbot County, Maryland. Throughout the 18th century the descendants of this couple were concentrated in Anne Arundel and Frederick Counties, Maryland. Second, and much smaller, is the North Carolina Family, who descended from Theophilus Spurrier. He appears in the 1790 census of Rockingham County, North Carolina. The smallest family is comprised of the Pennsylvania Spurriers. They descend from an immigrant ancestor, William Atwell Spurrier, who settled in Lancaster County, Pennsylvania.".]

STACY-STACEY

Aaron Stacy was born in 1760 in St. Mary's County, Maryland and lived in Granville County, North Carolina at the time of his enlistment in the militia during the Revolutionary War. He married Nancy Bullock on December 13, 1779 in Halifax County, North Carolina and afterwards lived in Virginia (county not stated). In 1821 they moved to Burke County, North Carolina where Aaron applied for a pension on January 30, 1833. He died on June 17, 1834 and his widow applied for a pension (W19118) in Burke County in 1843, aged 80. [Ref: *Genealogical Abstracts of Revolutionary War Pension Files, Volume III: N-Z*, by Virgil D. White (1990), p. 3286; *Roster of Soldiers from North Carolina in the American Revolution*, published by the North Carolina Daughters of the American Revolution (Durham, 1932), pp. 422, 585.]

Richard Stacy and William Stacy or Stacey (with wife Enne Stacey) and Martha Stacy were transported to Maryland in 1661. Sarah Stacy was transported to

Maryland in 1662. Simon Stacy and wife Mary immigrated to Calvert County in 1674. Edward Stacy was transported to Maryland by 1678. [Ref: *The Early Settlers of Maryland*, by Gust Skordas (1968), pp. 435-436; *A Supplement to The Early Settlers of Maryland*, by Carson Gibb, Ph.D. (1997), p. 207.]

Richard Stacey, of Patuxent Manor in Calvert County, died testate in May, 1674, leaving personalty to William Stacey and his (William's) wife Mary Stacey, executrix. [Ref: *Maryland Calendar of Wills, Volume I, 1635-1685*, p. 80.]

John Stacey witnessed the will of Thomas Cooke of St. Mary's County on June 3, 1715. [Ref: *Maryland Calendar of Wills, Volume IV, 1713-1720*, p. 71.] However, it must be noted that no one named Stacy or Stacey died testate in Maryland after 1675, i.e., none died leaving a will during the colonial period.

STANTON

On February 2, 1788, in Dorchester County, Maryland, George Stanton and wife Mary Stanton, alias Mary Hackett, of the County of Rockingham and State of North Carolina, conveyed to Ann Ennalls, widow and executrix of Henry Ennalls, deceased, of Dorchester County, Maryland, part of tracts called *Theophilus Choice* and *Travers's Purchase* or *Lott*, containing 94 acres more or less. Witnesses: John Hallam and John Webster. [Ref: *Abstracts of the Land Records of Dorchester County, Maryland, Volume 29 (Liber HD#2)*, by James A. McAllister, Jr. (1967), p. 11.]

STEELE

On July 13, 1798, William Steele, of Bertie County, North Carolina, conveyed to Samuel Phillips and Mary Phillips his wife, part of a tract called *Ragged Point*, formerly the property of William Steele, deceased, father of the said William Steele and Mary Phillips, on the Bay Shore and Brooks Creek, containing 130 acres. Witnesses were Joh Reed and Levin Woolford, Justices of Dorchester County, Maryland. On that same date, William Steele, of Bertie County, North Carolina, and Samuel Phillips and Mary his wife, of Dorchester County, Maryland, conveyed to Edward Hardy, of Currituck County, North Carolina, part of *Ragged Point*. Witnesses were John Reed and Levin Woolford, Justices of Dorchester County. [Ref: *Abstracts of the Land Records of Dorchester County, Maryland, Volume 36 (Liber HD#14)*, by James A. McAllister, Jr. (1967), pp. 8-9.]

STEVENSON

"The family of William Stevenson was living on Maryland's Eastern Shore as early as 1672 [at which time a William Stevenson witnessed the will of William Durand in Talbot County.] It is probable that few families contributed a greater number of persons to the southward movement than the Stevensons. Andrew, David, James, Thomas, John, and William Stevenson were all in the valley of Virginia between 1740 and 1755." From there they migrated into western North Carolina.

[Ref: *Carolina Cradle*, by Robert W. Ramsey (1964), p. 96, citing Lyman Chalkley's *Chronicles of the Scotch-Irish Settlements in Virginia, Extracted from the Original Court Records of Augusta County, 1745-1800* (Rosslyn, VA: Commonwealth Printing Co., 1912), III:7, 29, 39, 264, 276.]

There was also a William Stevenson in Somerset County in July, 1685, at which time "John Wallis, Sr., of Ireland and Monokin River, Somerset County, Maryland" left him a legacy in his will. [Ref: *Maryland Calendar of Wills, Volume I, 1635-1685*, p. 160.]

Also, there was a number of Stevensons who were transported into Maryland from Virginia in 1665, specifically Elizabeth, Katherine, Philip, Sarah, and Thomas. [Ref: *The Early Settlers of Maryland*, by Gust Skordas (1968), p. 441.]

One James Stevenson applied for a pension (no file number was given) in Cabarrus County, North Carolina on August 18, 1832, aged 87, stating that he lived in Cecil County, Maryland at the time of his first enlistment. He later went to Philadelphia, Pennsylvania and also enlisted there, and later enlisted a third time in York District, South Carolina. He died on February 5, 1833 and a son John Stevenson lived in Iredell County, North Carolina where he made affidavit on July 20, 1833. [Ref: *Genealogical Abstracts of Revolutionary War Pension Files, Volume III: N-Z*, by Virgil D. White (1990), p. 3330.]

James Stevenson was a private in Capt. John Ogilvie's Company in Cecil County, Maryland on July 25, 1776. One James Stevenson married Abigal Wilson by license dated February 25, 1789. [Ref: *Revolutionary Patriots of Cecil County, Maryland*, by Henry C. Peden, Jr. (1991), p. 108.]

STROUP-STRAUB

Adam Stroup, son of Jacob Straub or Stroup, was born in 1746 three miles from the City of Baltimore and was "boarded out" at the age of 8 years (indentured) because, it is indicated, he could not get along with his new step-mother, Catharine Masters. Adam lived in Lincoln County, North Carolina at the time of his enlistment and he applied for a pension (S7628) on July 24, 1834. No Stroup family information was given in his pension application, so "Adam's family is purely a reconstruction; however, four of the children are proven by letters of daughter Elizabeth Stroup Head." They were as follows:

(1) Catherine Stroup (born circa 1770 in Lincoln County, North Carolina, married Philip Dellinger, and died after 1820 in Wayne or Madison County, Missouri);

(2) Jacob D. Stroup (born March 18, 1771, married first to Elizabeth Dellinger, second to Hannah Hoyle Rhyne, third to Sarah Feuell, and died in Cass County, Georgia on October 8, 1846);

(3) John Stroup (may have married Barbara Masters in 1796);

(4) Joseph Stroup (born May 2, 1776, married Catherine Creasman in 1798, and died August 14, 1851 in Buncombe County, North Carolina);

(5) Margaret Elizabeth Stroup (married Alexander Spencer Head in 1800 and died after August, 1858 in Carter County, Tennessee);

(6) Andrew Stroup (married Catherine Link in 1803);

(7) David Stroup (married first to Hannah Goodson in 1803 and second to Margaret Inglefinger in 1806);

(8) Peter Stroup (supposedly married Elizabeth ---- and moved to Missouri);

(9) Solomon Stroup (married Nancy Haskins in 1816 and died testate in 1871 in North Carolina); and,

(10) Nancy Stroup (married Jesse Ross in Jefferson County, Kentucky in 1811).

The siblings of Adam Stroup (1746-c1835) were Frances (Stroup) Ecard, Jacob Stroup, Jr., Barbara (Stroup) Dellinger, George Stroup, Mary (Stroup) Reed, Philip Stroup, Hannah (Stroup) Posten, John Stroup, Daniel Stroup, Michael Stroup, and Elizabeth Stroup. [Ref: *German Speaking People West of the Catawba River in North Carolina, 1750-1800*, by Lorena Shell Eaker (1994), pp. 439-443.]

Jacob Stroup, the father of Adam and the above mentioned children, owned land called *Jacob's Lot* (20 acres) and *Major's Choice* (140 acres) in Baltimore County by 1750. [Ref: *Baltimore County Families, 1659-1759*, by Robert W. Barnes (1989), p. 616.]

SUMMERS

William Summers was born April 22, 1726 in Prince George's County, Maryland and married first on February 10, 1745 to Mary Wheat (September 20, 1727 - December 6, 1797). She appears to be the daughter of William Wheat and Mary Wall. Prince George's Land Records Book RR:142 records the following on July 10, 1761: "Mary Wall, of Prince George's County, for natural love and affection I bear to my beloved grandchildren Mary Summers, wife of William Summers, William Wheat, Jr., and Sarah Nabis, wife of John Nabis, after my decease and the decease of my daughter Amy Wheat, all the estate, property and interest except my negro man Thane which I give to granddaughter Mary Summers to be equally divided among my said grandchildren ... William Wheat, husband of said Amy, shall have no property after her decease." Frederick County Will Book A:287 records the will of William Wheat written on January 7, 1767 and probated on March 18, 1767, as follows, in part: "To daughter Mary Wheat, wife of William Summers, one negro woman named Chloe and her child Sam and all belonging to me ..." However, it should be noted that *The Heritage of Rowan County, North Carolina*, by Katherine Sanford Petrucelli (page 600), identifies Mary Wheat Summers as the daughter of William Wheat and Sarah Pardue. Therefore, additional research will be necessary before drawing conclusions.

William Summers' married second to Cassandra Ellis, daughter of Samuel Ellis. He is mentioned numerous times in the records of Frederick County (the part that became Montgomery County in 1776), including the 1760 list of sundry inhabitants of All Saints Parish in Frederick County, the 1776 census of Lower Potomack

Hundred in Frederick County, the 1783 assessment list in Sugarland Hundred in Montgomery County, and various land conveyances involving land tracts called *Strawberry Patch* and *Brandy* and *Wolf's Cow*. He moved from Montgomery County, Maryland to Iredell County, North Carolina sometime between 1783 and 1789 when he acquired land on Hunting Creek.

The children of William Summers and Mary Wheat were as follows:

(1) Anney (Amy) Summers (born May 11, 1746 and married William Howard);

(2) John Summers (born March 7, 1746 [sic], married Ann Claggett on December 8, 1774, and rose to the rank of captain in the Revolutionary War in Montgomery County, Maryland);

(3) Linney Summers (unmarried in 1799); Biney Summers (married ---- Belt by 1799);

(4) William Summers, Jr. (born circa 1751, married Rebecca Jacob on October 1, 1778, and acquired land on the South Yadkin River in Rowan County, North Carolina in 1790);

(5) Mary Summers (born 1750 and married Edward Jacob or Jacobs on October 28, 1779);

(6) Darkus or Dorcas Summers (born 1752 and married Zacharius Jacob or Jacobs on August 5, 1779);

(7) Bitha, Bertha or Tabitha Summers (born August 12, 1770, married John Tombelson or Tomlinson and migrated with his parents to Rowan, now Iredell, County, North Carolina);

(8) Basil Summers (married Ann Ellis, daughter of Samuel Ellis, on February 12, 1788 in Rowan County, North Carolina); and,

(9) Thomas Summers (died by 1799).

William Summers died testate after June 4, 1799 in Iredell County, North Carolina.

Thomas Summers was born in Prince George's County, Maryland, married Rachel Talbot by 1754, and died in Iredell County, North Carolina by August 21, 1799. Their children were as follows:

(1) George Summers (born by 1754 and was in Iredell County, North Carolina by 1798 when he purchased land);

(2) Thomas Summers; John Dent Summers (baptized July 13, 1754);

(3) Paul Talbutt Summers (baptized in January, 1762, married Sarah Bruce in Bedford County, Virginia in 1789, and bought land on Fifth Creek in Iredell County, North Carolina in 1798);

(4) Zachariah Summers (born 1763, married Sarah Dawson in Bedford County, Virginia on March 1, 1768 with the consent of his mother, and migrated to Iredell County, North Carolina, settling on Fifth Creek); and,

(5) Benjamin Summers (born 1772, married Verlinda Lovelace, and settled on the Yadkin River in Iredell County, North Carolina by 1799 when he acquired land).

Zachariah Summers was born in 1763 in that part of Frederick County, Maryland that became Montgomery County in 1777. A stone cutter by trade, he migrated to Iredell County, North Carolina where he died on September 3, 1848 and was buried in the Lewis Graveyard. See "Lewis" family section herein.

Joseph Summers was born circa 1730 in Prince George's County, Maryland and married by 1756 to Eleanor Clary, daughter of Daniel Clary and Eleanor Deveron, and died testate by January 16, 1809 in Newberry County, South Carolina. Their children were as follows:

(1) William Summers (born August 10, 1756 in Maryland, married Susannah Teague in 1777, and died October 12, 1823 in Newberry County, South Carolina);

(2) Mary Summers (born October 10, 1758 in Maryland, married Giles Chapman on September 14, 1775, and died October 15, 1813 in Newberry County, South Carolina);

(3) John Summers (born June 20, 1763 in Maryland, married Rosanna Waters, and died March 22, 1836 in Newberry County, South Carolina);

(4) Ruth Summers (baptized on December 6, 1765 and appears to have died young);

(5) Jesse Summers (born in 1775 in Newberry County, South Carolina, married Sarah Coate, and died testate by January 11, 1837 in Charles County, Alabama);

(6) James Summers (married Elizabeth ---- and died testate by August, 1826 in Edgefield County, South Carolina);

(7) Ellenor or Nelly Summers (married Thomas W. Waters in South Carolina and apparently died prior the writing of her father's will in 1802);

(8) Cassandra Summers (married --- Riggs and apparently died prior to the writing of her father's will in 1802);

(9) Ann or Annie Summers (married James Wells and died in Edgefield District, South Carolina); and,

(10) Dorcas Summers (married Griffin Coleman after the writing of her father's will in 1802, and died on March 20, 1837 in Newberry County, South Carolina).

[Ref: Above information compiled before 1998 by Rosemary B. Dodd, 2 Oak Lane SW, Glen Burnie, Maryland 21061-3461, which was then published in *The First Three Generations of John Summers of Prince George's County, Maryland*, by Rosemary B. Dodd and Helen Summers Holweck.]

The Summers family also lived in Baltimore County, Maryland. John Summers appears in the debt books in 1754 as owning tracts called *Summer Dear Park*, *Franklin's Choice*, and part of *Hills Camp*. [Ref: *Inhabitants of Baltimore County, 1692-1763*, by F. Edward Wright (1987), p. 55.]

On "13 Jan 1764, Richard Summers (elder brother son (sic) and heir John Summers, of Northampton Co., North Carolina to Richard Williams, of Baltimore Co., Maryland, £10, 100 acres ... north side of the little falls of Gunpowder ... patented, 1732, by John Summers, uncle of said Richard. Signed: Richard

Summers. Wit: John (x) James and Paul Williams." [Ref: *Baltimore County, Maryland, Deed Records, Volume Three, 1755-1767*, by John Davis (1996), p. 267.]

TATE

Samuel Tate originated in Baltimore County, Maryland, moved westward and southward, and settled on the Yadkin River in Rowan County, North Carolina between 1752 and 1762. [Ref: *Carolina Cradle*, by Robert W. Ramsey (1964), p. 83, citing Rowan County Deeds V:134, and Testamentary Proceedings 33:49.]

In Baltimore County on July 3, 1752, Samuel Tate administered on the estate of Henry Smith (weaver) who had died by October 16, 1749 when Tate posted an administration bond with Robert Brierly. Also, Isaac Smith, age 9 on September 1, 1758, son of Joseph Smith, was bound to Samuel Tate in June, 1759. Samuel may have been related to James Tate who sold some livestock to Thomas Rutter in Baltimore County in March, 1734. [Ref: *Baltimore County Families, 1659-1759*, by Robert W. Barnes (1989), pp. 590-591; *Baltimore County Deed Records, Volume Two: 1727-1757*, by John Davis (1996), p. 46.]

TAYLOR

In the deposition of John Greer in Baltimore County on July 25, 1743, age about 55, he states that about 30 years ago John Taylor, who then lived on the south side of the Gunpowder River near the ferry and afterwards went to Carolina and if living would be about 78 years old, showed him the bounds of *Thompson's Lott* and the second tree of a tract called *Adventure Addition*. [Ref: *Abstracts of Baltimore County Land Commissions, 1727-1762*, by the Baltimore County Genealogical Society (1989), p. 24.]

The aforementioned John Taylor, son of Arthur and Margaret, gave his age as 21 in 1692. Arthur Taylor was brought into Maryland by his father John Taylor by 1659. John Taylor, grandson of John, was mentioned in a deposition made by his nephew John Greer in 1732 as having been a Deputy Surveyor. John married first to Jane ---- and second to the widow Elizabeth Peckett. His known children were Arthur (born 1728) and Avarilla, who married first to Edward Day and second to Patrick Lynch. [Ref: *Baltimore County Families, 1659-1759*, by Robert W. Barnes (Baltimore: Genealogical Publishing Co. (1989), p. 624.]

TENNANT

James Tennant migrated to Rowan County, North Carolina from Kent County, Maryland and settled in the Davidson's Creek Settlement in 1754 where he purchased land from William Morrison. He moved to Orange County, North Carolina before 1765. [Ref: *Carolina Cradle*, by Robert W. Ramsey (1964), pp. 102-103, citing Rowan County Deeds III:23, VI:71.]

The debt books of Kent County list James Tennant (who paid taxes on a tract called *Debtford* and a lot in Charlestown beginning in 1747), Capt. John Tennant (who paid taxes on *Debtford* and a lot in Charleston between 1733 and 1747), and Moses Tennant (who paid taxes on *Debtford* and *Buck Hill* beginning in 1736). [Ref: *Inhabitants of Kent County, Maryland, 1637-1787*, by Henry C. Peden, Jr. (1994), p. 35.]

THARP

On October 6, 1721, Mable Tharp, wife of Richard Tharp, conveyed to James Tucker, a gift of all her chattels within the realm of North Carolina. On November 7, 1721, she also made over 400 acres called *Ireland* in Somerset County, Maryland, located between Broad Creek and Deep Creek. [Ref: Talbot County, Maryland Land Records, Volume 13, p. 20.]

THOMPSON-THOMSON

"Benjamin Thomson migrated from Charles County, Maryland" to western North Carolina and settled on the forks of the Yadkin River in Rowan County circa 1750. There was also a John Thompson who settled on Davidson's Creek. Others by that surname settled in the Irish Settlement prior to 1762 and they may have originated in Dorchester and Baltimore Counties. [Ref: *Carolina Cradle*, by Robert W. Ramsey (1964), pp. 83, 105, 124, citing Maryland Warrants LG#C:256-257, North Carolina Land Grants VI:201, XIII:21, XIII:116, Testamentary Proceedings 32:50, and Maryland Calendar of Wills IV:106, VII:121, VIII:67.]

It should be noted, however, that although there was a John Thomson or Thompson in Charles County who was a son of John who died in 1733, there is no mention of any Benjamin Thompson or Thomson in his will, or in *Early Charles County, Maryland Settlers, 1658-1745*, by Marlene Strawser Bates and F. Edward Wright (1995), or in *Charles County Gentry*, by Harry Wright Newman (1940).

TRACY-TRACEY

Thady or Teague Tracey was in Maryland by 1694 when he married Mary James on November 3, 1694 in St. James Parish, Anne Arundel County, and died in Baltimore County by June 18, 1712 when his estate was inventoried. James Tracey, son of Teague and Mary, was born on April 18, 1700 in St. James Parish and on November 4, 1724 he sold *Tracey's Park*, adjoining *James Meadows*, to his stepfather George Hitchcock. By March 1745/6 he had moved to Craven County, North Carolina when he appointed John Ensor his attorney to convey *James Meadows* and *Teague's Park* to John Cole [as noted above.] James' siblings were Dinah (born December 18, 1695), Sarah (born April 7, 1698), Teague (born April 18, 1703), and possibly Basil. James may have been the father of James and Nathaniel Tracey, two soldiers in the Revolutionary War in North Carolina, but this has not been proved.

[Ref: *Baltimore County Families, 1659-1759*, by Robert W. Barnes (1989), p. 649.]

On "29 Mar 1746, James Tracy, of Paris, Craven Co., North Carolina, power of attorney to John Ensor, of Patapsco Parish, Baltimore Co., Maryland to pass deed to John Cole Jr. Signed: James Tracy. Wit: Robert Howard, Mary (x) Brown and Rebecca (x) Brown." [Ref: *Baltimore County, Maryland Deed Records, Volume Two: 1727-1757*, by John Davis (1996), p. 244.]

Regarding the foregoing, please consider the following:

"29 March 1745/6: James Tracey of Craven Co., NC, appoints John Ensor of Patapsco Parish, his atty. to acknowledge deed to John Cole, Jr. for *James Meadow* and *Teague's Park* (TB#D:248)."

"29 March 1745/6: James Tracey of Craven Co., NC, gives p/a to John Ensor to sell *Teague's Park* and *James Meadow* to John Cole, Jr. (TB#E:248)."

Also: "9 Sep 1709: Teague Tracey, of BA Co, cooper, conv. 100 a. pt. of *James' Meadow*, on Briton Ridge, to Mordecai Price, of AA Co., planter. TT's wife Mary signed (TRA#A:146)." [Ref: *Baltimore County, Maryland, Deed Abstracts, 1659-1750*, by Robert Barnes (1996), pp. 111, 203.]

On "31 Jan 1765, John Ensor, Sr. (attorney for James Tracey, of Craven Co., North Carolina to sell to John Cole) and Thomas Sligh (attorney for John Cole), of Baltimore Co., Maryland, to George Haile, of same, £20, 100 acres. Signed: John Ensor and Thomas Sligh. Wit: William Smith and Moses Galloway." [Ref: *Baltimore County, Maryland, Deed Records, Volume Three: 1755-1767*, by John Davis (1996), p. 294.]

TRIPPE

Henry Trippe, of Dorchester County, Maryland, died leaving a will dated September 12, 1693 and proved March 21, 1697. The heirs named were: To wife Elizabeth, executrix, tract *Sark* and part of *Trippe's Neglect*. To eldest son Henry, land aforesaid at the death of his mother. To son John, 200-acre tract *Nemcock*. To son Edward, tract *Trippelow's Forest* and 40-acre tract *Addition to Trippelow's Forest*. To son William, 200-acre tract *Apperley*. To eldest son Henry and second son John, three parcels in Cason's Neck, viz., 100-acre *Dale's Delight*, 50-acre *Exchange*, and 100-acre *Dale's Addition*. To daughter Henrietta, personalty. [Ref: *Maryland Calendar of Wills, Volume II, 1685-1702*, p. 130.]

On June 16, 1720, John Trippe, of North Caroline *[sic]*, Gent., conveyed to Henry Trippe, Gent., of Dorchester County, Maryland, a tract called *Nemcock* on Armstrong's Bay, adjoining land laid out for Francis Armstrong called *Sark* and containing 200 acres more or less. Also, *Trippe's Neglect* near Trippes Bay, between two tracts of Henry Trippe, deceased, called *Sark* and *Nemcock* and containing 200 acres more or less. Excepting a small part of *Trippe's Neglect* devised by said Henry Trippe, Sr., deceased, to his said son Henry Trippe by his last will and testament. Witnesses: Phil. Feddeman, John Lawson, and Nehemiah Beckwith. Acknowledged on June 26, 1721 before Henry Ennalls and John Robson, Justices. [Ref: *Abstracts from Land Records of Dorchester County, Maryland, Volume B, 1689-1733*, by James A. McAllister, Jr. (1960), p. 97.]

TURNER

On October 6, 1742, Gilbert Turner, of Carteret County, North Carolina and Lewis Trott, of Onslow County, conveyed to George Baynard, in consideration of 3,000 pounds of tobacco, 200 acres called *Hacker's Forest* on the west side of Tuckahoe Creek [in Queen Anne's County, Maryland] adjoining *Branford*, formerly laid out for Col. William Digges, being so much due to John Hacker, of Talbot County, Maryland, by assignment from William Coursey, the assignee of William Hemsley, being part of a warrant for 620 acres granted to the said Hemsley, December 6, 1696, as appears by a patent granted to John Hacker, October 10, 1707. Witnesses were W. Jumpe and Henry Casson. Lewis Trott acknowledged the deed October 6, 1742 before Henry Casson. Henry Feddeman witnesses Trott's receipt to George Baynard. [Ref: *Queen Anne's County Land Records, Book Three, 1738-1747*, by R. Bernice Leonard (1993), p. 46.]

On July 12, 1742, Gilbert Turner, sometime of Talbot County, Maryland, now of Carteret County, North Carolina, planter, granted to Lewis Trott, of Onslow County, North Carolina, planter, power of attorney to sell *Hacker's Forest*, 200 acres in Queen Anne's County, Maryland, on the west side of Tuckahoe Creek, bequeathed to him (Turner) by his deceased uncle, John Rogers. Witnesses were Joseph Watts and Elizabeth Dudley. [Ref: Leonard, *loc. cit.*; Will of John Rogers, of Talbot County, dated August 8, 1726 and proved July 17, 1728 - *Maryland Calendar of Wills, Volume VI, 1726-1732*, p. 79.]

VOLKER-VOGELI

"Eighteen-year-old Peter Vögeli landed at Philadelphia in 1736. Thirteen years later, he and Jacob Völker were in Frederick County, Maryland. In 1756, Völker obtained a 656-acre tract (adjoining Squire Boone) in the forks of the Yadkin [in Rowan County, North Carolina] from Jacob Henkel. In 1761, Vögeli obtained 200 acres on Potts Creek, a short distance east of the Yadkin." [Ref: *Carolina Cradle*, by Robert W. Ramsey (1964), p. 75, citing Frederick County Court Judgments, 1748-1759, pp. 317, 432.]

WALL

On September 14, 1742, Joshua Wall, of North Carolina, planter, conveyed to Allen Thomas, of Dorchester County, Maryland, planter, in consideration of £25 current money paid by David Melvell, a tract called *Welcom* on a branch of Ingrams Creek in the freshes of Great Choptank River, containing 71 acres more or less, part of said land having been taken away by an elder survey called *Morfields* now in the possession of Thomas Foster. Witnesses: Henry Hooper and Henry Hooper, Jr. Acknowledged before Henry Hooper on September 15, 1742. [Ref: *Abstracts from*

Land Records of Dorchester County, Maryland, Volume C, 1732-1745, by James A. McAllister, Jr. (1962), p. 88.]

WALLACE

James Wallace, Sr., of Frederick County, Maryland, recorded on November 18, 1761, a deed made August 28, 1761 to him by James Wallace, son of William, of the Province of Carolina, for £43.6.8 current money of Maryland, for a tract called *Brother's Industry*, beginning at the dividing line that divided the aforesaid tract between William Wallace, Sr., deceased, and the aforesaid James Wallace, Sr., and on the south side of a branch being a fork of Captain [Cabin] John's Branch, and to run in the said William Wallace, Sr.'s land, a to include the plantation that the foresaid James Wallace, son of William, settled, and as much land as will make in the whole 100 acres on the south side of said branch, agreeable to the last will and testament of the said William Wallace, Sr., together with the dwelling houses, out houses, orchards, improvements, belonging thereto. Signed by James Wallace before J. Hepburn and Hume Moodie. James Wallace, son of William, acknowledged. [Ref: *Frederick County, Maryland, Land Records Liber G & H Abstracts, 1762-1763*, by Patricia Abelard Andersen (1996), p. 25.]

WALTON

Richard Walton settled in the Trading Camp Settlement in western North Carolina sometime between 1750 and 1762. "Richard Walton, a tanner, evidently originated among the Waltons of Somerset County, Maryland, who settled there before 1686." [Ref: *Carolina Cradle*, by Robert W. Ramsey (1964), p. 111, which stated "It is possible that Walton originated in Philadelphia.".]

As for Maryland, however, a Richard Wallton, of Somerset, was married and lived in Indian Cabin Neck, on the seaboard side of the county, in 1686. Also, William Wallton died testate there in August, 1686, and John Walton died in February, 1716/7, but neither mentioned a son Richard in his will. [Ref: *Old Somerset on the Eastern Shore of Maryland*, by Clayton Torrence (1935), p. 289; *Maryland Calendar of Wills, Volume II, 1685-1702*, p. 7; *Maryland Calendar of Wills, Volume IV, 1713-1720*, p. 105.]

Further, William Walton owned 1,400 acres in Somerset County in 1679 (plus another 100 acres in 1680), John Walton owned 200 acres in 1686, William Walton owned 450 acres in 1708, and John Walton owned 50 acres in 1743. [Ref: *Settlers of Maryland, 1679-1700*, by Peter Wilson Coldham (1995), p. 179; *Settlers of Maryland, 1701-1730*, by Coldham (1996), p. 163; *Settlers of Maryland, 1731-1750*, by Coldham (1996), p. 235.]

WATTS-WATT

"The Watt family was in Kent and St. Mary's Counties, Maryland, before 1722. William and James Watt, probably brothers, made their way to Carolina by way of the Cumberland Valley" circa 1752 or earlier. [Ref: *Carolina Cradle*, by Robert W. Ramsey (1964), pp. 94-95.]

Actually, the name was spelled "Watts" in both counties. John Watts died testate in Kent County in March, 1710/1, leaving his entire estate "to child named John Watts, born of Elinor Thomas." Peter Watts, gentleman, died testate in St. Mary's County in July, 1719, naming James Watts and his son James Watts, a Major William Watts, and brother Stephen Watts, among other persons. Also, in St. Mary's County, Catherine Watts (wife of William Watts) died testate in August, 1722, Thomas Watts died testate in November, 1723, William Watts died testate in January, 1723/4, William Watts died testate in March, 1745 (mentioning his sons William, Thomas, George, and Daniel), Stephen Watts died testate in March, 1751 (mentioning his cousin James Watts who was under age 21 in 1750), and Thomas Watts, Jr. died testate in July, 1752 (mentioning his brothers William and George). [Ref: *Maryland Calendar of Wills, Volume III, 1703-1713*, p. 189; *Volume IV, 1713-1720*, p. 208; *Volume V, 1720-1726*, pp. 109, 151, 155; *Volume 9, 1744-1749*, p. 16; *Volume 10, 1748-1753*, pp. 143, 236.]

WAY

Martha Duvall, of Prince George's County, Maryland, left a will dated May 2, 1729 (proved November 22, 1739). To her cousins Mary Whitehead, Ann Carrick and Elizabeth Denune, she bequeathed personalty. The residue of her estate went to her sister Ann Way, of South Carolina. [Ref: *Maryland Calendar of Wills, Volume VIII, 1738-1743*, p. 51.]

WHITAKER-WHITEACRE

Mark Whitaker was in Frederick County, Maryland sometime between 1749 and 1754. "The records of the Monthly Meeting of Friends in Dublin, Ireland, reveal that in 1719 'William Whitaker, formerly of Timahoe, but now of this city, desires a certificate to Pennsylvania.' Three years later, Katherine Whitaker of Dublin Meeting requested a certificate to America. James Whitaker was living in Bradford or Chichester Township, Chester County, as early as 1716. In 1738, the will of William Whitaker was proved in Queen Anne's County, Maryland. Joshua Whitaker, son of William, settled near Penn Creek on the east side of the Yadkin [in western North Carolina], while his kinsmen William and Mark Whitaker established themselves in the forks of the Yadkin." [Ref: *Carolina Cradle*, by Robert W. Ramsey (1964), pp. 76-79, citing Frederick County Judgments, 1752, p. 349; Chester County Deeds L:466; Probate Records 22:32; Tombstone of Joshua Whitaker, Jersey Church Cemetery, Linwood, North Carolina; Marriage of Joshua Whitaker and Mary Reed in Rowan County on September 12, 1764; North Carolina Land Grants VI:230; Rowan County Deeds III:106, V:329.]

One James Whiteacre served on a jury in Frederick County, Maryland in 1755. [Ref: *This Was The Life: Excerpts from the Judgment Records of Frederick County, Maryland, 1748-1765*, by Millard Milburn Rice (1979), p. 169.]

Mark Whitaker, formerly of Frederick County, Maryland, but now of Roan [Rowan] County, North Carolina, granted power of attorney to John Cary on June 23, 1767, giving him full power and authority to act in his behalf concerning matters in Frederick County. Signed by Mark Whitaker before Thomas Price and Henry Johnson. [Ref: *Frederick County, Maryland, Land Records Liber K Abstracts, 1765-1768*, by Patricia Abelard Andersen (1997), p. 110.]

WHITE

Joseph White, planter, of Spotsylvania County, Virginia, wrote his will on December 11, 1741. At the time of the writing he was a soldier in the King's Service, Goodu's Regiment, Capt. Loyd's Company, fighting the Spaniards. He wrote his will while on board the Neptune Hospital Ship at Kingston, Jamaica. The will was probated in Somerset County, Maryland on June 22, 1743. Joseph named Charles Stuart as his executor and left him his entire estate, including 260 acres in North Carolina near Bear Island, and his personal estate, including prize money or pay due him as a soldier. [Ref: *Maryland Calendar of Wills, Volume VIII, 1738-1743*, p. 218.]

WILCOCKSON

Isaac Wilcockson and John Wilcockson originated in the Delaware Valley and migrated either from Burlington County, New Jersey or Bucks County, Pennsylvania to Frederick County, Maryland by 1749 at which time John Wilcockson made application "to keep an ordinary, or House of Entertainment." They later migrated to the forks of the Yadkin River in western North Carolina. [Ref: *Carolina Cradle*, by Robert W. Ramsey (1964), p. 76, citing *Calendar of New Jersey Wills*, First Series, XXX:374; Frederick County Judgments, 1749, p. 389; North Carolina Land Grants VI:233.]

WILKINSON

William Wilkinson immigrated to Maryland by 1696 and settled in Charles County where he possibly married Rebecca (last name not known). Their children were: Francis Wilkinson, who married Ann Smith (1694-1759), daughter of Walter Smith and Rachel Hall, and Ann Wilkinson married second to Thomas Truman Greenfield (1682-1733); and, Sophie Wilkinson, who married James Wilson by 1726. "The origins of William Wilkinson are uncertain. He may have been the William Wilkinson, or his son, who was in Albemarle, North Carolina by the late 1670's, sat on the council there, but was banished as a result of political problems in the early 1690's. This man had earlier slain a servant in St. Mary's County, Maryland, had a wife from Cecil County, Maryland, and knew Nehemiah Blakiston." William

Wilkinson was in England, 1700-1701, served in the Lower House, Charles County, until 1711 and was a justice between 1699 and 1710. He died testate by August 29, 1726 (date of probate). [Ref: *A Biographical Dictionary of the Maryland Legislature, 1635-1789, Volume I*, by Edward C. Papenfuse, et al. (1985), p. 889.]

"William Wilkinson [our 7th great-grandfather], merchant of Charles County, drafted his will on 4th November, 1725. It did not mention his wife (name unknown), who presumably predeceased him. His son Francis [our 6th great-grandfather] had died earlier the same year, and Francis' widow Anne (Smith) Wilkinson was already remarried to William's acquaintance Thomas Truman Greenfield of nearby "Trent Hall." William's will provided that his daughter Sophia "alias Sophia Hicks" was to get 172 acres in Prince George's County and divide "the revenue of the mill" with grandson William. Sophia was also to divide with Francis' three children 600 acres on the Patuxent called *The Enclosure*. Sophia and a Thomas Grant were to be executors. A codicil of August 17, 1726 revoked a legacy to grandson William. The will was proved in Charles County just 9 days later, on 29th August 1726. Apparently Sophia was the wife or widow of a Mr. Hicks in November, 1725, but nothing more is known of him. Papenfuse says that by 1726 she was married to James Wilson, said to be a son of Major Josiah and Margaret (Lingan) Wilson of "The Ridge," Calvert County. Sophia had 5 Wilson children, and may have lived in Prince George's County. When Francis Wilkinson [our 6th great-grandfather], merchant of Calvert County, drafted his will 4th January 1725, he made his dear and loving wife Anne Wilkinson sole executrix and left her one-third of his personal property. He also left her his dwelling plantation (name and location unknown) until her death or the day of her marriage, which turned out to be just a few months later. As the will had provided, the dwelling plantation then went to son William, who married his second cousin Barbara Mackall. He left to Francis [our 5th great-grandfather] a house and lot in Lower Marlboro. The remainder of his personal estate was to be divided among William, Francis and Susanna, who would eventually marry her first cousin John Addison. The administration account of Francis Wilkinson, deceased, was submitted to the Prerogative Court 11th July 1726 by Thomas Truman Greenfield and Ann his wife, executors."

[Ref: Information compiled in 1998 by Barbara Marvin, 4629 Tilden Street, N.W., Washington, D. C. 20016-5617, who seeks information on what became of William Wilkinson of Albemarle, South Carolina.]

WILLEN-WILLIN

On April 25, 1791, in Dorchester County, Maryland, John Willen, of Pitt County, North Carolina, planter, conveyed to Levin McNamara and Shadrick Wingate, of Dorchester County, Maryland, planters, the following tracts: part of *Fair Dealing*, adjoining *Wadle's Desire* near the head of Goose Creek, adjoining *Wingate's Inclosure* and *Steple Bumstead*; *Addition to Fair Dealing*; *Timber Swamp* on the west side of Goose Creek which issues out of Fishing Bay; and, *Addition to Timber Swamp*. [Ref: *Abstracts of the Land Records of Dorchester County, Maryland, Volume 30 (Liber HD#3)*, by James A. McAllister, Jr. (1967), p. 25.]

On July 30, 1792, as recorded in Dorchester County, Maryland, Thomas Willin, of Pitt County, North Carolina, granted power of attorney to his brother John Willin. Witnessed by Shadrack Allen and Stephen Brook. On June 28, 1794, Thomas Willin, of Pitt County, North Carolina, farmer, conveyed to Levi Willin, of Dorchester County, Maryland, farmer, a bond concerning land sold by said Thomas to the said Levi. Witnesses were Benjamin Todd, Jr. and Robert Evans. [Ref: *Abstracts of the Land Records of Dorchester County, Maryland, Volume 32 (HD#6)*, by James A. McAllister, Jr. (1967), p. 60.]

WILLEY

Edward W. Willey, of Dorchester County, Maryland, died leaving a will dated July 5, 1792 and probated in Guilford County, North Carolina in August, 1793. His named heirs were: "To brothers John and Thomas W. Willey, all my right and claim to the land willed me by my father Prichard Willey, deceased, near the town of Cunna(?) on the Eastern Shore of Maryland. To sister Emelia Willey, money remaining after debts, given to them at discretion of Aunt Sarah White residing on Great Choptank River" in Dorchester County. The witnesses were Richard Sanford, John Van Storre and Cathren Van Storre. [Ref: *Guilford County, North Carolina, Will Abstracts, 1771-1841*, compiled, indexed and published by Irene B. Webster, p. 86, citing Wills Liber A, folio 398.]

"Prichard Willey" was the father of the Edward W. Willey, as noted in Edward's will in North Carolina in 1792. "Pritchet Willey" took the Oath of Allegiance in Dorchester County, Maryland in 1778. "Pritch Wille" was the head of household in 1776 in Nanacoake [Nanticoke] Hundred, aged between 30 and 40, with one male aged between 20 and 30, one male aged between 10 and 16, two males under age 10, two females aged between 21 and 30, one female aged between 10 and 16, and one female under age 10, plus 5 negroes. [Ref: *Revolutionary Patriots of Dorchester County, Maryland, 1775-1783*, by Henry C. Peden, Jr. (1998), p. 264.] It should be noted that there was another Edward Willey who was a son of Francis Willey (who died testate in 1745) in Dorchester County. [Ref: *Maryland Calendar of Wills, Volume 9, 1744-1749*, p. 62.]

On June 29, 1790, in Dorchester County, Maryland, Frederick Willey, Amelia Smith, and Sarah Willey conveyed to George Willey, bond to survey land of Rachel Willey, their mother, deceased, called *Timber Swamp*. Witnesses: Levi Foxwell and William Carroll. [Ref: *Abstracts of the Land Records of Dorchester County, Maryland, Volume 39 (Liber HD#3)*, by James A. McAllister, Jr. (1967), p. 51.]

WILLIAMS

On August 13, 1772, Solomon Williams, of North Carolina, son and heir of Giles Williams and Rachel his wife who formerly lived in Dorchester County, Maryland, but died lately in North Carolina, conveyed to James Pattison, son of John Pattison, Jr., of Dorchester County, half of a tract on Crab Cove on James Island and on the western side of Little Choptank River, laid out for Francis Armstrong and formerly called *Long Point*, but by a resurvey made by John Pattison, grandfather of said James Pattison, now called *Venture*, containing 75 acres more or less. Witnesses were Dan Sulivane and Thomas White, Justices of Dorchester County. [Ref: *Abstracts from Land Records of Dorchester County, Maryland, Volume H, 1772-1775*, by James A. McAllister, Jr. (1964), p. 27.]

Richard Colegate, merchant, of Petapsicoe [Patapsco] River, Baltimore County, Maryland, wrote his will on August 8, 1721 and it was proved on February 16, 1721/2. Among his heirs he mentioned his daughters Patience and Temperance to whom he left a 500-acre tract called *Friend's Discovery* in Baltimore County and "also all land bought of Edward Williams, of North Carolina, not bequeathed to daughter Prudence." One should see the actual will and perhaps do additional research since there is no indication as to whether or not they moved to North Carolina. [Ref: *Maryland Calendar of Wills, Volume V, 1720-1726*, p. 104.]

WILLSON

Recorded in the land records of Dorchester County, Maryland is the power of attorney granted on February 8, 1724 by Benjamin Small, of Nancemond *[sic]* County, Virginia, to Robert Willson, of North Carolina. Witnesses: John Young and Benjamin Gregry *[sic.]* The document was proved March 22, 1724 by oaths of the witnesses before Henry Ennalls and Thomas Taylor, Justices of Dorchester County. [Ref: *Abstracts from Land Records of Dorchester County, Maryland, Volume B, 1689-1733*, by James A. McAllister, Jr. (1960), p. 74.]

WINSLEY-WINSLY

Benjamin Winsley lived in Cecil County, Maryland as early as 1731 through at least 1740 when he and John Winsley served as privates in the militia in Capt. Zebulon Hollingsworth's Company of Foot. The debt books of Cecil County indicate that Benjamin Winsly owned a tract of land called *New Munster* on which he paid taxes in 1739, and Thomas Winsley owned *Winsley's Lott* on which he paid taxes in 1734, 1755, and 1760. Benjamin migrated to Rowan County, North Carolina and died in the Davidson's Settlement in 1759. [Ref: *Carolina Cradle*, by Robert W. Ramsey (1964), p. 71, citing Cecil County Judgments SK#4 (1736-1741), p. 132, and Rowan County Wills A:164. *Inhabitants of Cecil County, Maryland, 1649-1774*, by Henry C. Peden, Jr. (1993), pp. 51, 52, 121.]

A descendant, Anne J. M. Strupp, lived at 307 Walnut Grove, Peachtree, Georgia 30269, but a letter to her in April, 1998, was returned as "undeliverable as addressed; forwarding order expired." [Ref: Information obtained in 1997 from James A. L. Miller, Jr., 2810-K Carriage Drive, Winston-Salem, North Carolina 27106-5328.]

WINSUIT-WIMSATT

Abraham Winsuit and Richard Winsuit went from St. Mary's County, Maryland to the forks of the Yadkin River in Rowan County, North Carolina circa 1750. [Ref: *Carolina Cradle*, by Robert W. Ramsey (1964), pp. 77-78, citing Rowan County Deeds VI:435 and Anson County Deeds 1:319-320.]

One Richard Wimsatt lived in St. Mary's County by December 25, 1742 when he leased land on His Lordship's Manor at Beaverdam. [Ref: *Catholic Families of Southern Maryland*, by Timothy J. O'Rourke (1981), p. 47.]

WRIGHT

Hynson Wright, County of Beaufort, Province of North Carolina, planter, and Sarah his wife, in consideration of £250 current money of Pennsylvania, conveyed to Christopher Cox, gentleman, on March 20, 1755, 300 acres of land called *Low's Arcadia* on a branch of Island Creek [in Queen Anne's County, Maryland.] Witnesses were George Johnston, H. B. Whiteford, and William Carruthers, Jr. In North Carolina, on March 20, 1755, before James Hassell, Chief Justice of the Province, at Newbern, Hynson Wright and Sarah his wife (she being privately examined) acknowledged their deed. Justice Hassell certified by Arthur Dobbs, Governor of the Province. [Ref: *Queen Anne's County Land Records, Book Four, 1743-1755*, by R. Bernice Leonard (1994), p. 94.]

On November 9, 1781, in Dorchester County, Maryland, a deed was recorded in which James Wright, of North Carolina, planter, conveyed to John Stewart, son of Ann, of Dorchester County, planter, parts of tracts called *Wright's Venture* (containing 141 acres), *Taylor's Neglect* (containing 263 acres), and *Connoley's Chance* (containing 10 acres), all three tracts adjoining each other and being the dwelling plantation where the said James Wright formerly lived. Witnesses: William Ennalls and Robert Harrison, Justices of Dorchester County. [Ref: *Abstracts from the Land Records of Dorchester County, Maryland, Volume 24 (Liber 28 Old)*, by James A. McAllister, Jr. (1965), p. 52.]

Edward Wright applied for a pension (S7977) in Montgomery County, North Carolina on October 4, 1832, stating that he was born in 1758 in Maryland and lived at Guilford, North Carolina at the time of his enlistment. He married shortly after his first tour of duty (name of wife was not given) and lived in Guilford County about 7 years. No further family information was given. [Ref: *Genealogical Abstracts of Revolutionary War Pension Files, Volume III: N-Z*, by Virgil D. White (1990), p. 3968.]

YOUNG

Sewell Young, son of John Young and Elizabeth Sewell, was baptized on April 12, 1710 in St. Anne's Parish, Anne Arundel County, Maryland. "Suel Young" married Margaret Acton on January 13, 1736 in St. Paul's Parish, Baltimore County, Maryland. Sewell first appears in Rowan County, North Carolina on a 1768 tax list along with sons Joshua, Henry and Acton. On November 27, 1771 a petition for the formation of a new county (Burke) shows: Sewell Young, Sr. and Jr.; Joshua Young, as well as two other sons, Philip and Vachel. Land records for Burke County, North Carolina in 1778 reveal that Sewell Young, Senr. owned 250 acres on "Youngs fork of Muddy Creek." Murtie June Clark's *Loyalists in the Southern Campaign of the Revolutionary War, Vol. I*, lists four of the sons serving with the Loyalist forces: Acton, Sewell, Philip and Vachel Young. [Ref: Information compiled in 1998 by Carol L. Porter, 2928 Putty Hill Avenue, Baltimore, Maryland 21234-4643.]

John Young (referred to as "Capt." in 1717) and Elizabeth Sewell were married circa 1707 and he appears to have been the John Young who married Elizabeth Frances on February 10, 1714/15 in Anne Arundel County, Maryland. His children, born in St. Anne's Parish, were as follows:

Edward Young, baptized June 29, 1708;
Sewill Young, baptized April 12, 1710;
James Young, born July 31, 1714;
Joshua Young, born March 25, 1717, baptized June 23, 1717;
Margaret Young, baptized September 3, 1722;
Lurana Young, baptized September 3, 1722.

[Ref: *Anne Arundel County Church Records of the 17th and 18th Centuries*, by F. Edward Wright (Westminster, Maryland: Family Line Publications, 1990), pp. 34, 66, 69, 74, 75, 76, 79, 80, 146.]

Sewell Young married Margaret Acton, daughter of Richard Acton and Anne Sewell, of Anne Arundel County, Maryland. His sons Henry Young and Richard Young were mentioned in the will of their grandfather [Richard Acton] which was written on October 8, 1740 and probated on May 6, 1741. In November, 1753, Samuel and Martha Shipley conveyed part of *Meton's Resolution* (225 acres) and *Addition to Greenbury's Grove* (72 acres) to Sewell Young. Also, Joshua Sewell died by August 22, 1763 when his administration bond was witnessed by Christopher Sewell, W. Sewell Young, and William Towson. Christopher Sewell was administrator of the estate in 1764. [Ref: *Baltimore County Families, 1659-1759*, by Robert W. Barnes (Baltimore: Genealogical Publishing Company, 1989), pp. 2, 572, 578, 714.]

INDEX

-A-

ACTON, Anne, 136; Margaret, 136; Richard, 136
ADAMS, Macnemarrow, 1; Peter, 42; Sarah, 1; William, 1
ADDISON, John, 132; Susanna, 132
AGNIS, Thomas, 58
AKER, Barbara, 65
ALBRIGHT, George, 15
ALCOCK, Humphry, 31; John, 31
ALDERSON, Simond, 116
ALEXANDER, Robert, 89
ALLEN, Joseph, 20; Shadrack, 133
ALLISON, Rebekah, 51
ALLNUTT, Elizabeth, 34
ALMOND, Nancy Lee, 75
ANDERSEN, Patricia Abelard, 53, 63, 64, 92, 111, 129, 131
ANDERSON, Patricia Abelard, 14, 22, 45, 77, 84
ANDREW, Benjamin, 47; Davis, 1; Dennis, 1; Elizabeth, 47; James, 1; John, 1; Mary, 1; Nathaniel, 1; Patrick, 1
ANDREWS, 1; E., 48
ANSELL, 50
ANSELT, Margaret, 49
ANTHONY, Anna Maria, 112
ARCHIBALD, John, 1; Martha, 78; William, 1, 78, 105
ARICK, Christian McCoy, 97
ARMSTRONG, Francis, 127, 134
ARNETT, James, 2; Valentine, 2
ARTERBERRY, Nancy, 4; William, 3
ARTERBURY, Mary, 5; Thomas, 5
ASHFORD, Esther, 54
ATTABERRY, Anney, 3; Bridget, 3; Elijah, 3; Ellender, 3; James, 3; Mary, 3; Nathan, 3; Sary, 3; Thomas, 3; William, 3
ATTABERY, Brigget, 3; Thomas, 3
ATTEBERRY, Susan A., 4
ATTEBERY, Thomas, 3
ATTEBURY, Betsy, 4; Bridget, 3; Charity, 4, 5; Elijah, 4, 5; Eliza Jane, 4; Elizabeth, 4; Ellen, 4; Family, 3; Greenberry, 4; Harriet, 4; Isaac Newton, 4; James, 4, 5; Josephine, 4; Martha Jane, 4; Mary, 4; Mary Taylor, 5; Nancy, 4; Nathan, 4, 5; Sarah, 4; Seaman, 4; Stephen, 4; Susan A., 4; Susannah, 3; Thomas, 3, 4; Thompson, 4; William, 3, 4; William Pain, 4; Zephaniah, 4; Zephaniah Murray, 3, 4
ATTERBARY, Sarah, 5
ATTERBERRY, Betsy, 4; Elizabeth, 4; James, 4; Martha Jane, 4; Sally, 4; Stephen, 4; Thomas, 4; William, 4; William Pain, 4
ATTERBURY, Dorcas, 6; Edward, 5; James, 5, 6; Mary, 6; Sarah, 5, 6; William, 6
AULD, Daniel, 6; Edward, 6; James, 6; John, 6, 7; Mary, 6; Philemon, 6; Rosanna, 6; Sarah, 6
AUSTIN, Henry, 101; Lydia, 101; Robert H., 101
AVERY, John, 56

-B-

BAIN, Lydia, 67; William, 67
BAIRD, Ellis, Mrs., 118; Jonathan, 68; Lorine, 118
BAKER, Barbara, 7; Henry, 7; Isaac, 44; John, 7, 59; Nathan, 7; Peter, 7
BAKER Family, 40
BANKER, Jacob, 14
BARKER, Milly, 104
BARNES, Caleb, 40; Nicodemus, 38, 40; Robert, 20, 21, 40, 58; Robert W., 23, 26, 37, 48, 49, 58, 64, 66, 67, 88, 89, 96, 101, 115, 122, 125, 127, 136; Samuel, 72
BARNETT, Jacob, 8
BARNEY, John, 113
BARNS, Moses, 102
BARONS, John, 9
BARRON, Abraham, 9; Adam, 9; Alexander, 8, 9; Catharine, 8;

Dorcas, 9; Elizabeth, 10; James, 8, 9; James Alexander, 9; Jane, 9, 87; John, 7, 8, 9, 10, 87; Joseph, 10; Margaret, 7, 8, 87; Martha, 9; Samuel, 9; Sarah, 8, 10
BARRONS, Elizabeth, 10; Joseph, 10
BARROW, Anne, 10; James, 9, 10; John, 9, 10; Margaret, 10; Susanna, 9; Thomas, 10
BARRY, Andrew, 10; Catherine, 10; Hugh, 8; Samuel, 8
BARTON, Benjamin, 10, 23; John, 10, 35; Joshua, 23
BARWICK, Alice, 11; Edward, 11; John, 11; Joshua, 11; Nathan, 11; Solomon, 11
BASHFORD, Anne, 11; Thomas, 11, 52
BASS, Sarah, 34
BATES, Marlene Strawser, 59, 96, 126
BAYARD, Peter, 9, 71
BAYNARD, George, 128; Thomas, 106
BEALL, Brooke, 12; Catherine, 78; Eleanor, 36; George, 35; James, 78; Jane, 12; Margaret, 78; Nancy, 12; Nancy Begley, 12; Robert, 12; Samuel, 36; Thomas, 35, 84; Verlinder, 36; Zadock, 12
BEARD, Andrew, 12; John, 12; Matthew, 12; Rachel, 12; Susannah, 12
BEATTY, Susanna, 84; William, 23
BEAVER, Bernard, 16; James, 16
BECK, James, 28; Rev., 63
BECKWITH, Nehemiah, 127
BEDDINGFIELD, James Decatur, 93; Mary Carolyn Moser, 93
BEGGS, Samuel, 54
BEGLEY, Nancy, 12
BELL, Abigail, 13; Anthony, 13; Catherine, 13; Family, 12; Jane, 13; John, 13; Richard, 13; Thomas, 13
BELT, ---, 123; Elizabeth, 76; Margery, 27
BENCKER, Jacob, 63
BENHAM, Samuel, 13; Tamlason, 13
BENNET, William, 14
BENNETT, Richard, 18
BENTLEY, Hannah, 14; Thomas, 14

BENTLY, Thomas, 14
BERNARD, Elizabeth, 4
BERRY, Benjamin, 14; Catherine, 10; Hugh, 116; James, 14; John, 14; Joseph, 14; Loretta, 20; Mary, 96; Sarah, 14; Thomas, 14; William, 10, 14
BEST, Catharine, 70; Sarah, 70; Sebastian, 70
BILLETER, Anna, 14; Zebdiah, 14
BILLETOR, James, 15; Joseph, 15; Zebdiah, 15
BILLITOR, James, 15; Joseph, 15; Zebdiah, 15
BINKLEY, Maria Sarah, 93
BIRMINGHAM, Elizabeth, 110; John, 110; Margaret, 110
BISHOP, David W., 51
BLAKISTON, Nehemiah, 132
BLOOMFIELD, John, 57
BLOUNT, Capt., 77
BLOWERS, Ann, 33
BLUME, Lewis, 2
BODRAY, Elizabeth, 15; John, 15
BOISE, Bostian, 63
BOLICK, David "Foote", 98; Elizabeth, 61, 98; Maria Margaret, 61; Sebastian, 61
BONAR, James, 24
BOND, Samuel, 13
BONDY, Elizabeth, 15; John, 15
BONNEDY, John, 15
BONWELL, McKeel, 86
BOONE, Family, 104; Jonathan, 67; Squire, 128
BOSTICK, James, 15; John, 15; Mary, 15; Nathan, 15; Rebecca, 15; Sary, 15; Solomon, 15; Tamar, 15; Thomas, 15; William, 15
BOSTOCK, Elizabeth, 15; James, 15; Jane, 15; John, 15; Mary, 15; Samuel, 15; Sarah, 15; Susannah, 15; Thomas, 15
BOTT, Anna Catharine Gertrude, 111
BOUCHELLE, Peter, 31
BOUDY, Elizabeth, 15; John, 15
BOUTELL, William, 72

BOWEN, Benjmin, 115; Josias, 115; Solomon, 115
BOWER, James, 16
BOWERS, Barbara, 7; Bernard, 16; Daniel, 16; James, 7, 16; Nicholas, 16
BOYCE, Cornelius, 58
BOYDSTON, Betsy, 4; John, 4
BOYDTSEEN, Betsy, 4; John, 4
BOYER, Ann Lynch, 55, 109
BRADLEY, Nathan, 2
BRAKEFIELD, Lila Ann, 38; Margaret, 38; Martha, 38
BRALY, John, 111
BRAMBLE, David, 16; Elizabeth, 16; Eton, 16; Hackett, 16; Levin, 16; William, 16
BRANDON, Anne, 11; Cenith, 12; David, 12; James, 11; John, 11; William, 11, 12
BRANNOCK, David, 16; Edmund, 80
BRATTON, Col., 8; William, 8
BRAWLEY, James S., 12, 46, 53
BREDING, Mary, 17
BREEDEN, John, 17, 98; Mary, 17
BREVARD, John, 17; Robert, 17; Zebulon, 17
BREWSTER, Walter Whatley, 43
BRIERLY, Robert, 125
BRIGHT, Elizabeth, 119
BROAD, Barbara, 37
BROOK, Stephen, 133
BROOKE, Eleanor, 36; Mary, 36
BROOKS, William, 17
BROWN, Capt., 35; David, 110; Elizabeth, 110; Helen W., 97; John, 40; Jonas, 40; Mary, 127; Rebecca, 127; Thomas, 90; William, 36
BROWNE, Benjamin, 28; Mary, 28; Thomas, 90
BROWNING, John, 18; Mary, 18; Sarah Gooding, 18; Thomas, 18; William, 18
BRUCE, A. B., 80; Abner B., 80; Sarah, 123
BRUMBAUGH, Gaius M., 84
BRYAN, 24; Mary, 48; Morgan, 45, 48

BULL, William, 67
BULLOCK, Nancy, 119
BUNDERICK, Nicholas, 18
BUNDRICH, A. M., 18
BUNDRICK, Anna Maria, 18, 19; Bunch, 19; J. Nicholas, 18; Johan Nicholaus, 18; Nicholas, 18, 19
BURCH, Elizabeth, 19; Family, 20; James, 19, 20; John, 19; Mary, 19; Richard, 19; Sarah, 19; Thomas F., 20; William, 19
BURCHFIELD, Adam, 21; Ann, 20; Betsey, 22; Elizabeth, 20, 22; Elizabeth Justice, 20; James, 21; Joanna, 21; John, 21, 22; Joseph, 21; Kitty, 22; Lydia, 20, 21; Mary, 20, 21, 22; Meshack, 22; Nancy, 22; Nathaniel, 21; Robert, 20, 21, 22; Sally, 22; Sarah, 21; Thomas, 21
BURGES, John, 22
BURGESS, Joseph, 81, 82; Susannah, 5; Ursula, 5; William, 5
BURK, James, 22; Thomas, 22
BURKE, Mary, 54; Thomas, 23
BURMINGHAM, Margaret, 110
BURNDRAKE, Nicholas, 19
BURR, Horace, 114
BUSH, Elizabeth, 47; Thomas, 48
BUTTNER, Adam, 23; Anna, 23; Catherine, 23; James, 23; Leah, 23; Martha, 23; Peter, 23

-C-

CAIN, Elizabeth, 95
CALDWELL, 23; John, 23, 54; Spencer, 23
CALVERT, Charles, 72
CAMBRIDGE, Christopher, 72
CAMP, Joseph, 68
CAMPBELL, ---, 36; John, 23, 106; Mary, 23; Mollie, 36; Moses, 23, 24; Rebecca, 23; Walter, 16; William, 23
CANADAY, Elizabeth, 70; John, 70; Margaret, 70
CANNADAY, Elizabeth, 70; John, 70
CANNON, Rebecca, 96
CARMACK, John, 23

CAROTHERS, Bettie Stirling, 91
CARRICK, Ann, 130
CARROLL, Charles, 14; James, 74;
    William, 133
CARRUTHERS, William, 135
CARTER, Dinah, 25; Edward, 13; James,
    24, 25, 41; Mary, 25; Susannah, 24
CARY, John, 131
CASSON, Henry, 128
CATHER, George, 103
CATHEY, Alexander, 25; Andrew, 25;
    George, 25, 56, 79; Hannah, 56;
    James, 13, 25, 52; John, 25; William,
    25
CATOR, Levin, 56
CAUSEY, Isabell, 73; Nehemiah, 73
CESAR, Bartell, 63
CHALKLEY, Lyman, 121
CHAMBERS, Henry, 25
CHAMNESS, Anthony, 26; Joseph, 26;
    Sarah, 26
CHAMNIS, Anthony, 26; Sarah, 26
CHAMPION, Margaret, 8; Richard, 8
CHANCE, Samuel, 26
CHAPLINE, Moses, 22
CHAPMAN, Giles, 124; Mary, 124
CHARLES, 27
CHARLESTON, Charles, 96; Dorothy,
    96
CHASE, Samuel, 89
CHEREL, 113
CHEW, Elizabeth, 27; Henry, 26; Joseph,
    27; Thomas, 27; Thomas S., 26;
    Thomas Sheredine, 27
CLAGGETT, Ann, 123
CLARK, ---, 33; Ann, 20; Daniel, 27;
    Eleanor, 28; Kesia, 76; Murtie June,
    19, 29, 136; Richard, 27; Ruth, 28;
    Thomas, 27; William, 27, 28
CLARKSON, Henry, 110; John, 64
CLARY, Ann, 28; Basil, 28; Benjamin,
    28; Daniel, 28, 29, 124; Eleanor, 29,
    124; John, 28, 29; Kasandra, 28;
    Levine, 28; Linny, 28; Mary, 28, 29;
    Ruth, 29; Sarah, 28; Vachel, 28;
    William, 29
CLAYTON, Solomon, 68

CLEMENTS, S. Eugene, 33, 92, 106, 110
CLEMMONS, Susannah, 3
CLIMER, Family, 29
CLOCKER, Daniel, 57
CLUBB, Elizabeth, 60
CLYMER, Cain, 29; James, 29; Sara, 29
CLYMOR, Family, 29
COALE, Sarah, 26
COATE, Sarah, 124
COATES, Mary, 72; Thomas, 72
COBB, Charity, 117; James, 117;
    Rebecca, 117
COFFELL, Joseph, 94
COLDHAM, Peter Wilson, 37, 54, 72,
    78, 82, 88, 99, 102, 116, 129
COLE, Dolly, 98; George, 17, 98; John,
    126, 127; Joseph, 26; Mary, 17;
    Sarah, 26; William, 26
COLEGATE, Patience, 134; Prudence,
    134; Richard, 134; Temperance, 134
COLEMAN, Dorcas, 124; Griffin, 124
COLLIER, John, 57
COLLINSON, Edward, 68
COLLISON, Benjamin, 68
COMMINS, Harmon, 30; Harmond, 30
COMMONDS, Harmond, 30
CONNOLLY, Terrence, 90
CONRAD, Mary, 111
COOK, Elizabeth, 30; Jesse, 30, 32; John
    C., 30; Lucinda, 30; Pheba, 30;
    Phoebe, 30; Prudence, 30, 32; Sarah,
    30
COOKE, Benjamin, 72; Thomas, 120
COONSE, Margaret, 42; William, 42
CORBIN, Elizabeth, 35
CORKRAN, Timothy, 68
COURSEY, William, 128
COURTS, John, 67
COVINGTON, Hannah, 31; John, 31;
    Sarah, 31
COX, Christopher, 135; Susanna, 88
CRAGE, Arcabil, 31; Archabil, 31;
    Elizabeth, 31; Mary, 31; William, 31
CRAGH Family, 31
CRAIG, Archibald, 31; Family, 31, 59;
    James, 31; Mary, 31
CRAIGE, James, 31, 111

CRANER, Charles, 32; Dorcas, 32; Elizabeth, 32; Lucresey, 32; Mary, 32; Moses, 32; Samuel, 32; Thomas, 32
CRANOR, Elizabeth, 32; Hannah, 32; Jane, 32; John, 32; Joseph, 32; Joshua, 32; Moses, 30, 31, 32; Phebe, 32; Prudence, 30, 32; Sarah, 30, 32; Thomas, 32; William, 32
CRANOR FAMILY, 31
CRAVEN, Jane, 103
CRAWFORD, James, 86
CREASMAN, Catherine, 121
CRESAP, Thomas, 93
CROSBY, Ann, 96; Dennis, 96; Frances P., 97; Hannah, 96; Margaret, 97; Stephen, 97
CRUMBECKER, Jacob, 20
CUBBAGE, George, 80
CULVER, Francis B., 27, 89
CUMMIN, Harmon, 30
CUMMINGS, William, 84
CUMMINS, Harman, 30
CUNNINGHAM, Francis, 21; I..., 20
CURRY, Sally Ann, 89
CURTIS, Thomas, 11
CUSACK, George, 32; Michael, 32
CUSHMAN, Elizabeth, 30
CUSICK, Edward, 32; Nicholas, 2

-D-

DABNEY, Josephine, 4; Mary, 4
DARBY, Aden, 33; Ann, 33; Anna, 33; Anne, 33; Asa, 33, 34; Basil, 33, 34; Caleb, 33, 34; Dorcas, 33; Drusillar, 33; Elizabeth, 33, 34; George, 33; James, 33; John, 33; Leonora, 33; Mary, 33; Mary Ann, 33; Nancy, 33; Rada, 33; Rezin, 33, 34; Samuel, 33; Thomas, 33; William Jeffrson, 33; Zadock, 33
DAVID, John, 13, 46
DAVIDSON, Family, 17
DAVIES, John, 72
DAVIS, Edward, 34; Jane, 60; John, 24, 26, 37, 48, 57, 58, 64, 66, 67, 89, 100, 115, 125, 127; Phillip, 34;
Samuel, 34; William, 22
DAWSEY, Patience, 40
DAWSON, Benjamin, 123; Cornelius, 37; Richard, 114; Sarah, 123
DAY, Avarilla, 125; Edward, 125; Mary Ann, 69; Samuel, 69
DEACON, Elizabeth, 34; James, 34, 63; Thomas, 34
DEADMAN, Edmund, 35; Elizabeth, 35; Sarah, 35; Thomas, 35
DEAN, James, 3
DEAVER, Margaret, 96
DEDMAN, Nathaniel, 35
DEDMON, Edward, 35
DELANEY, Anthony, 72
DELL, John, 36; Mary, 36; William, 36
DELLINGER, Barbara, 122; Catherine, 121; Elizabeth, 121; Philip, 121
DEMMETT, James, 37
DEMPSEY, Ann, 109
DENNISTON, Ann, 51; Daniel, 51; Sarah, 51
DENT, Ann, 36; Mary, 36; Mollie, 36; Peter, 36; Verlinder, 36; William, 35, 36
DENUNE, Elizabeth, 130
DEVALINGER, Leon, 32
DEVERN, Eleanor, 28; William, 28
DEVERON, Eleanor, 28, 29, 124; William, 28, 29
DICKEY, John, 36
DICKINSON, H., 3, 68; John, 56, 79, 86; Roger, 96
DICKSON, J., 77; Walter, 102; William, 44
DIGGES, William, 128
DILL, James, 36; John, 36, 37; Mary, 36, 37; Peter, 36; Sarah, 36; Thomas, 37
DILL Family, 36
DIMMITT, Athaliah, 37; Barbara, 37; Elizabeth, 37; Elizabeth Ann, 37; James, 37; Mary, 37; William, 37
DOAK, Nancy Ann, 73
DOBBINS, Alexander, 11
DOBBS, Arthur, 135
DOBSON, Elizabeth, 73; Rebecca, 73
DODD, Rosemary B., 19, 29, 124

DODDY, Elizabeth, 4
DOETSCH, Vicki, 5
DONOHUE, Mathew, 24
DOOM, Georg Michael, 63
DORCEY, Cornelius, 40
DORRIS, Angell, 80; John, 80
DORSEY, Alexander, 37, 38, 41;
    Andrew, 38, 39, 40; Ann, 39; Arah, 38; Bazil, 40; Beal, 39; Charles, 39; Cornelius, 37, 38, 39, 40; David, 38; Deborah, 39; Edward, 39; Elisha, 40; Elizabeth, 39, 40; Endemean, 39; Endymon, 39; George, 40; Henry C., 39; Indimion, 39, 40; Indimon, 40; Indymon, 39; James, 38, 40; John, 37, 38, 39; John Hood, 39; Lanslot, 39; Luke, 39; Margaret, 38; Martha, 38; Mary, 39; Nacey, 40; Nancy, 40; Nicholas, 39; Orlando, 39; Orlando G., 39, 40; Patience, 39, 40; Patsy, 38; Peggy, 37, 38; Rebecca, 38; Robert Walker, 38, 40; Vachel, 39; Wesley, 38
DORSEY Family, 37
DOUGE, Elizabeth, 70
DOWDEN, Elizabeth, 54; Esther, 54; John, 54
DOWDY, Elizabeth, 4
DOWNES, Henry, 106
DRAYTON, William Henry, 96
DUDLEY, Elizabeth, 128
DUNCAN, John, 9
DUNHAM, Lucresey, 110; Lucretia, 110; Mary, 110
DUNN, 24; John, 34, 41
DURAND, Andrew, 120; David, 120; James, 120; John, 120; Thomas, 120; William, 120
DUVALL, Martha, 130
DWIER, Thomas, 42
DWIGANS, Daniel, 41; James, 41; John, 41; Lydia, 41; Nathan, 41; Robert, 41; Samuel, 41
DWIGENS, Daniel, 41; Samuel, 41
DWIGGANS, James, 41; John, 41; Nathan, 41
DWIGGINS, Lydia, 41; Robert, 41
DWIRE, Thomas, 41, 42
DWYER, Thomas, 42

-E-

EAKER, Lorena Shell, 43, 47, 49, 60, 61, 65, 70, 93, 98, 113, 115, 122; Mrs., 50
EARLE, James, 68
EARLEY, Mary, 37
EATON, John, 42
ECARD, Frances, 122
ECCLESTON, John, 57, 86, 92
ECKERT, Adam, 42, 98; Anna Maria, 42, 98; Barbara, 42; Catherine, 42; Daniel, 43; Elizabeth, 98; Eva, 42; Hans Adam, 43; Magdalen, 43; Margaret, 42; Maria Elizabeth, 42; Martin, 42; Peter, 42; Simon, 42
EDERINGTON, Francis H., 97; Precious Anne, 97
EDMONDSON, William, 86
EDMONSTON, Margaret, 78
EDRINGTON Family, 97
EDWARD, Sarah, 115
EDWARDS, Benjamin, 43; J., 27; James Crumton, 44; Jarrott, 43; John, 43; Joseph, 43; Mark, 43; Mary, 43, 44; Maryan, 43; Matthew, 43; Stourton, 43
EDWARDS Family, 43
ELDER, John, 113
ELLIOTT, Edward, 6; George, 44; Nancy, 73; Sarah, 6
ELLIS, Ann, 123; Cassandra, 122; Catherine, 89; Martha Jane, 4; Samuel, 122, 123
ELROADE, Jeremiah, 23
ELTINGE, Isaac, 44
EMERSON, Family, 20, 45; George, 44, 45; James, 44; John, 44; Mary, 44, 45; Richard, 44
EMMERSON, Anney, 44; Catherine, 44; Elizabeth, 19; Family, 45; George, 44; John, 44; Phendle, 44; Richard, 44; Sarah, 44; William, 44
EMORY, Arthur, 68; Rebecca, 101
EMSON, James, 117; Rebecca, 117

143

ENDSLEY, Delilah, 89
ENNALLS, Bartholomew, 45; Henry, 127, 134; Joseph, 45
ENNALS, Ann, 120; Henry, 120; William, 135
ENOCHS, Enoch, 45; Gabriel, 45
ENSOR, John, 115, 126, 127; Joseph, 26
ENYART, John, 45; Silas, 45
ERWIN, Christopher, 46; George, 46; William, 46
ERWIN Family, 46
ESTES, Elizabeth, 33; Thomas, 33
EVANS, Robert, 133; Thomas, 46; William, 46
EVERETT, Laurence, 102

-F-

FAIGLIN, Johannes, 46
FAIGLINS, Johannes, 46; Ursula, 46
FARRAR, Field, 103
FEDDEMAN, Henry, 128; Phil., 127
FEE, John, 14
FEIGLEE, Peter, 47
FEIGLEY, Anna Catherine, 111; Anna Ursula, 111; Catherine Schell, 46; Johannes, 46, 111; John, 46; Ursula, 46
FELLOW, John, 47; Pheby, 47; Robert, 47; Sarah, 47
FELLOWS, John, 47
FELTMATT, Theodore, 11
FENTRESS, John Milton, 73; Mary Molly, 73
FEUELL, Sarah, 121
FEW, Benjamin, 47; Catherine, 47; Elizabeth, 47; Hannah, 47, 48; Ignatius, 48; Isaac, 47; James, 47; Mary, 47, 48; William, 47, 48
FIELDS, Charlottey, 73; Peter, 73; Ruhamah, 73; Tabitha, 72
FIGELY, George, 47; Johannes, 46; John, 47
FIGLEE, John, 47
FIGLEY, Peter, 47
FIKELE, Johannes, 46
FINCHER, Francis, 96; Hannah, 96
FISHER, Ann, 72

FITCH, Henry, 27
FITZGERALD, Cenith, 12; David, 12; Elizabeth, 74; Henry, 12, 76; Margaret, 12, 76; Nancy Begley, 12
FLETCHALL, Thomas, 48
FOOKES, William, 14
FOOTE, Leonora, 33
FORBES Family, 48
FORBUSH, 24; Bathshaba, 48; George, 34, 48; Isaac, 48; Mary, 48
FORD, Elizabeth, 32; Henry, 32; Prudence, 32; Thomas, 32
FORSTER, Hugh, 91
FORTNEY, Patricia A., 49
FOSTER, Thomas, 128
FOWLER, Miss, 95
FOXWELL, Levi, 133
FOY, Enoch E., 49; James, 49; John, 49; Joseph Franklin, 49; Marinda, 49; Rebecca, 49; Rebekah, 49; Thomas, 49
FRANCES, Elizabeth, 136
FRANKLIN, Thomas, 67
FREEBORNE, Priscilla, 64
FREY, Elizabeth, 49; Hannah, 49; Johannes, 49; Johannes Nicolaus, 49; Mary Elizabeth, 49; Nicholaus, 49
FRIE, Elizabeth, 50
FRIZLE, Jason, 39
FROHOCK, John, 67
FRONEBARGER, Mary, 70; William, 70
FRY, Catharine, 49; Elizabeth, 50; Margaret, 49; Nicholas, 49; Nicholaus, 50

-G-

GAITHER Family, 40
GALLION, Elizabeth, 50; Hanna, 50; Joseph, 57, 58; Rachel, 50; Sarah, 58
GALLOWAY, Moses, 127
GAMBLE, Robert, 24
GARDINER Family, 59
GARDNER, Nicholas, 37
GARNER, George, 103; John, 51; Miss, 51
GARRETT, Amos, 64; Henry, 13; Isaac, 13; Mary, 13

GATHER, John, 16
GEORGE, Mary, 60
GHISELON, Reverdy, 63
GIBB, Carson, 1, 36, 82, 120
GIBBENS, John, 50
GIBBON, Edmond, 50; Francis, 50; George, 50
GIBSON, George, 40; James, 40; William, 39, 40
GILES, Ann, 51; Elijah, 51; Elizabeth, 64; Jacob, 64, 100; Lewis F., 51; Nathaniel, 51, 100; Thomas, 51
GILES Family, 51
GILL, Lydia, 96; Robert, 96
GILLESPIE, Ann, 51; Catherine, 51; Elizabeth, 51, 52; George, 51; James, 52; John, 52; Joseph, 52; Margaret, 53; Naomi, 52; Patrick, 51; Rebekah, 51; Robert, 11, 51, 52; Rollin Wilson, 52; Ruth, 52; Thomas, 13, 25, 34, 52; Widow, 53; William, 52
GILLIAM, Christina, 30; James B., 30; Pheba, 30; Phoebe, 30; William, 30
GILMORE, Stephen, 53
GIVAN Family, 53
James, 53
GIVEN, Edward, 54; Family, 53; James, 54; John, 54; Michael, 54; Robert, 54; Samuel, 54; William, 54
GIVVINS, Robert, 54
GLAZEBROOK, Susan A., 4
GOAR, Dorcas, 33
GOBBLE, M., 119
GODWIN, Daniel, 57
GOFORTH, William, 90
GOHUNK, Elizabeth, 2
GOLDER, Capt., 35
GOLDSBOROUGH, Howes, 6; Rosanna, 6
GOODEN, Alexander, 77; Tabitha, 77
GOODIN, Alexander, 77; Tabitha, 77
GOODING, Sarah, 18
GOODMAN, Hattie S., 73
GOODRIDGE, Nicholas, 72
GOODSON, Hannah, 122
GOODU, 131
GOORE, Dorcas, 33

GORDON, Arramenta, 94
GORE, Clement, 55; Clemsias, 108; Davis, 55; Dorcas, 33; Easter, 55, 108; Eleazar, 55; Elizabeth, 55; Elizabeth Dowden, 54; Esther, 55; Fillinda, 55; James, 54, 55, 108; James Manning, 55; John Ashford, 55; Mary, 54, 55, 108; Mary Sanders, 108; Michael, 55, 108; Michael Dowden, 55; Thomas, 55, 108
GOULT, William, 14
GRAFTON, Aquila, 56; Casander, 55; Cassandra, 56; Daniel, 56; Margaret, 56; Nathaniel, 56; Priscilla, 56; Samuel, 56; Sarah, 55, 56; William, 55, 56
GRAHAM, Hannah, 56; James, 56; John, 56; Richard, 56
GRANGER, Benjamin, 56, 57; John, 57; Mary, 57
GRANT, Thomas, 132
GRAY, William, 98
GREEN, Henry, 57; Karen Mauer, 29; Priscilla, 57; Samuel, 76
GREENFIELD, Ann, 131; Anne, 132; Thomas Truman, 131, 132
GREER, John, 125
GREGORY, Christian Nevitt, 97; Forrest G., 29
GREGRY, Benjamin, 134
GRIFFIS, Alan, 15
GRIFFITH, Sarah, 35
GROGAN, Nancy, 4
GROOM, John, 1; Samuel, 72
GULLEDGE, Martha, 110
GULLICK, John, 67
GUNNELL, Edward, 57, 58; Elizabeth, 107, 108; George, 57, 58; Sarah, 107, 108; William, 58, 107
GWATHMEY, John H., 30, 75, 83

-H-
HACKER, John, 128
HACKETT, Mary, 120; Oliver, 72; Rosannah, 72
HADLEY, Rebecca, 15

HAFNER, Jacob, 61
HAHN, Elizabeth, 60, 112; John, 63
HAILE, George, 49, 127
HALL, Aquila, 38, 113; John, 58; Joseph, 58; Leut, 103; Nancy, 4; Polly, 103; Rachel, 131; William, 4
HALLAM, John, 120
HALLEY, Elizabeth, 44
HALLOWELL, Benjamin, 68, 69
HALY, Elizabeth, 28
HAMBLETON, Archibald, 59; Mary, 6
HAMILTON, Archibald, 58; John, 98
HAMLIN, Gertrude, 119; John, 119
HAMMOND, Charles, 28; Nicholas, 68
HAMPTON, David, 59; John, 59
HAMPTON Family, 59
HANNA, Robert, 71, 86
HANSON, Dorothy, 59
HARDMAN, Henry, 47
HARDY, Edward, 120
HARLAN, John, 53, 92
HARMAN, Georg, 63
HARMON, John, 59
HARPER, Irma, 32, 102
HARRIS, Ann, 51; Frances, 51; Isaac, 51; Jacob, 51; John, 55; William, 51
HARRISON, Dorothy, 59; Joseph, 59; Mary, 67; Richard, 59; Robert, 135; William, 59
HARRISON Family, 59
HART, Richard, 14
HARTLE, ---, 42; Elizabeth, 60; George, 60; Jacob, 60; Jane, 60; Jesse, 60; Joseph, 60; Margaret, 60; Mary, 60; Michael, 60; Peter, 60; Sarah, 60; Sarah Ann, 60; Simon, 60; Solomon, 60
HARTLIE, ---, 42
HASKINS, Nancy, 122; William, 66
HASSELL, James, 135
HATHAWAY, John, 57
HAUER, Michael, 49
HAUSER, Daniel, 2, 3
HAWN, Christian, 111
HEAD, Alexander Spencer, 122; Elizabeth Stroup, 121; Margaret Elizabeth, 122

HEATH, James, 24; James Paul, 24
HECKEL, Virginia, 37, 41
HEDRICK, Magdalena, 98; Margaret, 98; Solomon, 98
HEFNER, Anna Maria, 60, 61; Barbara, 98; Catherine, 61; Dorothea, 61; Elias, 98; Elizabeth, 61; Jacob, 61; John, 61; Maria Catherine, 61; Maria Margaret, 61; Melchoir, 60, 61; Michael, 98; Philip, 61; Sarah, 98
HELME, John, 62; Penelope, 62; Sarah, 62
HELMES, John, 62; Mary, 62
HELMS, Gerald, 62; Ira, 62; John, 61; Jonathan, 61; Moses, 61; Tilman, 61
HEMSLEY, William, 128
HENDERSON, Mary, 3; Willson, 3
HENDRICK, James, 71
HENDRICKS, Henry, 71, 72; Mary, 71, 72
HENKEL, Jacob, 128
HENRICKS, Hendnay, 71
HENRY, Hugh, 62; James, 20; John, 62; Mary, 62; Robert Jenkins, 62
HEPBURN, J., 129
HEPNER, Adam, 2
HERMAN, George, 63; Mary, 63
HERMANN, George, 63
HERNDON, John G., 17
HICKMAN, Arthur, 44; Henry, 44; William, 44, 66
HICKS, Sophia, 132
HIDE, Elizabeth, 72
HILL, Elizabeth, 20, 22
HILLHOUSE, Sarah, 8; William, 8, 9; William Minter, 8
HILLIN, Hannah, 49
HINDS, Charles, 66; James, 66; John, 66; Mary, 66; Nathaniel, 66; Thomas, 66; Vincent, 66
HITCH, 23
HITCHCOCK, George, 126
HITE, Joist, 94
HOEFERIN, Anna Maria, 61
HOLCOMB, Brent, 22, 117; Brent H., 40, 70
HOLDER, Harriet, 4

HOLDMAN, Isaac, 63
HOLLINGSWORTH, Zebulon, 10, 25, 59, 134
HOLMAN, Betsey, 104; Ebenezer, 104
HOLMES, Jennet, 13; John, 13, 70
HOLWECK, Helen Summers, 124
HOOPER, Henry, 82, 128
HOOPS, Adam, 44
HOPE, James, 8, 9, 87; James Madison, 8, 87; Jane, 9
HOPKINS, Gerard, 100; Mary, 6
HOPKINSON, Joshua, 67
HOPPER, Sarah, 31
HORAH, Henry, 11, 63, 64
HORNE, William, 72
HOSKINS, William, 66
HOWARD, Amy, 123; Anney, 123; Benjamin, 16, 64; Cornelius, 16, 64; Hannah, 48; John, 31, 64, 67, 84; Lydia, 64; Martin, 11; Mathew, 64; Nancy, 40; Philip, 64; Phillip, 40; Rhesa, 48; Robert, 127; William, 123
HOWARD Family, 40
HOWELL, Aquila, 64; Daniel, 64; Frenella, 64; Job, 64; Mordecai, 64; Phebe, 64; Priscilla, 64; Samuel, 64
HOYLE, Catharine, 70
HUCHISON, Mary, 69
HUFFMAN, Anna Barbara, 65; Anna Maria, 65; Barbara, 65; George, 65; Henry, 65; Martin, 64, 65; Polly, 65
HUFMAN, Barbara, 64; Elizabeth, 65; Hannah, 65; John, 65; Joseph, 65; Martain, 64; Martin, 64; Mary, 65
HUGHES, 24; Edward, 34; William, 24
HUGHSON, Rebecca, 23
HUGHSTON, Elizabeth, 23; Jane, 23; John, 23; Rebecca, 23; Thomas Waltham, 23
HUMPHREY, William, 52
HUMPHRIES, ---, 33; Mary, 33
HUNT, Jonathan, 45; Jonathon, 111
HUNTER, C. L., 53
HURDLE, Hardy, 80
HUSBAND, Harman, 66; Herman, 66; William, 66, 100
HUSBANDS, Harman, 66; James, 66; William, 66
HUTCHISON, Mary, 69; Robert, 69
HYATT, Ezekiah, 20; Mary, 20
HYCKLYN, Rachel, 95
HYNDS, James, 66

-I-

IAMS, Elizabeth, 28; George, 27, 28; Richard, 27
INGLEFINGER, Margaret, 122
INNES, Isabella, 83
IRELAND, John, 66; Mary, 66; Samuel, 67; William, 66, 67
ISAAC, Richard, 27

-J-

JACK, George, 44
JACOB, Darkus, 123; Dorcas, 123; Edward, 123; Mary, 123; Rebecca, 123; Zacharius, 123
JACOBS, Darkus, 123; Dorcas, 123; Edward, 123; Mary, 123; Zacharius, 123
JAMES, Abraham, 90; John, 47; Mary, 47, 126
JENKINS, Casander, 55; Francis, 55; Ursulla, 99
JESTER, Lucresey, 32
JETTON, Abraham, 67
JEWELL, Moses, 44
JOHNSON, Amos, 67; Henry, 131; Lydia, 67; Thomas, 89; William, 67
JOHNSTON, George, 74, 135; John, 101
JONES, Catherine, 68; David, 35, 45, 67; Delitha, 68; Elijah, 68; Elisha, 68, 117; Griffith, 67; Henry, 67; John, 45, 68; Lucretia, 67; Mary, 67, 68; Phebe, 68; Ralph, 67, 68; Richard, 72; Sarah, 68; Thomas, 2, 57, 68, 80, 81; Widow, 1; William, 68
JONES Family, 68
JORDAN, Charity, 69; Jane, 69; John, 68, 69; Mary Ann, 69
JORDINE, John, 69; Mary, 69
JOURDAN, Elise Greenup, 28, 36, 60, 62, 67, 96, 114

JUMPE, W., 128
JURICIC, Andrea K., 110
JUSTICE, Elizabeth, 20; Hans, 20, 21; John, 20; Joseph, 40

-K-
KALLENDER, Thomas, 102
KATHI, Hannah, 56
KAYSER, John Adam, 69; Lorentz, 69
KEENE, Benjamin, 57; John, 81
KEISER, Hans Adam, 69; Lawrence, 69
KELLER, Elizabeth, 61
KELLY, Mary, 96; Sally, 22; Thomas, 22, 96
KENNEDY, Felix, 70; John, 70
KERSHAW, Joseph, 85
KEY, Sarah, 110
KIDD, Mary, 33
KILLPATRICK, John, 71
KILPATRICK, John, 71
KING, Elizabeth, 19; Family, 20; Francis, 9; James, 19; John, 80
KIRKHAM, 72
KIRKMAN, Ann, 72; Comfort, 72; Donna, 72, 73; Eleanor, 71; Elijah, 71, 72; Elisha, 71, 72; Elizabeth, 72, 73; George, 71, 72; Isabell, 73; James, 71, 72, 73; John, 71; Joseph, 73; Letitia, 73; Levin, 92; Lucinda, 73; Mary, 71, 72; Mary Molly, 73; Nancy, 73; Nancy Ann, 73; Nancy Letitia, 73; Peter, 71; Rebecca, 73; Rhoda, 72; Robert, 73; Roddy D., 73; Rodger, 71; Roger, 72, 73; Rosannah, 72; Ruhamah, 73; Samuel Edward, 73; Sarah, 71, 72, 73; Sarah Wood, 73; Tabitha, 72; Thomas, 73; Thomas Sherwood, 71, 72; William, 71, 72, 73; Zebedee, 73
KIRKMAN Family, 71, 72
KIRKMON, 72
KISER, Adam, 69, 70; Ca..., 70; Christina, 70; Elizabeth, 70; George, 69; Joseph, 69; Laurence, 69; Lawrence, 69; Lorance, 69; Lorentz, 69; Mary, 70; Sarah, 69
KIZER, Ca..., 70; Joseph, 69; Lawrence, 69
KNOX, Ann, 73; John, 73; Mark, 73; Samuel, 73; William, 73
KOCHER, Maria, 93
KRAUS, Dorothea, 65; Theodorous, 65
KYSAR, Lawrence, 69
KYSER, Adam, 70; Lawrence, 69; Sarah, 70

-L-
LACEY, Col., 86; Zelpha, 89
LACY, Col., 38; Edward, 38
LAMAR, Robert, 44, 84
LAMASTER, Joseph, 74
LAMASTERS, Joseph, 75
LAMBDIN, Sarah, 6; William, 6
LAMBERT, Robert S., 29
LANAY, Isaac, 8
LANGSDEN, William, 54
LAWSON, Hugh, 73; John, 127; Roger, 73, 74
LAZENBY, Elizabeth, 74; Henry, 74; James, 74; Joshua, 74; Keziah, 74; Margaret, 74; Margery, 76; Mary Elinor, 12, 74, 76, 79, 105; Polly, 74; Rezin, 74; Robert, 74, 76; Robert Lewis, 74; Susan, 74; Talitha C., 74; Venelia, 76
LEDGERWOOD, Sarah, 21
LEE, Elizabeth, 47; Greenberry, 47; Harry, 15; Temperance, 101; Thomas Sim, 35
LEMASTER, Benjamin, 75; Cathryne, 75; Charity, 75; Charlott Rebakah, 75; Elizabeth, 75; Isaac, 74, 75; James Knox Polk, 75; John Brown, 75; John Waddell, 75; Joseph, 74, 75; Marcus Lafayett, 75; Mary, 74, 75; Mary Elizabeth, 75; Mary Waddell, 75; Nancy Lee, 75; Rebecca, 75; Richard, 75; Saphrona Ann, 75; Thomas, 75
LENKIN, Dickinson, 77
LEONARD, R. Bernice, 10, 69, 80, 90, 101, 114, 128, 135
LESTER, Memory A., 33
LESURE, Nancy Pearre, 39

LETHERHOOD, Edward, 20
LEVERTON, John, 82
LEWIS, Aaron, 1, 17, 98; Abraham, 1, 17, 98; Amey, 76; Ann, 76; Anne, 76; Daniel, 35, 75, 76; Elizabeth, 76; John, 59, 63, 76; Margery, 75, 76; Richard, 76
LIMBAUGH, Catherine, 60
LINDSAY, Alice, 76; Anthony, 76; Samuel, 76; Walter, 76
LINDSEY, James, 22; John, 22
LINGAN, Margaret, 132
LINGLE, Walter L., 52
LINK, Catherine, 122
LINN, Andrew, 79, 80; David, 80; Elizabeth, 80; James, 79, 80; Jo White, 16, 39, 63, 100, 111; John, 79; Joseph, 80
LINVILLE, 24
LISCHY, Jacob, 93
LISTER, ---, 32; Mary, 32; Sarah, 32
LISTOR, Joseph, 32
LIVEZEY, Jon Harlan, 90
LLOYD, John, 77
LOGAN, Joseph, 68
LOMACK, William, 77
LOMAX, Amy, 77; Benjamin, 78; Blanch, 78; Clayborn, 78; Cleborne, 78; Cornelius, 77; John, 77; John A., 77; Nancy, 77; Polly, 77; Tabitha, 77; Wesley, 77; West, 77; William, 77, 78
LOMAX Family, 78
LOVE, John, 55
LOVELACE, Amelia, 79; Ann, 104; Archibald, 78, 79; Catherine, 78; Charles, 78; Eleanor, 78, 79, 104; Elias, 78, 79, 104; Isaac, 78, 104; John, 79; John Baptist, 78, 79, 104; Luke, 78; Margaret, 78; Mary Ann, 78, 79; Milicent, 79; Millicent, 78; Sarah, 104; Thomas, 79; Vachel, 78, 79; Vechtel, 78; Verlinda, 123; William, 78
LOW, Hannah, 110; James, 58
LOWE, Isaac, 79, 92; Vincent, 57
LOWIS, Richard, 76

LOYD, Capt., 131
LUX, Darby, 89; William, 37
LYNCH, Avarilla, 125; Patrick, 125
LYNN, Andrew, 79; James, 79; John, 79

-M-
MCALLISTER, 3; ---, 81; Anne W., 65; Henrietta, 85; James A., 1, 2, 11, 14, 17, 45, 57, 68, 79, 80, 82, 86, 92, 98, 102, 106, 120, 128, 129, 133, 134, 135; William, 85
MACATEE, Mary, 97
MCBEE, May Wilson, 10, 85
MCCAIN, Lucinda, 73
MCCALL, Margaret, 112
MCCALLISTER, Henrietta, 85; William, 85
MCCAULEY, William, 80
MCCLANAHAN, Alexander, 29; Andrew, 40; Phillip, 29; Thomas Marshall, 29
MCCLAREN, Daniel, 8; Mary Stephenson, 8
MCCLARON, Daniel, 87; Mary, 87
MCCLURRE, John, 85
MCCOLLISTER, Jeremiah, 85; Vachel, 85
MCCOLLISTER Family, 85
MCCOLLUM, Jane, 118
MCCORKLE, Margaret, 53; Samuel Eusebius, 53
MACCOY, Margaret, 101
MCCULLOCH, Elizabeth, 73
MCDOWELL, Charles, 85; John, 85, 97; Joseph, 85
MACE, Angell, 80; Ezekiel, 80; Josias, 80
MCGARITY, James, 86; Patrick, 86; William, 85
MCGEE, Andrew, 86; John, 86; Samuel, 86
MCGHEE, Alexander, 86; Andrew, 86; Isabell, 86; John, 86; Joseph, 86; Mary, 86; Samuel, 86; William, 86
MCGOWIN, William, 8
MCGRAW, Phebe, 68
MACKALL, Barbara, 132

MCKAY, Rebecca, 75
MACKEY (McKey), Elinor, 81; Ezabella, 81; Hezekiah, 81; Lylius, 81; Martha, 81; Mary, 81; Philip, 81; Rachel, 81; Robert, 81; Sarah, 81; William, 81
MCKINKEY, John, 30; Prudence, 30
MACKNAUL, Mary, 18
MCKNITT, John, 17
MCLENDON, Jessie, 110; Sarah, 110
MCMANUS, James, 34
MCNAMARA, Levin, 132
MCNEELY, Robert N., 70, 79
MCPHERSON, James, 15; Robert, 86, 87
MCQUARY, Lucinda, 30
MCREE, Capt., 77
MCSHAINE, David, 100; Elizabeth, 100
MCSWAIN, David, 100; Hannah, 100
MCWHORTER, Hugh, 87; Jeremiah, 89
MAID, Thomas, 82
MAINYARD, 84
MALLOY, Mary Gordon, 34
MANARD, 84
MANLEY, Robert, 81, 82
MANLOVE, Absalom, 30; Prudence, 30; Prudence Cook, 30; William, 30
MANUEL, Janet D., 34
MANYARD, 84
MARDERS, Edward, 82
MAREN, Jonathan, 88; Kezia, 88
MARIEN, Jonathan, 88; Kezia, 88
MARINE, Zorobabel, 88
MARLEY, Francis, 82
MARLIN, Alexander, 82; James, 82; John, 82
MARLING, Francis, 82; Isaac, 82; Jacob, 82
MARSHALL, Benjamin, 82, 83
MARTIN, Abraham, 92; Hannah, 112; Isaac, 112; Isabella, 83; Jane, 84; Jennet, 83; John, 23; John Peter, 83; John Stanwood, 19, 84, 87, 111; Moses, 2; Rachel, 112; Samuel, 83, 84
MARVIN, Barbara, 132
MASTERS, Barbara, 121; Catharine, 121; Elizabeth, 60; Jacob, 60; Sarah, 60
MATZGER, George Valentine, 18
MAUNEY, Catherine, 70; Valentine, 70
MAXWELL, Elizabeth, 51
MAYNARD, Nathan, 84; Susanna, 84
MEAKS, John, 62; Sarah, 62
MEEK, Adam, 8, 87; Jane, 8, 87; William, 87
MEEKES, John, 62
MELOXEN, John, 2, 3
MELVELL, David, 128
MEREDITH, Ann, 88; Henry, 87, 88; Isabell, 73; John, 88; Kivett, 73; Susanna, 88; Thomas, 88
MERIDETH, Catherine, 68
MERINE, Charles, 88; David, 88; Esther, 88; James, 88; Janet, 88; Jenett, 88; John, 88; Mary, 88; Matthew, 88; William, 88; Zorobabel, 88
MERRICK, Elizabeth, 10; James, 10
MERRYMAN, Charles, 89
MERRYMAN Family, 89
MEYER, Sarah, 2
MEYERS, Sarah, 2
MICHAEL, Ann, 89; Baltsher, 90; Bennett, 89; Betsy, 89; Catherine, 89; Daniel, 89; Delilah, 89; Elizabeth, 89; George Baltsher, 89; George W., 89; Margaret, 89; Sally Ann, 89; Sarah, 89; William, 89
MICHEL, Ann, 89; George Baltsher, 89; Johann Jacob, 89; Mary Philippina, 89
MIDDLETON, George, 13
MILES, James, 57; Joanna Garner, 103; Peter, 67; Priscilla, 97
MILLAR, 90
MILLER, ---, 42; Anna Maria, 18, 19; Elizabeth, 60, 90, 91; Family, 90; James, 90; James A. L., 135; John, 103; Joseph, 60; Mary, 6, 90, 112; Michael, 90; Robert, 90, 91; Susanna, 90; William, 90
MILLS, James, 58; John, 62; Mary, 62; Peter, 72
MILNER, Benjamin, 7
MINNER, Edward, 91; Elisha, 91;

William, 91
MINOR, Elijah, 91; William, 91
MINTER, William, 8
MINTERS, 8
MISSIONARY, John Sargent, 3
MITCHEL, Elizabeth, 5; John, 5; Mary Lee, 5
MITCHELL, David, 5; Dora W., 72, 73; Elizabeth, 5; James, 106; John, 5, 91; Sarah, 5, 6; Solomon, 92; Susannah, 5
MONEY, F., 17
MONRONEY, Catherine, 89; Sylvester, 89
MONTAGUE, Charity, 101
MONTGOMERY, Hugh, 7; James, 9; Margaret, 9
MOODIE, Hume, 129
MOORE, Ann, 36; Eliza Jane, 4; James, 102; Mollie, 36; Mordecai, 5; Risdon, 36; Sarah, 92; Smythe, 36; Thomas, 92; Ursula, 5; William, 92
MORGAN, Brigr. Genl., 35; Cassandra, 27; Daniel, 36; Edward, 100; Elizabeth, 27, 46; William, 27, 56
MORRISON, William, 125
MORTON, Jacob, 80
MOSER, Ann Elizabeth, 93; Christian, 93; Claude Rankin, 93; Elizabeth, 93; Frances, 93; Francis, 92, 93; Henry, 93; Jacob, 93, 94; John, 93; John Michael, 93; Joseph, 93; Leonard, 92, 93; Maria, 93; Maria Sarah, 93; Mary, 93; Michael, 93; Samuel, 93; Sarah, 92, 93
MOUNTICUE, Elisabeth, 101
MOXLEY, Ann, 94; Daniel, 94
MUCKELDORY, Rachel, 100
MUIR, Adam, 17
MULL, Anna Maria, 112; Frances, 112; John, 112
MULLER, Gottlob, 61
MULLERIN, Anna Maria, 18, 19
MUREIGN, Stephen, 80
MURRAY, Bridget, 3; Catherine, 51; William, 3
MUSE, Walker, 109

MUSGRAVE, Cuthbert, 96
MUSGROVE, Ann, 94, 96; Arramenta, 94; Calpernia, 95; Coleman, 95; Cuthbert, 94, 96; Dorothy, 96; Edward, 94, 95, 96; Edward Beaks, 96; Edward G., 95; Edward Gordon, 95; Elizabeth, 95; Francis Asbury, 95; Gilbert, 94; Hannah, 96; John, 94, 95; John Tate, 95; John W., 95; John William, 94, 95; Joseph, 95; Larkin C., 95; Larkin Cuthbert, 95; Leah, 96; Liney, 96; Linney, 94; Louisa, 95; Lycurgus, 95; Lydia, 96; Margaret, 94, 96; Mary, 94, 96; Minty, 95; Missouri, 95; Nancy, 95; Philip M., 95; Rachel, 95, 96; Rebecca, 96; William, 94, 95, 96; William H., 95; William Henry, 95
MUSGROVE Family, 96; Anthony, 96; Charles, 96; Jane, 96
MUSGROVES, Anthony, 96; Margaret, 96
MUSHGROVE, Mary, 96
MYERS, Abraham, 5

-N-

NABIS, John, 122; Sarah, 122
NANTICOKE, Billy, 2; Elizabeth, 2
NEGRO, Ben, 115; Bett, 87; Ceasar, 55; Chloe, 122; Easter, 55; Hannah, 55; Jack, 37, 55; Joe, 115; Judy, 37; Nam, 55; Rose, 86; Sall, 55; Salt, 55; Sam, 122; Sambo, 84; Thane, 122; Toby, 64; Tom, 55; Will, 115
NEILL, Andrew, 97; James, 97; William, 97
NEILL Family, 97
NEVITT, Benjamin, 97; Christian, 97; Cornelius, 97; Cornelius Q., 97; Elizabeth, 97; Elizabth, 97; Frances P., 97; John, 97; John M., 97; Joseph K., 97; Kellis, 97; Margaret, 97; Precious Anne, 97; Priscilla, 97; Richard, 97; Sallie, 97; William, 97; William Miles, 97
NEWMAN, Harry Wright, 6, 59, 63, 64, 126

NIBLET, Solomon, 98
NICHOLS, Daniel, 1; Dolly, 98; Isaac, 17, 98; Simon, 84
NICHOLSON, Catherine, 47
NICKELSON, George, 22
NISWONGER, Catherine, 60; Joseph, 60; Mary, 60
NIXON, Alfred, 19; John, 85
NOLAND, Augustine, 24; Elizabeth, 55
NOLL, Barbara, 98; Catharina, 98; Christina, 98; Elizabeth, 98; Jacob, 98; John, 98; Magdalena, 98; Margaret, 98; Mary, 98; Peter, 98; Sarah, 98
NORRIS, Thomas, 110
NORWARD, Nathaniel, 5
NULL, Christine, 98; Elizabeth, 98; Jacob, 98; John, 42, 98; Magdalena, 98; Margaret, 98; Maria Elizabeth, 42; Sarah, 98

-O-
OCKERT, Anita L., 29
OGDEN, Nehemiah, 44
OGILVIE, John, 121
OLIPHANT, John, 20
O'NEAL, Betsey, 22
ONSELL, 50; Margaret, 49
O'ROURKE, Timothy J., 135
OSBORN, Ann, 89; Thomas, 89; William, 58
OTTEY, William, 113
OTTLEY, Donna J., 31, 32
OVERTON, Jane, 58; Thomas, 58
OWINGS, Sarah, 23
OZBURN, Thomas, 89

-P-
PABST, Henry, 49; Mary Elizabeth, 49
PAPENFUSE, Edward C., 6, 91, 132
PAPSTIN, Elizabeth, 49
PARDUE, Sarah, 122
PARKER, Elmer O., 40; Elmer Oris, 9, 87
PARKINS, Daniel, 114; David, 114
PARSONS, George, 99; John, 99; Joseph, 99; Joshua, 99; Mary, 99; Nelly, 99; Peter, 99; Ursulla, 99; William, 99
PASINGER, John, 35
PATTISON, James, 134; John, 134; Richard, 80, 102
PATTON, Robert, 85
PAYNE, John, 79
PEACH, Joseph, 27
PEARKINS, Daniel, 114; Daniell, 114; David, 114
PEARSONS, Sarah, 68
PECKETT, Elizabeth, 125
PEDEN, Henry C., 1, 7, 9, 10, 13, 15, 16, 17, 25, 33, 34, 35, 41, 47, 49, 54, 59, 62, 66, 70, 71, 74, 76, 81, 83, 84, 86, 87, 90, 91, 93, 103, 109, 111, 113, 116, 121, 126, 133, 134
PENDRAKE, Nicholas, 19
PENDRIACK, Nicholas, 19
PENDRICK, Nicholas, 19
PENN Family, 74
PERKINS, Benjamin, 100; Charles, 100; Elisha, 100; Moses, 100; Reuben, 100; Richard, 100; Rubin, 100; Sebert, 100; William, 100
PERRINE, Peter, 48; William, 48
PETEET, Rebecca, 49
PETRUCELLI, Katherine Sanford, 122
PHELPS, Avanto, 101; Avinton, 100; Rachel, 100; Rosanna, 100; Rose, 100; Thomas, 100, 101; Vinton, 100
PHILIPS, John, 46
PHILLIPS, Francis, 115; James, 58; Mary, 120; Samuel, 120
PICKENS, Andrew, 70
PIPEN, Benjamin, 101; John, 101; Joseph, 101; Rebecca, 101; Robert, 101; Solomon, 101
PIPER, Michael, 6; Rosanna, 6; Rose Ann, 6
PIPPEN, Benjamin, 101; Charity, 101; Joseph, 101; Lydia, 101; Margaret, 101; Martha, 101; Nancy, 101; Richard, 101; Robert, 101; Temperance, 101
PIPPIN, Derias, 102; Elisabeth, 101; John, 101, 102; Joseph, 102; Solomon, 101

PLONK, Barbara, 115; Elizabeth, 70; Mary, 115; Nancy, 115; Peter, 70, 115
PLOWMAN, Jonathan, 113
PLUMMER, Micajah, 23
PLUNK, Barbara, 115; Mary, 115; Nancy, 115; Peter, 115
PLUNKETT, Letitia, 73
POLK, James Knox, 52
POOL, Elizabeth, 73
POOR, James, 24
PORTER, Carol L., 136; Martha, 101
POSTEN, Hannah, 122
POTEE, Rebecca, 49
POTEET, Peter, 49; Rebecca, 49
POTTS, Henry, 102; James, 102; John, 102; Thomas, 102
POWERS, Ruth Blakely, 55
PRATHER, Thomas, 22, 110
PRESTON, John, 90
PRICE, Mordecai, 127; Thomas, 14, 77, 131
PRITCHETT, Arthur, 1; Edward, 102
PUDDINGTON, Ursula, 5
PUNDRICK, Nicholas, 19

-Q-
QUINN, Hugh, 8; Peter, 8

-R-
RAGAN, Charles, 19
RAGEN, William, 67
RAGH, Thomas, 66
RAMSEY, Robert W., 1, 7, 10, 12, 13, 14, 16, 17, 22, 23, 25, 31, 32, 34, 36, 41, 42, 44, 45, 46, 48, 52, 53, 56, 58, 59, 63, 64, 66, 67, 70, 71, 73, 74, 76, 79, 81, 82, 85, 87, 90, 91, 97, 99, 102, 103, 104, 105, 113, 114, 116, 121, 125, 126, 128, 129, 130, 131, 134, 135
RANDALL, Mary, 19
RATCLIF, John, 47
RATCLIFFE, Sarah, 47
RATCLIFFE Family, 47
RAUB, Anna Maria, 60; Johann Michael, 60

RAUH, Anna Maria, 61; Elizabeth, 61; Jacob, 61; Johann Michael, 61; Maria Ursula, 61
RAWLINGS, Anthony, 72; John, 72
RAY, Asa, 33; George Washington, 33; James, 33; Martha Ann, 33; William Alford, 33; Worth, 22
READ, Joseph, 103; Richard, 103
REAMY, Martha, 26
REDING, Comfort, 72
REED, Jane, 103; Johannes, 120; John, 1, 2, 3, 120; Joseph, 103; Mary, 103, 122, 130; Richard, 102, 103; Robert, 103; Shadrick, 18
REEVES, Edward, 58
REID, Joanna Garner, 103; Joseph, 103; Richard, 102; Robert, 103
REISZ, Eva, 42
REITER, Elizabeth, 60
REMY, Mary, 107
RENEAU, Martha Powell, 5
RHOADES, Nelson Osgood, 88
RHYNE, Hannah Hoyle, 121
RICE, Eva, 42; Millard Milburn, 19, 23, 44, 48, 55, 74, 80, 109, 131
RICH, Christoph, 2
RICHARDSON, Joseph, 15, 45, 56, 68, 79; Peter, 86
RICHMAN, John, 72
RIDDLE, John, 104; Margaret, 104; Stephen, 103, 104
RIDGELY, Charles, 115
RIGGS, ---, 124
RISINGER, Faight, 19
ROBBS, Alexander, 80
ROBERTS, Edward, 104; Mary, 22; William, 104
ROBERTSON, David, 21
ROBEY, Absalom, 104; Ann, 104; Anne, 104; Barton, 104; Basil, 104; Berry, 104; Betsey, 104; Cynthia, 104; Ede, 104; Eleanor, 79, 104; Elizabth, 104; Esther, 104; Greenberry, 104; James, 104; John, 104; John Boswell, 104; John Randolph, 104; Leonard, 104; Martha, 104; Mary, 104; Matilda, 104; Milly, 104; Nathan, 104; Patta,

104; Polly, 104; Prior Smallwood, 75, 104, 105; Rachel, 104; Sarah, 104; Thomas, 78, 104, 105; Tobias, 104
ROBEY Family, 105
ROBINSON, Amos, 105; Charity, 105, 117; Ezekiel, 105; George, 105; Henry, 105; James A., 105; Job, 105, 117; John, 105; Martha, 105; Mary, 105; Richard, 105; Samuel, 105; William, 105; Zacariah, 105
ROBISON, Richard, 105
ROBSON, John, 127
ROGERS, Benjamin, 37; John, 128; Sarah, 6
ROSEBROUGH, James, 105; John, 78, 104; Margaret, 78
ROSS, Bobby Gilmer, 30, 83, 103, 106; Bobby Gilmor, 86, 88; Charles, 106; Jesse, 122; Nancy, 122
ROTHWELL, Thomas, 24
ROWLAND, Ralph Shearer, 29; Star Wilson, 29
RUDDLE, Stephen, 103
RUMPLE, Jethro, 41
RUMSEY, William, 24, 41
RUTTER, Thomas, 125
RUTTY, Daniel, 102
RYAL, David, 106; William, 106; Young, 106
RYALL, Daniel, 106; John, 106; William, 106
RYALS, David, 106; John, 106; Joseph, 106; William, 106
RYER---, Peter, 53
RYLE, John, 53
RYLE Family, 106

-S-

SANDERS, Aaron, 108; Barbara, 108; Easter, 108; Elias, 108; Elizabeth, 55, 107; Hardy, 108; Hendrey, 108; Hendry, 107; Henry, 108; James, 55, 107, 108; Jared Young, 108; John, 107, 108; John Hyde, 109; Lewis, 108; Lynus, 108; Mary, 55, 107, 108; Mary Elizabeth, 107, 108;

153

Philip, 107; Phillip, 106, 107; Presly, 108; Robert, 108; Sarah, 107, 108; Ursula, 107; Ursulee, 107; William, 107; William Gunnell, 108
SANFORD, 23; Richard, 133
SARGENT, John, 3
SAUNDERS, Anne, 33; Thomas, 33
SCHARF, J. Thomas, 114
SCHELL, Anna Catharine Gertrude, 111; Anna Catherine, 111; Anna Maagdalena, 112; Anna Maria, 112; Carl Frederick, 112; Caspar, 111, 112; Catherina, 112; Charles Frederick, 112; Elizabeth, 112; Frances, 112; Gertrude, 112; Henry, 112; Johanna Caspar, 111; Johannes, 111; Johannes Casper, 111; Michael, 112; Sarah, 112
SCHILDKNECHHT, Calvin E., 93
SCHILDKNECHT, C. E., 19
SCHMID, Maria Margaretha, 115
SCHNEBLEY, Henry, 47
SCHNECKENBERGER, Anna Ursula, 111; Christian, 46, 47; Ursula, 46
SCHNECTOR, Catharine, 49
SCHNEGENBERGER, Christian, 47
SCHOMAKER, Conrad, 28
SCOTT, James, 25
SCOTTEN, Sarah, 15
SEABAUGH, Christopher, 60; Mary, 60; Sarah, 60
SEAGO, Abraham, 109, 110; Ann, 109; Benjamin Horton, 109; Elender, 109; Elizabeth, 109; Ellender, 110; Hannah, 110; James, 109, 110; John, 109, 110; John O., 110; Joseph, 110; Lucresey, 110; Lucretia, 110; Margaret, 109, 110; Martha, 110; Mary, 110; Nancy, 110; Robert, 109, 110; Sarah, 109, 110; Thomas, 109; William, 109; William Crain, 110
SEALY, Edward, 33; Nancy, 33
SEEGAR Family, 110
SEEGO, Thomas, 109
SEGO, Benjamin, 109, 110; Elender, 109; John, 109; Robert, 109
SEGORE, John, 109

SEIB, Johann Paul, 115; Maria Margaretha, 115
SEIP, Johann Paul, 115; Paulus, 115; Philip, 115
SELIVAN, Elizabeth, 30
SELVIN, Elizabeth, 30
SELWARD, Betsy, 89; Henry, 89
SERGEANT, John, 2
SERGO, Thomas, 109
SEWALL, Samuel, 113
SEWARD, Anna, 14
SEWEL, Christopher, 20
SEWELL, Anne, 136; Christopher, 113, 136; Comfort, 113; Elizabeth, 136; Joshua, 113, 136; Mary, 72; Samuel, 113
SHARP, Peter, 16; Thomas, 34
SHAW, James, 45; Mary Ann, 79; Robert, 104
SHELBY, Evan, 111; Isaac, 111; John, 111; Letitia, 111; Moses, 110
SHELL, ---, 112; Anna Catharine Gertrude, 111; Charles, 112; Charles Frederick, 111; Christian, 112; Daniel L., 112; Hannah, 112; Henry, 111; Johannes Casper, 111; John, 47, 112; Margaret, 112; Mary, 112; Rachel, 112
SHEPARD, Marinda, 49
SHERIL, Elisha, 20
SHERRILL, Adam, 113; Rudil, 113; Samuel, 113; Ute, 113; William, 113, 114; Yont, 113
SHERRILL Family, 113
SHERWOOD, Daniel, 6; Mary, 6, 72
SHIELDS, David, 82
SHIPLEY, Henrietta, 85; Martha, 136; Samuel, 136
SHIRRELL, Adam, 114
SHOBER, Gottlieb, 2
SIGLEY, Johanna, 114
SILL, Elizabeth, 114; Family, 114; John, 114; Joseph, 114; Thomas, 114
SIMPER, Thomas, 76
SIMPERS, Ann, 76; Nathaniel, 76; Thomas, 76
SINGLETON, John, 72

SIPE, Abraham, 115; Daniel, 115; Henry, 115; Jacob, 115; Johann Paul, 115; Mary, 93, 115; Nancy, 115; Paul, 115; Sarah, 115; Susannah, 115; William, 93
SIPES, Daniel, 115; Johann Paul, 115; Paul, 115
SKILLINGTON, Kenelm, 14
SKINNER, V. L., 59; Vernon L., 78, 88
SKORDAS, Gust, 1, 35, 36, 54, 72, 78, 82, 96, 99, 120, 121
SKYCER, Lawrence, 69
SLIGH, Thomas, 127
SMALL, Benjamin, 134
SMITH, ---, 58; Amelia, 133; Ann, 96, 131; Anne, 132; Daniel, 60; David, 96; Ede, 104; Elizabeth, 60; Elizabth, 97; Henry, 125; Isaac, 125; Jerome, 72; Jessie, 110; John, 82; Joseph, 125; Kitty, 22; Margaret, 55; Mary, 99, 110; Mary Ann, 33; Matthew, 72; Nancy Letitia, 73; Nathaniel, 94; Philip, 60; Rachel, 131; Robert, 68; Sarah, 60; Sarah Ann, 60; Thomas, 55, 56; Walter, 131; William, 73, 127
SMOOT, Barton, 48; Edward, 48; John, 48
SMYTH, James, 114; Robert, 114
SOLLERS, Family, 115; James, 115; Sabret, 115
SPARKES, Edward, 116; William, 116
SPARKS, Jonas, 116; Matthew, 116; Solomon, 116; William, 116
SPARROWS, Elizabeth, 116; John, 116; Kensey, 116; Matilda, 116; Solomon, 116; Thomas, 116
SPEDDEN, Robert, 10
SPENCER, Charity, 105, 117; William, 82, 116, 117; Zachariah, 105, 117; Zechariah, 116
SPRAGUE, Stuart Seely, 6
SPRIGG, Thomas, 27
SPURRIER, Anna Amanda, 119; Daniel, 118; Edward, 109; Elbert, 118; Elizabeth, 118, 119; Family, 117; Frances, 118; Frances D., 118;

Green, 117; Harry Thomas, 118; J.
M., 117, 119; James Laid, 118; Jane,
118; John, 117, 118, 119; Lorine,
118; M., 119; Margaret, 119;
Martha, 118; Mary, 118; Mary Jane,
118; Nancy, 119; Rachel, 118;
Rachel Cawood, 119; Samuel, 118;
Sarah E., 119; Theophilus, 117, 118;
Thomas, 117, 118; Thomas W., 119;
William, 118, 119; William Atwell,
119; William G., 119
STAB, Mary Philippina, 89
STACEY, Enne, 119; John, 120; Mary,
120; Richard, 119, 120; William,
119, 120
STACY, Aaron, 119; Edward, 120;
Martha, 119; Mary, 120; Nancy,
119; Richard, 119; Sarah, 10, 119;
Simon, 120; William, 119
STAINTON, Benson, 11
STANFIELD, Hannah, 47
STANTON, George, 120; Mary, 120
STEELE, John, 53; Ninean, 76; William,
52, 53, 120
STEPHENS, Edward, 108
STEPHENSON, Dorcas, 9; Jane, 8, 9;
John, 8; Margaret, 9; Mary, 8, 87;
Robert, 8, 9; Samuel, 9
STERN, Daniel, 63
STEVENS, John, 1; R., 57, 92; Robert J.,
96; Thomas, 26
STEVENSON, Abigal, 121; Edward, 58;
Elizabeth, 121; James, 121; John,
121; Katherine, 121; Philip, 121;
Sarah, 121; Thomas, 121; William,
120, 121
STEWART, Ann, 135; John, 135
STILWELL, Elias, 111
STOCKDALE, Arah, 38
STONE, Benjamin, 22
STRATTON, Col., 86
STRAUB, Catharine, 121; Jacob, 121
STROUD, Ellen, 4
STROUP, Adam, 121, 122; Andrew, 122;
Barbara, 121, 122; Catharine, 121;
Catherine, 121, 122; Daniel, 122;
David, 122; Elizabeth, 121, 122;
Frances, 122; George, 122; Hannah,
122; Hannah Hoyle, 121; Jacob, 121,
122; Jacob D., 121; John, 121, 122;
Joseph, 121; Margaret, 122;
Margaret Elizabeth, 122; Mary, 122;
Michael, 122; Nancy, 122; Peter,
122; Philip, 122; Sarah, 121;
Solomon, 122
STRUPP, Anne J. M., 134
STUART, Charles, 131
STUDES, Thomas, 50
STUMP, John, 100
SULIVANE, Dan, 134
SULLIVAN, Rhoda, 72
SUMERS, Marget, 70
SUMMERS, Amy, 123; Ann, 123, 124;
Anney, 123; Annie, 124; Basil, 123;
Bertha, 123; Biney, 123; Bitha, 123;
Cassandra, 122, 124; Darkus, 123;
Dorcas, 123, 124; Eleanor, 28, 124;
Elizabeth, 124; Ellenor, 124; Family,
124; George, 123; James, 124; Jesse,
124; John, 123, 124; John Dent, 123;
Joseph, 28, 124; Linney, 123;
Margaret, 70; Mary, 122, 123, 124;
Mary Wheat, 122; Nelly, 124; Paul
Talbutt, 123; Rachel, 123; Rebecca,
123; Richard, 124, 125; Riggs, 124;
Rosanna, 124; Ruth, 124; Sarah,
123, 124; Susannah, 124; Tabitha,
123; Thomas, 123; Verlinda, 123;
William, 122, 123, 124; Zachariah,
75, 123, 124
SWEARINGEN, Massom, 28; Samuel,
28; Sarah, 28
SWEEN, Jane C., 34
SWEENY, David, 64
SWIFT, ---, 100
SYMPERS, Ann, 76; Nathaniel, 76

-T-

TALBOT, Edmund, 48; John, 48; Rachel,
123
TATE, James, 125; Nancy, 95; Samuel,
125; Thomas, 8; William, 8
TATUM, Max L., 19
TAYLOR, Absalom, 40; Arthur, 125;

Avarilla, 125; Elizabeth, 125; Isaac, 4; Jane, 125; John, 57, 125; Joseph, 115; Margret, 125; Mary, 4; Thomas, 134; Ursulee, 107
TEAGUE, Susannah, 124
TEMPLETON, Family, 17
TENNANT, James, 125, 126; John, 126; Moses, 126
TEVIS Family, 39
THARP, Mable, 126; Richard, 126
THOMAS, Allen, 128; Elinor, 130; Kasandra, 28; Timothy, 28
THOMPSON, Benjamin, 126; James, 8; John, 105, 126; Naomi, 52
THOMSON, Benjamin, 126; John, 126; William, 85
TICE, David, 45
TILGHMAN, ---, 61; Christopher, 62; Elizabeth, 62; Family, 62; Gideon, 62; Matthew, 6, 7, 91; Richard, 61, 62, 68
TILLMAN, Stephen, 62
TILMAN, John, 62; Tobias, 62
TODD, Benjamin, 133
TODD FAMILY, 40
TOLLSON, Francis, 76
TOMBELSON, Bertha, 123; Bitha, 123; John, 123; Tabitha, 123
TOMLINSON, Bertha, 123; Bitha, 123; John, 123; Mary Burke Gore, 54; Tabitha, 123
TORRENCE, Clayton, 99, 129
TOWNSEND, Leah, 68
TOWSON, William, 136
TRACEY, Basil, 126; Dinah, 126; James, 126, 127; Mary, 126, 127; Nathaniel, 126; Sarah, 126; Teague, 126; Thady, 126
TRACY, James, 127
TRAFFENSTAAT, Catherine, 42
TRAVERSE, Matthias, 57
TREWHER, William, 27
TRIPPE, Edward, 127; Elizabeth, 127; Henrietta, 127; Henry, 127; John, 127; William, 127
TROSPER, Nicholas, 20
TROTT, Lewis, 128

TROTTER, Hannah, 32; Jane, 32
TRUNKER, William, 27
TUCKER, Esther, 104; James, 126; Mary, 104
TURBUTT, Richard, 114
TURNER, Elizabeth, 119; Gilbert, 128
TWYFORD, Ann, 72; John, 72
TYLER, John, 94; Margaret, 94
TYRON, Will, 11

-U-

UNSELD, 50
UNSELT, 50

-V-

VALENTINE, Elizabeth, 50; Henrich, 50
VAN STORRE, Cathren, 133; John, 133
VENABLES, 23
VICKREY, Charlottey, 73
VOGELI, Peter, 128
VOLKER, Jacob, 128

-W-

WADDELL, Elizabeth, 75; George, 75; James, 75; Jane, 75; John, 74, 75; Mary, 74, 75; William, 75
WAGGAMAN, Henry, 68
WALKER, Alexander, 38; Charles, 37; J. Richard, 6; Leakin, 38; Margaret, 6, 40; Martha, 38; Phillip, 40; Robert, 38, 40; Thomas, 72
WALL, Joshua, 128; Mary, 122
WALLACE, Elizabeth, 119; James, 129; William, 129
WALLIS, John, 121
WALLTON, Richard, 129; William, 129
WALTON, John, 129; Richard, 129; William, 129
WAMACK, Abram, 19
WARD, Mary, 18; Nancy, 101; William, 13
WARDE, Jane, 15
WATERS, Ellenor, 124; Margery, 75, 76; Nelly, 124; Philemon, 95; Rosanna, 124; Thomas, 95; Thomas W., 124
WATT, Family, 129; James, 129; William, 129

WATTS, 130; Catherine, 130; Daniel, 130; Elinor, 130; George, 130; James, 130; John, 130; Joseph, 128; Peter, 130; Stephen, 130; William, 130
WAY, Ann, 130
WAYLAND, John W., 48, 87
WEATHERFORD, Nancy, 4
WEBSTER, Irene B., 32, 71, 133; John, 120
WEINER, Barbara, 65
WELLS, Ann, 124; Annie, 124; Charles, 58; James, 124
WELSH, James, 13
WETHERELL, George, 54, 114
WHARTON, Ellender, 110
WHEAT, Amy, 122; Mary, 122, 123; Sarah, 122; William, 122
WHEATLEY, William, 2
WHEELER, Benjamin, 47; Mary, 47; Robert, 96
WHELAND, Benjamin, 14; William, 13
WHITAIN, Nancy, 22
WHITAKER, James, 130; Joshua, 130; Katherine, 130; Mark, 130, 131; Mary, 130; William, 130
WHITAM, Nancy, 22
WHITE, Henry, 1; Jacob, 48; Jo Linn, 35, 84; Joseph, 131; Louisa, 95; Margaret, 55; Mary, 72; Sarah, 133; Thomas, 11, 106, 134; Virgil D., 9, 15, 16, 17, 22, 26, 30, 42, 75, 77, 83, 84, 85, 86, 88, 92, 101, 102, 103, 106, 109, 119, 121, 135
WHITEACRE, James, 131
WHITEFORD, H. B., 135
WHITEHEAD, Mary, 130
WHITTINGTON, John, 114
WHORTON, Elender, 109
WIEMAR, Jacob, 60
WIGLEY, William, 114
WILCOCKSON, Isaac, 131; John, 131
WILFONG, John, 47
WILKERSON, Dorcas, 6
WILKIE, Will, 40; William, 40
WILKINS, Thomas, 64
WILKINSON, Ann, 131; Anne, 132; Barbara, 132; Francis, 131, 132; Rebecca, 131; Sophia, 132; Sophie, 131; Susanna, 132; William, 131, 132
WILLE, Pritch, 133
WILLEN, John, 132
WILLEY, Edward, 133; Edward W., 133; Emelia, 133; Francis, 133; Frederick, 133; George, 133; John, 133; Prichard, 133; Pritchet, 133; Rachel, 133; Sarah, 133; Thomas W., 133
WILLIAMS, Edward, 134; Giles, 134; James, 125; John, 2, 125; Mary, 15; Paul, 125; Rachel, 134; Richard, 124; Robert, 2; Solomon, 134; T.J.C., 87, 111; William, 24, 53, 91
WILLIAMSON, Arthur, 4; Sally, 4; Sarah, 4
WILLIN, John, 133; Levi, 133; Thomas, 133
WILLINGHAM, Mary, 68
WILLIOCKSON, John, 35
WILLSON, Robert, 134
WILSON, Abigal, 121; Catherine, 13; Howard M., 25, 87; James, 131, 132; Jennet, 13; Josiah, 132; Margaret, 132; Minty, 95; Robert, 13; Sophia, 132; Sophie, 131
WIMSATT, Richard, 135
WINDLY, Sarah, 73
WINEBARGER, Margaret, 98; William, 98
WINEBERGER, Christine, 98; Jacob, 98
WINFIELD, J., 17
WINGATE, Shadrick, 132
WINN, John, 85; Richard, 85
WINNEBARGER, Christina, 98; Jacob, 98
WINSLEY, Benjamin, 134; John, 134; Thomas, 134
WINSLY, Benjamin, 134
WINSUIT, Abraham, 135; Richard, 135
WISE, Philip, 60; Sarah, 60
WOMACK, Abram, 19
WOOD, Easter, 55; Easter Sanders, 55; Esther, 55; Isabell, 73; Joseph, 14, 45, 53, 92; Mary, 73; Robert, 53, 92;

Sarah, 72; Zebedee, 73
WOODRING, Daniel, 115; Susannah, 115
WOODS, John, 66
WOOLFORD, Levin, 2, 3, 80, 102, 120
WOOLSEY, Mel T., 3
WORNELL, Sarah, 55
WORTHINGTON, Samuel, 82
WRIGHT, C. Milton, 100; Edward, 135; Elisha, 86; F. Edward, 6, 10, 13, 31, 33, 35, 36, 37, 49, 59, 66, 69, 70, 71, 81, 90, 91, 92, 96, 98, 99, 101, 103, 106, 110, 113, 114, 124, 126, 136; Henry, 67; Hynson, 135; Jacob, 86; James, 135; Margaret, 89; Sarah, 135; Thomas Hynson, 68
WYAND, Florence L., 63; Jeffrey A., 63
WYATT, Bethlehem, 116; James, 116
WYLIE, Joseph Alexander, 67; Lucretia, 67

-Y-

YACKLEY, Robert, 6
YAXLEY, Elizabeth, 5; Robert, 6; Sarah Mitchell, 6
YOE, Sary, 15
YOUNG, Acton, 136; Edward, 136; Elizabeth, 136; Henry, 136; James, 136; John, 134, 136; Joshua, 136; Luana, 136; Margaret, 136; Mary, 108; Philip, 136; Ray A., 50, 52, 94, 117; Richard, 136; Sewell, 136; Sewill, 136; Suel, 136; Thomas, 20; Vachel, 136; W. Sewell, 136; William, 28
YOUNT, Ray A., 20, 21, 44, 61, 65, 105

-Z-

ZUG, Leinhard, 63